Oxford Shakespeare Topics

Shakespeare and the English-speaking Cinema

OXFORD SHAKESPEARE TOPICS

Published and Forthcoming Titles Include:

Oxford Shakespeare Topics

Shakespeare and the English-speaking Cinema

RUSSELL JACKSON

OXFORD
UNIVERSITY PRESS

Great Clarendon Street, Oxford, OX2 6DP,
United Kingdom

Oxford University Press is a department of the University of Oxford.
It furthers the University's objective of excellence in research, scholarship,
and education by publishing worldwide. Oxford is a registered trade mark of
Oxford University Press in the UK and in certain other countries

First Edition published in 2014

Published in the United States of America by Oxford University Press
198 Madison Avenue, New York, NY 10016, United States of America

British Library Cataloguing in Publication Data

Data available

Library of Congress Control Number: 2014934902

ISBN 978-0-19-965946-3

To the memory of
Kenneth S. Rothwell and Bernice W. Kliman,
scholars, critics, friends

Preface

The organization of this book is 'horizontal', in that, rather than offer a chronological account of its subject, or one divided strictly according to genres, its chapters approach films from a number of different perspectives. Excellent historical accounts, in particular Kenneth S. Rothwell's *History of Shakespeare on Screen* (2nd edition, 2004), provide alternative and comprehensive introductions. Although considerations of dramatic genre hover over some chapters more than others, in general I have tried to reflect our sense, as playgoers and readers as well as cinemagoers, of a compromise between dramatic and cinematic genres. The first chapter, 'places', deals with the realization of the locations of the action and the choice of historical period; this leads to 'people', a discussion of the ways in which individual characters and relationships have been influenced by these decisions. The third and fourth chapters consider the part played by the erotic in comedy and tragedy respectively; the fifth deals with politics – 'power plays'– in films from plays of a range of dramatic genres; and the sixth with films that adapt more radically or make significant use of Shakespearian 'originals'.

In order to keep the book to an appropriate length, I have quoted sparingly from the very considerable body of informed, perceptive, and challenging critical commentary that has appeared since the 1970s. The brief conclusion, 'Rewind', suggests some ways in which the reader may wish to take the book's subject further. The suggestions for 'Further Reading' (pp. 177–184) include scholarship and commentary that I would have liked to engage with, but which in any case will provide the reader with ideas, arguments, and information to take back to the films and, I hope, what I have written here. The restriction to 'English-speaking' cinema precludes discussion of such influential films as Akira Kurosawa's *Throne of Blood* (1957, from *Macbeth*) and *Ran* (1987, from *King Lear*), but I have allowed myself comparisons in a few instances with Grigori Kozintsev's Russian versions of *Hamlet* (1964) and *King Lear* (1969).

In the text and filmography, directors' names are used to identify films, not out of a dogmatic devotion to the *auteur* theory, but because it is a term of convenience in common use. In order to keep my text tidy, the nationality of films is indicated in the filmography but not within the body of the text. References to the plays are to the act, scene, and line numbering of the *Complete Works*, edited by Stanley Wells and Gary Taylor (2nd edition, Oxford, 1986).

Acknowledgements

I am grateful to my colleagues in the department of Drama and Theatre Arts at the University of Birmingham for their support during a period of study leave that enabled me to complete this book. I have benefitted from insights gleaned from discussions with students in study options on its subject, and from other scholars and critics in conferences and symposia. Like all those engaged in the study of Shakespeare on film, I owe an incalculable debt to Kenneth S. Rothwell and Bernice W. Kliman, to whose memory this book is dedicated, for their collegial engagement in debate and the example of their published work. Patricia Lennox, who has shared in the viewing and discussion that lies behind this book, and Peter Holland and Stanley Wells, who commissioned it, have been acute and encouraging in their comments on its drafts.

RJ

Birmingham
June 2013

Contents

Illustrations

Introduction: Legalized Plagiarism and the Rewards of Adaptation

Jean Renoir, discussing his 1936 film adaptation of a short story by Guy de Maupassant, 'Une Partie de campagne', insisted that he truly believed in the idea of 'a framework within which one embroiders':

It's a question of plagiarism. I must admit something: I'm absolutely in favour of plagiarism. I believe that if we want to bring about a great period, a new renaissance of arts and letters, the government should encourage plagiarism . . . I'm not kidding, because the great authors did nothing but plagiarism, and it served them well. Shakespeare spent his time writing stories that had already been written by little-known Italian authors and by others.

Apologizing for what may seem a digression in his commentary on the film in question, Renoir points out that borrowing of this kind 'frees you from the unimportant aspect', to concentrate on 'the way you tell the story . . . the details, the development of the characters and the situations'.[1] The sense of freedom that Renoir enjoys in his reworking of the story can be paralleled in the suggestion by Julie Sanders that 'it is usually at the very point of infidelity that the most creative acts of interpretation take place'.[2] Deborah Cartmell suggests a convenient classification of adaptations from text to screen: transposition, commentary, and analogue.[3] It is possible to go further. In *Film Adaptation and Its Discontents* (2007) Thomas Leitch, having surveyed various taxonomies of adaptation, proposes a list of ten strategies: celebration, adjustment, (neoclassical) imitation, revision, colonization, deconstruction, analogy, parody (and pastiche), imitation (secondary, tertiary, and quaternary), and allusion.[4] All, he suggests, are present in Baz Luhrmann's *William Shakespeare's Romeo+Juliet* (1996).

Discussion of adaptation has problematized the terms 'original' and 'fidelity', partly motivated by a desire to avoid a hierarchy of texts and in response to the alleged death of the author, but it remains current in the thinking of those who work on screen (or stage) versions, and is an appropriate and convenient word for their raw material. The redirection of emphasis from the author – a concept defined variously even in the time when the plays were written – has been a salutary element in critical thinking, but authorship is still invoked by the makers and distributors of films, notably in the appropriate legally and professionally significant credits on scripts. 'Fidelity' to the original, though, is not a quality prized implicitly or explicitly in the present work, but it should be acknowledged that, for better or worse, this concept, however discredited in theoretical writing on adaptation, continues to have currency in the popular reception of films. Colin McCabe, introducing *True to the Spirit* (2011), a collection of essays addressing the problematic nature of these concepts in relation to specific examples, observes that in recent theoretical writing '[t]he endless attacks on fidelity . . . meant that [critics] were ill equipped and unwilling to sketch that particular form of productivity that preserves identity at the same moments that it multiplies it'.[5] 'Circulation' and engagement with the audience's pleasure in recognizing and enjoying changes by invoking the source texts may be a more useful way of describing the interplay between audience, film, and original: current advertising (spring 2013) for a tie-in edition of J.R.R. Tolkien's *The Hobbit* promises 'the book that inspired the film'. In a sense, what we are dealing with is the (re)circulation of originals that are themselves revisiting existing plays, novellas, or chronicles. This having been said, and for all one's desire to see the 'original' retrieved as faithful to audience perceptions, it is important to acknowledge that, in Linda Hutcheon's words, 'to be second is not to be secondary or inferior; likewise, to be first is not to be originary or authoritative'. The source may be seen or read after the adaptation – as the publishers of Tolkien clearly hope – and '[m]ultiple versions exist laterally, not vertically'.[6]

Some Definitions: 'Shakespeare', 'English', and 'Cinema'

The title of this book includes terms whose significance may seem self-evident, but which call for some examination. What do we mean by 'Shakespeare', 'English-speaking', and 'cinema'?

The first is perhaps the easiest to define: we are considering the ways in which the plays in the Shakespeare canon have been adapted for a new medium and the processes and results identifiable in a number of examples. Invoking the canon carries with it the implication that all and any of the plays (and poems) in the various editions of the *Complete Works* might be in question, and that all of these are safely attributed to the sole authorship of Shakespeare. In practice, although some plays have been accepted as the product of collaboration – *Macbeth* is the prime example – so far as the general public is concerned, the participation of Thomas Middleton as a reviser is of little interest, and film-makers and their audiences have so far not shown any desire to make such matters a factor in their work or enjoyment. Given that the creation of a script from the 'raw material' of *King Lear* or *Hamlet* is itself an act of radical revision, the existence of different equally 'authentic' versions of the same play from the dramatist's own theatre and lifetime has not usually been a consideration: Kenneth Branagh's *Hamlet* (1996), with its claim to deliver the whole of the play's dialogue, nevertheless makes eclectic choices from First Folio and Second Quarto texts. Critical comment on the textual decisions made by all film-makers – what to include or exclude, and so on – informed by debate regarding meaning and significance of the original texts, is of course another matter. So, for pragmatic reasons, 'Shakespeare' here refers primarily to the plays commonly attributed to the dramatist, and the 'original' will denote the texts on which the screen versions are based.

As for 'English-speaking', the emphasis here is mainly linguistic, Shakespeare films in other languages being part of a diverse 'world cinema', but it also signifies the very fact of speech in films.[7] Before the advent in the late 1920s of synchronized sound for dialogue, the adaptation of storylines, episodes, and characters bore only limited responsibility for delivering the equivalents for the spoken words of the original texts. Before the talkies came along, moreover, the movies could speak to everyone, because the substitution of title cards in the language of the country where they were shown made films easy to export. *Hamlet*, with Sir Johnston Forbes-Robertson in the title role, released in 1913, was the most notable (surviving) British Shakespearian film of its era, but, as Judith Buchanan argues, has a less sophisticated interpretive agenda than the Italian film with Ruggero Ruggeri released in 1917: the former's origin in the dramatist's own country and the eminence of its principal actor as an exponent of the role in the original language do not guarantee its claim to artistic superiority.[8] The 'silent' cinema – even this term needs some qualification, as films were not watched without accompaniment of music and in some cases sound effects – had its own kinds of eloquence in acting, *mise-en-scène*, and editing, and there was usually little need to render dialogue in the intertitles. Relatively few survive of the total number of films made from Shakespeare's plays between 1899 and 1927, estimated at between 250 and 300. There was considerable variety in kinds of adaptation, from what might be the illustration of episodes in a familiar play (the 1910 *Richard III* with Frank Benson's company), to sophisticated revisionist versions such as *Hamlet, the Tragedy of Vengeance* (1920) in which the great star Asta Nielsen appears as a prince who is really a princess in disguise.[9] Silent films were more vulnerable to revision than talkies during their period of distribution, sometimes at the hands of exhibitors, occasionally by their creators. Among the silent Shakespeare films made after the First World War, the *Othello* made in Germany with American finance in 1922 and directed by Dmitri Buchowetski, seems to exist only in a version some twenty minutes shorter than when it was first shown.[10]

Sound films were not immune from this kind of revision, as the plethora of 'director's cuts' and the inclusion of 'missing scenes' as extras on DVDs attests. Sometimes alterations have been made to satisfy different censorship and certification regimes in the territories where they have been distributed, or the 'final cut' has been the privilege of a studio rather than the director. Mary Pickford, persuaded in the 1950s not to destroy the films she had made in the first decades of the century, had *The Taming of the Shrew* (1929) revised to alter some sequences and even shots, so that a medium or long shot might be rephotographed from the original footage to produce a closer shot on specific characters or action.[11] The fact that this was the first of the Shakespearian talkies, with a silent version provided for showing in cinemas not yet equipped for sound, suggests (as with the 1922 *Othello*) the need for further research on the textual aspects of these films.

This brings us to the third of the terms that need definition: 'cinema'. It has been chosen in preference to 'film' because it represents collectively the various regimes of production, distribution, and consumption within which the films exist and for which they have been conceived. The term also explicitly excludes work made exclusively for television or other video or online viewing. Moreover 'film' is commonly used to denote the medium itself, with an emphasis on its artistic qualities and potential, while the more colloquial 'movies' celebrates the show business and entertainment dimension. Even more dignified than 'film', which is after all the name of the coated celluloid itself, is 'the moving picture', and early attempts to settle on an appropriate term for the finished product included 'photoplay', which suggests kinship and equivalence with the theatrical drama.

In the text and filmography I have followed the convention of referring to films by the name of their director and the year of production. This corresponds to the way in which the various productions are commonly identified. However, the choice begs a number of questions. This is not the place for discussion of *auteur* theory, but some consideration should be given to the ways in which, for example, George Cukor's *Romeo and Juliet* (1936) or Orson Welles *Othello* (1952) reached the screen. At one end of the spectrum is the *Romeo and Juliet* made for Metro-Goldwyn-Mayer (MGM) in 1936. It can be attributed, conventionally, to Cukor as director, but he was a highly skilled artist working within a system that indicated directors in the credits with a degree of prominence that did not always reflect their executive power once the footage left the studio floor. Strictly speaking, the 1936 *Romeo and Juliet* should be thought of as being 'by' its studio, MGM, a so-called 'prestige' product designed to add lustre to the studio's reputation even if it did not do good business at the box office. (It didn't.)

Much of the work of Orson Welles, including his three completed Shakespeare films, represents the other end of the spectrum. Here the director/scriptwriter/actor – a classic 'triple threat' in film business parlance – was unquestionably the *auteur*. His career has even been construed as *'Despite the System'*, the title of a book by Clinton Heylin that describes Welles' struggles after the first fine flush of studio-supported independence represented by *Citizen Kane* (1941).[12] The difficulties encountered in securing finance for *Othello* can stand as symptomatic, albeit to an extreme degree, of the problems still faced by the independent film-maker; Welles had to interrupt the filming several times, going off to act in other people's films to make money to carry on, stopping and starting in a variety of locations, devoting his considerable energies to raising funds as well as to all the other responsibilities he characteristically took on himself. Typically, an independent company will now gather funding from a variety of sources, indicated one after another by their various 'idents' at the start of a film and their presence in the final crawl of credits; will have financed itself by selling distribution rights in advance; and will have had to secure guarantees (a completion bond) to cover these funds, as well as (in most cases with British and other European films) securing the participation of television companies. Canal+, Channel Four Films, the BBC, and other providers will all have their specific requirements, depending on the place the product may have in their own plans for exhibition. Sometimes this has included the framing of significant action within a 'safe' video area within wider-screen formats: in older VHS tapes it was not unusual to be told that a film had been 'reformatted', which usually meant that shots had been 'panned and scanned' to provide alternative angles on participants in dialogue who would otherwise disappear off the sides of the video frame.

Since the 1950s, production in the English-speaking cinema has been affected crucially by a number of factors: the move in Hollywood from production wholly by studios themselves to their participation in (and provision of facilities for) productions originating with agents, stars, and producers who put a package together; the rulings that divorced – with only partial effect – distribution and exhibition from the studios' production activities; the necessity for American studios to spend revenue from the export of their products in the country where it was earned; and the influence of television and various forms of domestic consumption, from videotape to DVD and now to digital streaming.[13] The initial opening in cinemas and the published grosses are now held to contribute more to a movie's reputation and attractiveness, and consequently its profitability in other media, than to the revenues it earns overall.

These factors have had a bearing on the techniques of film-making, notably in recent years and in view of the fact that the word 'film' is an anachronism when applied to work originated and shown by digital means. Meanwhile the cinema – the place of viewing usually designated as 'theatrical' in the trade – has been under threat, with respites in its much-publicized decline achieved either through the use of techniques (such as the various widescreen formats) best appreciated in appropriately equipped auditoria or through the less fathomable factor of the public's enjoyment of a night out. In this connection, it is important not to overlook the fact that the films discussed here were made to be shown in cinemas before an audience who brought their own kind of 'liveness' to the occasion. Such screenings are a very different experience from viewing movies in the home or a seminar room, let alone on a laptop. Quite apart from the size and quality of the image and sound – which may be approximated or even surpassed with HD screens and audio equipment – the social context of 'going to the movies' ought to be kept in mind. Although the films themselves may be the same as they were when they were first exhibited, private viewing of them in the digital age is often as far from that of the cinemas and picture palaces of the 1930s, or even art cinemas of the late twentieth century, as our theatre world is from that of Shakespeare's time.

Putting Shakespeare in his Place

Given the complexity of the contexts denoted by the word 'cinema' we might ask what place Shakespeare – the works rather than the dramatist – has occupied in it. Indeed, we should identify the places in the plural, because Shakespeare has served diverse purposes during the history of the medium. During the first decades of sound and the ascendancy of the major studios, from the 1920s through to the early 1950s, only a handful of Shakespeare films reached production in Hollywood. *The Taming of the Shrew*, directed by Sam Taylor in 1929, was followed by *A Midsummer Night's Dream* (directed by Max Reinhardt for Warner Bros, 1935), *Romeo and Juliet* (Cukor for MGM, 1936), *Macbeth* (Welles for Republic Pictures, 1948), and *Julius Caesar* (Joseph L. Mankiewicz for MGM, 1953). Meanwhile, in the UK, Paul Czinner directed *As You Like It* (Twentieth Century Fox, 1936) and Laurence Olivier followed his *Henry V* (Two Cities/Rank, 1944) with *Hamlet* (Rank, 1948). In 1952 Welles' *Othello* appeared from Mogador Films and Mercury Films, and Renato Castellani directed *Romeo and Juliet* in Italy for 'Verona Productions' in 1954. The names of the producing companies for the last two reflect the new basis for financing, with separate entities created for a specific production – a means of legal and taxation protection for backers – and Castellani's film, distributed in the UK by Rank, was a co-production with a required quota of local

Italian resources and a largely Anglophone cast. Olivier's plans for a *Macbeth*, prepared by him during and after work on his *Richard III* (London Film Productions, 1955), did not find the necessary funding: the financial groundwork already done formed the basis for an unadventurous film directed by George Schaefer (1960) and shown on television in America as part of the 'Hallmark Hall of Fame' series.[14]

After the interruption of its development during the Second World War, television had become widespread between the late 1940s and mid-1950s, more rapidly in the USA than in Great Britain and Europe. The effect of this on the film industry and the Hollywood studios in particular has often been described.[15] An accommodation was soon reached after an initial attempt to ignore the new medium, and the anxious striving to devise technical features (wider screens, 3-D, the more general use of colour, etc.) that would differentiate the movie-going experience from the box in the corner of the room. The more intimate relationship between the domestic medium and theatrical (i.e., cinema) exhibition had begun to develop with Olivier's *Richard III*, shown first on television in the USA but released only to cinemas in the UK. In subsequent decades, similar arrangements were made for Peter Hall's 1968 *A Midsummer Night's Dream* by British Home Entertainment (BHE), the company that produced the films derived from Peter Brook's 1962 *King Lear* for the Royal Shakespeare Company (filmed by the director himself, 1971), and the National Theatre's 1965 *Othello*, directed for the screen by Stuart Burge from John Dexter's theatre production. In the event, a further BHE film from an RSC production, Hall's RSC *Macbeth* (1962), failed to materialize. As for the *Dream*, in the UK it was screened only in cinemas and seems not to have reached the video market in its country of origin: at the time of writing it has been issued in the USA on VHS and subsequently DVD, but in a badly degraded print with poor colour and some jumps in continuity that cannot be explained as part of its claim for kinship with the European *avant-garde*.[16]

Other Shakespeare films of the 1960s and 1970s came from a variety of sources. Franco Zeffirelli's *Taming of the Shrew*, invested in largely by its stars Richard Burton and Elizabeth Taylor (Royal Films, 1967), was successful enough to facilitate his *Romeo and Juliet* (BHE/Dino de Laurentiis, 1968), and Hugh Hefner's Playboy Organisation funded Roman Polanski's *Macbeth* (1971). *The Tempest*, directed by Derek

Jarman (1980), was the first of a package of three projects financed by Channel 4 Films, and is, in many respects, the least countercultural of the director's works. If a pattern can be said to have emerged, it is probably one of wavering faith on the part of investors in Shakespeare as a prospect for success in this expensive medium, resulting in sporadic bursts of activity. The wide distribution of the BBC/Timelife series delivering the complete works in the course of the 1980s may have seemed to confirm the plays as more suitable for television – without theatrical distribution and cinematic production values – but Kenneth Branagh's *Henry V* (Renaissance Films, 1988) prompted a revival in optimism. Branagh's own *Much Ado About Nothing* (1993) was followed in the UK by his *Hamlet* (Castle Rock, 1996) in the 'epic' 70 mm format and offering the 'complete' text of the play, Oliver Parker's *Othello* (Rank/Castle Rock, 1995), and Trevor Nunn's *Twelfth Night* (Renaissance Films, 1995). *Richard III*, directed by Richard Loncraine and inspired by a National Theatre production (United Artists, 1995) and Baz Luhrmann's *William Shakespeare's Romeo+Juliet* (Twentieth Century Fox, 1996) suggested that filmed Shakespeare was once again viable, an impression supported by the reception of Julie Taymor's *Titus* (Fox Searchlight/Clear Blue Sky Productions, 1999) and furthered by the success in the Academy Awards and in global distribution of John Madden's *Shakespeare in Love* (Renaissance/Miramax,1999). In 1999 the Weinstein brothers' Miramax also co-produced Michael Almereyda's *Hamlet*, released and set (as its opening titles proclaim) in 'Manhattan, 2000' and determinedly unlike Branagh's 1996 film in its approach and production values. In the same year Branagh's *Love's Labour's Lost* (also a Miramax co-production, with partial funding from the Arts Council of Great Britain) failed to make much of an impression at the box office. This was the first of three titles announced by the Shakespeare Film Company formed by him and the producer David Barron. (Branagh left Renaissance after *Much Ado*.) The second of the new company's films, *As You Like It* (2006) was a co-production deal with the American cable channel HBO and had a limited theatrical release. Effectively, very brief exposure in cinemas has become the pattern even for such well-received productions as Michael Radford's handsome *Merchant of Venice* (2004). The currency of this and such films as Julie Taymor's *The Tempest* (2011) and Ralph Fiennes' *Coriolanus* (2011) now relies in part on a few television showings (where television money is involved), but mainly on distribution on DVD and internet streaming. Since the 1980s, the technology, picture quality, and size (including aspect ratio) of television screens have changed radically, decreasing the aesthetic distance between films watched in the cinema and at home.[17]

This summary, brief as it is, does reflect the fact that, relative to the total output of the various producers, there have not been many Shakespeare films in the English-speaking cinema. The inclusion of work outside the mainstream commercial industry, until recently the gatekeeper for distribution and availability, would add a few titles, but would not make a significant increase in the total number of films made and distributed since the 1930s. David Bradley's remarkable amateur *Julius Caesar* (USA, 1951) has been released on DVD, but there have been few opportunities to see Liz White's *Othello*, with an all-black cast (USA, 1980).[18] Had they been made in the past decade, they would undoubtedly have been generated on video and distributed via the internet: in the case of White's film, the scarcity of prints and fragility of the celluloid medium have (to date) kept it from a wider public.

In the present context, it is not possible to do more than indicate sketchily the complex world of film finance and production, in particular the part played by the relationship between independent ('indie') film-makers and companies specializing in the adoption of their product, either as independent entities in themselves or as designated wings of a parent company.[19] A general point can be made: financial dependence, even partial, has always brought with it responsibilities that are likely to affect the aesthetic and other choices made by the makers of films. In one respect, this can be seen to sanctify the maverick (such as Welles), but it also complicates the ways in which creative teams work and the kind of attention we pay to their products. Absolute independence and the integrity of authorship, justly valued by artists themselves, also support auteurist critical interpretations that identify kinship and thematic consistency across a range of films and side with (usually) the director in what is assumed to be a struggle for artistic control. But such control, even when it is achieved, is not the be-all and end-all of the bargaining process. Rather, this is a negotiation in which the director and the sources of the finance identify common ground: producers and financiers can also be imaginative and creative, with equal access to the quality identified as 'vision'. Orson Welles 'versus the system' is a romantic and largely true story, but it has not been the master narrative of all worthwhile or innovative film-making.

Crafting the Product

This account of Shakespearian films made for the English-speaking cinema may seem remote from the values that most viewers of the finished product are concerned with, which one might describe as the uses that are made of the plays. This last consideration lurks behind much of our response to a new film of, say, *Hamlet* or *Macbeth*. In fact, it may be one of the pleasures, guilty or otherwise, of discussing them. We enjoy discerning what has been added or taken away, and find the manner in which scripts have been manufactured as intriguing as other elements of the entertainment – the performances, décor, and so on. Douglas Lanier, in a discussion of 'unfaithful' adaptations of Shakespeare in pop culture, suggests that 'since popular culture privileges relevance and use-value over faithfulness to the Shakespearian text, Shakespop adaptations typically value interplay between pop conventions and the Shakespearian source, not passive reproduction of the Shakespearian text'.[20] Although Lanier is describing work that has no pretension to reproduce an original, and may merely allude to it or draw on elements of it – one of his examples, the science-fiction film *Forbidden Planet* (1956), is discussed in Chapter 6 – it is arguable that, with some adjustment of scale, the same might be said of the ways in which we enjoy films that do make such a claim. Peter Greenaway's *Prospero's Books* (1991), in which most of the dialogue – almost complete – is spoken by John Gielgud, is unique as a radical adaptation with what might be thought a slavish regard for its original's text. On the other hand, for an audience member to sit through any live performance with a copy of the play's text in hand is a deservedly thankless undertaking. Moreover, the 'text' of a play should be identified not only in the stricter sense of the words on the printed page, but also as the dramatic event realized when it is performed. The latter is so variable, and has shifted so much in techniques and their significance since the period of the play's first appearance, that no single approach can be regarded as authentic or authoritative. In any case, it is rare for a theatrical production to use every word of a play, and a long (and honourable) history of adaptation in the theatre has encompassed degrees of adaptation from simple adjustments of action and abbreviation of dialogue to wholesale reworkings, from those of the newly reopened theatres after 1660 to no less radical treatments by postmodernist directors.

Nevertheless, from the screenwriter's point of view, the immediate problem remains: how does a play of three to four thousand lines become a two-hour script for an entertainment that privileges images over language and can provide both greater intimacy and a grander scale than most stage performances? In general, the apparent proximity of theatre to film – the action is performed rather than narrated – is as much an embarrassment as an advantage, a relationship that has to be negotiated carefully and an influence that can be a source of anxiety. From the actor's point of view, the camera's ability to see their eyes makes for the most important distinction between stage and screen performance, but the same investment of imagination and emotional commitment underlies work in both media. Given that every author of a 'how to' book on writing for the cinema tells the reader to think in images, and warns that verbal eloquence – or even the mere quantity of dialogue — is a commodity to be used warily, how can Shakespeare's rhetorically organized and expressive theatrical text serve the film-maker's turn? The advent of sound suddenly brought with it responsibilities that some theorists and cineastes regarded as irrelevant to the 'art of the film'. Apart from questions of acting technique and vocal delivery – it was not long before subtler sound recording techniques reached the studios – the decision still had to be made as to which words from the plays should be selected in a script.[21]

One simple working assumption might seem to be that pictures would do the work of descriptive speeches, but giving an account of action not shown on stage is not merely a matter of efficient reportage: the manner in which the description is framed and the language in which it is expressed may also be important. Within dialogue, the development of a metaphor or a simile – or a series of similes – may invite cutting in the interests of efficiency, but (as in the preparing of acting versions for the stage) necessary questions of the play may be identifiable with this kind of elaboration, including characterization. Occasionally unusual or archaic words are altered for the sake of clarity – Olivier's *Hamlet* is a case in point – and familial and other relationships may be rendered by some more specific substitute for such words as 'coz'. Joss Whedon, in his contemporary and domestic *Much Ado About Nothing* (2013) leaves archaic language intact, presumably because the language is in general more patterned and elaborate than its modern equivalents, and there is no point in trying to apologize for the effect. Olivier's use of the Globe Theatre sequences at the beginning of his *Henry V* was in great part a consequence of his anxiety about creating a language barrier between his audience and the film. (The backstage dimension also helped, generating a sense of excitement and anticipation within the film that might convey itself to the cinema audience.)

Stanley Cavell, in his influential *Pursuits of Happiness* (1981), proposes a link between Shakespearian comedy and the brilliant 'comedies of remarriage' and singles out in the 'golden age' of the 1930s and 1940s, such as *His Girl Friday* (Howard Hawks, 1940) and *The Lady Eve* (Preston Sturges, 1941). Perhaps for the versions of *Much Ado* and *As You Like It*, the effect of smart talk among sophisticated people is close enough to some Hollywood comedy – especially from the 1930s – for the dialogue to be accepted as normal in its milieu, although Sarah Kozloff, in *Overhearing Film Dialogue*, points out that the immediate models for the styles of speech come from modern stage comedy, including Noël Coward, rather than Shakespeare. The repartee in *Bringing up Baby* (Howard Hawks, 1938) or *The Thin Man* (Hunt Stromberg, 1938) is often witty through smart delivery, pace, and rhythm rather than any sophistication in the statements being made by each participant, and the scripts use overlapping and interruptions, techniques of 'realism', to an extent beyond any equivalents in the Shakespearian texts.[22]

Film scripts often reorder scenes and sequences, shuffling elements of them so that they can seem to take place at the same time in different places – a privilege dear to the writers of screenplays. Thus, in his *Taming of the Shrew*, Zeffirelli splices parts of the storyline of Bianca and her suitors into the forward-moving narrative concerning Katherine and Petruchio; Almereyda and Zeffirelli both do without the first scene of *Hamlet*; Orson Welles moves freely (and often effectively) among the materials provided for him in the plays he adapts; Derek Jarman redistributes sections of Prospero's long speech of exposition in the second scene of *The Tempest*; and Richard Loncraine and Ian

McKellen divide the famous opening speech of *Richard III* between two distinct places: a ballroom and a gents' lavatory.

Apart from such wholesale revisions as those in Welles' films, where a radical cutting and reordering of action and dialogue serves a larger aesthetic purpose, most rearrangements of this kind are made in order to maintain the momentum of the film, whether the adapter is concerned about 'beats' in the manner of some schools of thought or governed by the kind of concern with the division into 'acts' that shapes screenplays in a quasi-Aristotelian manner. The *Poetics* have made regular appearances in books on screenwriting. An early example is Victor Oscar Freeburg's *The Art of the Photoplay* (1918), where the three-act structure of beginning, middle, and end is commended: 'no plot maker can say that he has a plot until he has arranged his characters and actions firmly into that framework, thus organising all his parts into that unity'.[23] A recent tribute to the practicality of the Athenian's advice is Michael Tierno's *Aristotle's 'Poetics' for Screenwriters* (2002), and Joseph McBride, in *Writing in Pictures* (2012), identifies the *Poetics* as 'the earliest how-to book on screenwriting'.[24] Apart from the tendency to prize this formal organization, the desire for a kind of character development (or trajectory) specific to a cinematic genre, especially in its resolution and the sequences leading up to it, sometimes motivates revision of the play's structure, and also requires in comedies the confirmation of endings unqualified by the kind of shadow Shakespeare likes to cast by leaving a character slightly aside from the general rejoicing: *Love's Labour's Lost*, for which Branagh's film provides a happy conclusion quite different from the final moments of the original, is probably the most remarkable example of this problem. It is notable that, at least to date, no major feature film of *All's Well That Ends Well*, *Measure for Measure*, or *Troilus and Cressida* has appeared (or at least achieved wide distribution), and that no one has tackled the less qualified optimism but looser plotting of *Pericles*, and *The Winter's Tale*.

The history plays may be thought to require knowledge of events beyond and before their narrative: in a film version any exposition within the play itself usually needs to supply such additional information to an extent uncommon in the theatre. This is not so much an assumption that theatre audiences are better informed or more intelligent, as an acknowledgement of the need for a film to be a self-contained narrative, intelligible in itself with perhaps a certain amount of prompting in the shape of preliminary titles. But any significant action needs to be shown rather than described, much as off-screen events should be witnessed by us rather than narrated by on-screen characters or a narrator. Thus, Welles introduces *Chimes at Midnight* (1964) with a voice-over narration from Holinshed, and Olivier opens *Richard III* with a scene confirming Edward III's place on the throne and identifying important characters, and then adds lines from 3 *Henry VI* to Richard's first soliloquy, which conveniently fulfils the office of a prologue in the play itself. Branagh, like Olivier, retains the Chorus in his *Henry V*, although unlike Olivier he includes flashbacks to make clear the significance of Henry's youthful relationship with Falstaff, borrowing lines from 2 *Henry IV* and even allowed himself a moment when Falstaff (Robbie Coltrane) tells his young friend 'We have heard the chimes at midnight, Master Harry'.[25] Juxtapositions of action taking place in different time frames – or simultaneously in different places – are a privilege of the medium that can also have the force of a responsibility. Both directors allow themselves an illustration of the death of Falstaff. Showing tableaux or silent action of this kind has its perils. In his *Hamlet* (1996), Branagh includes plenty of flashbacks and illustrations – too many for the taste of some critics – and originally scripted more, but (unlike Olivier and Zeffirelli) he decided not to show the death of Ophelia, leaving the screen to Julie Christie's Gertrude. (Oddly enough, at such moments, when a flashback has no dialogue or diegetic sound we are suddenly in the world of the silent film, where action was eloquence.)

* * * * * * * * * * *

The word 'original', discussed briefly above, is used here and throughout the following chapters as a convenient synonym for 'the play this film starts from'. It should not be taken as an indication that there is a hierarchy in which the play *Romeo and Juliet* is an ideal to be venerated or at least handled with extreme care at the expense of imaginative creativity. On the contrary, the arrangement of chapters that follow reflects a conviction that the transgressive, playful dimension of films that profit from Shakespeare – that go 'Beyond Shakespeare' in the title of the sixth chapter – is to be valued and celebrated. The spirit of the enquiry is to understand how the new work is functioning, and how its makers are negotiating the terms of their engagement with the exciting combinations of techniques and opportunities designated by both 'Shakespeare' and 'film'. At the end of *The Maltese Falcon* (John Huston, 1941), a police detective weighs the falcon in his hands and is told by Sam Spade (Humphrey Bogart) that it is 'the stuff dreams are made of [*sic*]', a line not in Dashiel Hammett's novel; James Bond (Daniel Craig), confronted in *Skyfall* (Sam Mendes, 2012) with the latest innovation supplied by the new 'Q' (Ben Whishaw), responds with 'Brave new world'; Shakespeare himself (Joseph Fiennes), walking down the street in *Shakespeare in Love* (John Madden, 1999), makes a mental note of a preacher calling down 'a plague on both your play houses'. From the briefest allusion to full-scale versions and appropriations of the plays, the cinema's engagement with Shakespeare has been varied and exciting.

1

Places

Setting the location of a film, in terms of period as well as physical surroundings, is a major priority in the cinema's treatment of any pre-existing text, but with Shakespeare's plays the distance between the means at the film-maker's disposal and those of the theatre of the dramatist's time make the choices especially significant. The decision to film on location or on studio sound stages (or even a back lot), as well as more general design strategies, will 'read' as part of the audience's perception of the finished product, sometimes complementing, sometimes deliberately or inadvertently at variance with signals sent out by the dialogue itself (and consequently calling for alterations to achieve consistency or, rarely and more radically, point up dislocation between word and image). Woodlands and forests are an appropriate starting point for a discussion of the ways in which film-makers have supplied settings for plays written for an open stage in which location was established by word of mouth ('So this is the forest of Arden'), the re-identification of a feature of the stage's architecture (as a box-tree or a bush), or a few appropriate props. Just as a bush, in the imagination of apprehensive, night-bound lovers within the play, might easily be supposed a bear, the stage-posts of the Globe could be accepted as trees with no great imaginative leap on the audience's part. Paradoxically, film, as well as its ability to render convincing images of natural environments, also offers opportunities for making even 'actual' woodlands strange, charged with atmosphere, and pleasingly self-conscious in their artifice. In the first decades of the twentieth century the cinema often seemed bent on improving on nature by challenging comparison not so much with Shakespeare's theatre as that of the nineteenth century.

In the plays, woods and forests can be a place of liberation and contact with the essential values of a life that has none of the responsibilities and hazards of the court. For those who have been obliged, like the exiled Duke in *As You Like It*, to 'throw into neglect the pompous court' and have the imagination to perceive the benefits of the new life, they furnish opportunities for moralizing and hunting, comfortable so long as there is appropriate shelter from the winter wind. Woods may also be a place of magic, the alleged domicile of magicians, old religious men (such as the one who converts the usurping Duke Frederick), or, in *A Midsummer Night's Dream*, fairies – and high-ranking ones at that. They may also harbour dangers: snakes and lions in the Forest of Arden and the possibility of 'the loose encounters of lascivious men', and (in the event) outlaws in *The Two Gentlemen of Verona*. In *Titus Andronicus*, the woods afford opportunities for the murder of Bassianus and the rape and mutilation of Lavinia. It is easy to get lost among the trees and undergrowth, as the lovers and Bottom do, or to be misled there by mischief or villainy. If, as in *Dream*, we are to believe that 'night and silence' prevail, the effect of such confusions is intensified, though moonlight will provide at least fitful illumination. In the less exotic daylight world of Arden, sheep-farming is the dominant rural industry, with deer available as the occasion of sport and source of victuals for aristocratic hunters. Many stage productions have marked the transition from winter to spring that seems to be indicated by the text, taking their cues from the campfire song 'Blow, blow, thou winter wind' in the final scene of 2.7, and the references to the springtime in 'It was a lover and his lass' in 5.3.

Cinematic realizations of the wood in *A Midsummer Night's Dream* have ranged from the claustrophobia of studio-built sets to the open air location filming of Peter Hall (1969). Standing apart from these is Adrian Noble's 1996 adaptation, which carries over the surrealistic, non-representational scenic style of his RSC stage production for interior and exterior scenes. In Max Reinhardt's spectacular film for Warner Bros. (1935), the most extensively laid out and elaborate of studio forests is introduced with brief location shots, and we see real parkland when Theseus and Hippolyta arrive at the edge of the wood and meet the bemused lovers. The film returns to the studio set for Bottom's awakening. Michael Hoffmann (1999), whose magic woodland resembles that of the 1935 film, but on a smaller scale, situates this liminal space – the nearest the mortal court gets to the magic realm – securely in the Tuscan countryside. Reinhardt's forest has some notable antecedents in theatre and film design, including his own successive productions of the play on stage and outdoors, and Puck (Mickey Rooney) rides what can only be described as a Shetland unicorn through towering tree trunks and shafts of light that recall Siegfried riding through the forest in Fritz Lang's *Die Nibelungen* (1926). Erich Wolfgang Korngold's score, adapting Mendelssohn's works, mainly but by no means exclusively his incidental music for the play, accompanies 116 of the film's 140 minutes, contributing to the effect that Daniel Albright has identified when he comments that 'the movie fascinates in that it represents a limit in the perverse evolution of *A Midsummer Night's Dream* toward masque'.[1] Hoffmann's imagery is more directly indebted to painting, specifically to Gustave Moreau and other symbolists and to J.W. Waterhouse's Victorian painting of alluring water nymphs. Christine Edzard's indoor forest for *The Children's Midsummer Night's Dream* (2001) is part of a general scheme of self-conscious artifice that reminds viewers – not that they need it – that they are watching a play performed by children, an additional layer of artificiality complemented by the ersatz foliage. Peter Hall, filming in and around the Warwickshire mansion of Compton Verney (then in a state of semi-decay), places his all but naked immortals in real woods and undergrowth, rendered magical by lighting and the use of coloured filters and trick shots.

Between them, the three feature films of *As You Like It* similarly encompass studio artifice (Paul Czinner, 1936), genuine woodland (Kenneth Branagh, 2006), and an urban wasteland (Christine Edzard, 1992). Czinner resembles Reinhardt in the creation of a version of the natural world that seems only marginally distinct from the fairy-tale castle inhabited by the court. During the wrestling, a throng of spectators – evidently peasants — presses against the gate of the usurper's domain, and it is through these that Orlando makes his way when he is dismissed. The exiled Duke seems to have camped out in the ruins of a castle or palace, with a gateway that separates it from the woodland: rejoicing country folk, preceded by a flock of sheep, will rush through it to celebrate the impending weddings and reconciliations.

In Branagh's *As You Like It* the forest scenes are filmed in a genuine woodland, dressed more or less plausibly as a 'Japanese' landscape. This complements the convincing interiors of the palace inhabited by Duke Senior, a European enthusiast for the more peaceful aesthetic pursuits of the country where he has settled, but where he is vulnerable to his usurping brother, who has cultivated the martial arts. The film hopes that audiences will go along with its 'dream of old Japan', but the epilogue, set in the unit's base camp, with Bryce Dallas Howard appearing now as herself rather than as Rosalind, does not break the illusion of the imagined Japan so much as that of the film as a whole. Edzard's refugees have fled from the corporate world (cold, soulless office architecture) to the inhospitable landscape of a vacant lot in London's as yet undeveloped docklands, where traffic noise and passing aircraft can be heard. Comfort is provided by a bivouac resembling those of the homeless, Audrey runs a snack bar from a caravan, deer are nowhere to be seen, and the sheep population is limited to one. This lonely animal contrasts with the dozen or so in Branagh's Arden and the considerable flocks that inhabit Czinner's, a film crowded with tame beasts, including ducks, chickens, geese, swans, a cow and a calf, rabbits, a stork, hunting dogs, and (in two shots) an Old English Sheepdog.

A Midsummer Night's Dream progresses from the palace, via the workmen's premises, to the woods, and *As You Like It* begins in an orchard, and reaches Arden after scenes in a palace. Designers are called on to provide some elements of the built environment, though the tendency in most of the films has been to achieve a degree of self-conscious artifice in realizing the woodlands. *The Tempest* would seem not to make any architectural demands, but two films – that directed by Derek Jarman (1980), and Peter Greenaway's *Prospero's Books* (1991) – place the principal action indoors, while a third, Julie Taymor's (2011), creates an elaborate 'cell' for the mage and produces a palace for the flashback illustrating the events that led to exile. Jarman has blue-tinted exterior sequences, including the emergence of the naked Ferdinand from the sea, but most of his *Tempest* is situated in a dilapidated mansion (the Georgian wing of Stoneleigh Abbey in Warwickshire, since restored) reminiscent of the 'old dark house' of gothic fiction and film. In one room, Caliban brings logs in a wheelbarrow across a floor carpeted with loam, and in another, its panelled walls decorated with cabbalistic signs, Prospero has drawn a magic circle on the bare boards of the floor. The house seems to have been 'occupied' as if by squatters, and commandeered by a wizard and his daughter, with the old retainer

(Caliban) kept on as a servant. Sycorax appears in a flashback as a grotesque maternal figure suckling her full-grown son, and Ariel wears white overalls resembling those of a garage mechanic. Transformation has taken place, so that the 'island' (represented by the dunes outside) has been made to invade the house. Jarman wrote that he 'needed an island of the mind, that opened mysteriously like Chinese boxes: an abstract landscape so that the delicate description in the poetry, full of sounds and sweet airs, would not be destroyed by any Martini lagoons', by which he meant the glamorously idyllic settings associated with the then current television advertising for the brand of vermouth.[2] As Pascale Aebischer observes, the film 'invoke[s] the trappings of period drama in order to dismantle them before our eyes'.[3]

The improvised nature of the setting with skimpily re-dressed rooms and flickering fire- or candle-light, parallels Jarman's own production values, as though Prospero and the director shared the same resources and goals. Yolanda Sonnabend, the costume designer, recalled the atmosphere of the filming: 'Like the dream of *The Tempest*, work and life were suspended. Derek, our Prospero, pulling the threads together, making us all willing conspirators in his vision. Some celestial harmony breathed on us for a while'.[4] The costuming and make-up of Heathcote Williams as Prospero and Toyah Willcox as Miranda would have passed as only mildly outré in the alternative lifestyles of the film's own time. Specifically, though, Miranda, Ferdinand, and the court appear to be from the *ancien régime*, while Prospero's costume is modelled on images of Robespierre; Caliban and Ariel seem to be nineteenth-century workmen. In his study of the director's films, William Pencak points out that 'Jarman makes sure that the clothes, thoughts and behaviour of each character suit an important group of people in modern history', so that the film's ninety minutes 'give us a whirlwind tour of Western civilisation since the Renaissance'.[5]

On Julie Taymor's island, her regendered Prospera (Helen Mirren), aided by an Ariel (Ben Whishaw) whose flittings sometimes resemble those of Disney's Tinkerbell, rules a domain achieved by using an exotic location – a Hawaiian island – enhanced by lavish manipulations of imagery through technical trickery, blue screens, and (for Caliban) elaborate make-up. Taymor has explained that here, as in her *Titus*, 'location is metaphor and represents the essence of the scene in a visual ideograph'.[6] One almost expects Prospera's cell to include an editing suite. *Prospero's Books*, in which (as was noted in the Introduction) most of the dialogue is spoken on- or off-screen by John Gielgud, confines the action of the play to an elaborate indoor set, a series of rooms in which tableaux appear that correspond to the leaves of the books in Prospero's library, and are responsive to the tome in which he is writing the play as he thinks and speaks it. Although it is an extreme example of self-reflective cinema, comparable with the surrealist avant-garde or Jean Cocteau's fantasies in *Orphée* and *La Belle et la bête*, Greenaway's film shares the approach of Jarman and Taymor in so far as all three directors have seen their chances and taken them in a play even more dominated by the supernatural than *A Midsummer Night's Dream*. In this they are following the playwright's lead, aligning the exercise of their own art with that of the illusionist within the play. Nevertheless, their approaches are distinguished by appeals to distinct cinematic genres: Jarman's to the alternative avant-garde of the 1970s and 1980s; Taymor's to the computer-enabled second worlds of contemporary fantasy; and Greenaway's to a tradition of art film that challenges the other graphic media and situates itself in relation to their heritage of images.

The 'magic' (or 'magicked') worlds of these *Tempest* films are of a different order from the artificial or adjusted environments created for most of the other Shakespeare films, including the versions of *A Midsummer Night's Dream* in which the mortals inhabit an Italian town and an adjacent villa (Hoffmann) or an English country house (Hall). But even these are of course more than the locations as found by the location scouts. They have been dressed, sometimes with additions to their architecture or the masking of inappropriate street furniture or other features, and they have become – as film crews will always refer to them – 'the set', a prepared environment which will be taken over by actors with their costumes and props and altered further by lighting, camerawork, and editing.

Royal or ducal courts, remote from the everyday experience of the majority of audiences but familiar in media representations (including the plays on stage), offer their own opportunities and challenges. Perhaps more acutely than other settings, these directly affect decisions about period, the etiquette of deference and ritual, and the consequences for character and action. Versions of the history plays encompass stylized evocations of medieval art (Olivier's 1944 *Henry V* and 1955 *Richard III*), studio-built naturalistic sets (Branagh's *Henry V*, 1989), atmospheric use of 'found' architecture (Welles' *Chimes at Midnight*, 1964), and carefully fabricated constructions of a 'parallel history' for the twentieth century (Loncraine and McKellen's *Richard III*, 1995). It would be relatively straightforward to devise appropriate behaviour within the first two of these environments: actors and audiences are familiar with the court's rules for approaching a royal presence and responding to the monarch and each other within the court's purlieus, and gestures of obeisance and other details are easily recognized.

The first court scenes in Olivier's *Henry V* are played in the Globe, with stylized gesture and vocal delivery congruent with a reconstruction of Elizabethan performance practices. This distances the action and 'naturalizes' the archaic language for the cinema audience, while preparing the way for the even more stylized settings of the central portions of the film. The duke himself is seen, reading this very manuscript; see Figure 1.1. The delicate architecture of the French court scenes, with their foreshortened perspectives and subtle colours, derives from the illustrations to the Duc de Berri's *Très riches heures*. Throughout the

Figure 1.1. *Henry V* (Laurence Olivier, 1944): the French court – the King (Harcourt Williams) and the Dauphin (Max Adrian, to his left) receive Henry's message from Exeter (Nicholas Hannen, second from left).

film, even in these 'medieval' central scenes, stylized gesture takes second place to naturalism, although Olivier as Henry carries over some of the physical language (the raised arm and hand, admonishing or urging action) from the 'Globe' scenes. The fairy-tale connotations of the French palaces put the main narrative at a safe remove from contemporary events, with images of an idealized France that even the battle of Agincourt, played out in bright sunshine in beautiful (Irish) countryside, does not compromise. With the exception of the arguments of the English common soldiers on the eve of the battle, and a brief glimpse of corpses on the field of battle, war is never allowed to be grim-visaged. So far as the courts themselves are concerned, the English one is seen only as represented at the Globe, while the French is either the stylized 'medieval' image or the tableau at the theatre to which the play's concluding lines return. In this last sequence, Katherine (Renée Asherson) is transformed to a boy player, perhaps the one seen backstage in an early scene stuffing an orange down his bodice in preparation for his entrance in the play. The tableau itself, with Henry and his Queen in the centre and courtiers kneeling at either side in stiff attitudes of prayer, suggests Tudor monumental sculpture rather than any of the medieval models, and it presents fleetingly yet another visual register. Olivier's sophisticated, multilayered film takes its leave of courtly, 'period' behaviour as it returns its audience by degrees to their own time by way of another shot of the London model.

The significance of this idealization in wartime is manifest, although Olivier's *Henry V* should not be pigeon-holed as simple propaganda. In his *Richard III* the evocation of medieval art is less pronounced, although it inspires a major element of its design: an extensive composite set of an open space in the London streets, a suite of ceremonial halls, and a royal presence chamber. (The Tower of London seems to be no more than a step away from Westminster, a geographically unsound but thematically appropriate arrangement.) Now the stylization comes not so much from the imitation of supposedly medieval patterns of behaviour – though the court ceremonial is simple and effective – but from the sense of the camera as a participant and privileged observer in the action, with long takes covering the interpolated opening scene (with dialogue from 3 *Henry VI*) showing the confirmation of Edward III on his throne, and subsequently following Richard from the door of the now empty presence chamber, into the adjacent room and then back again as he confides his plans. At one point he beckons the camera to come nearer to him, and even seems to take its (that is, our) arm as his confidences grow more specific and intense. This self-consciousness, a cinematic equivalent of the button-holing soliloquy, is of a different order from that of Olivier's *Henry V*. In his *Richard III* the patterning of the action seems more relaxed, less insistent, until we arrive at the coronation of Richard himself, a chilling ritual in which the declarations of good fellowship of the kind made among Edward III and his peers are not possible. The scenic space is used differently, with Richard's throne on a high dais, and the emptiness of the new king's claims for loyalty reflected in the more sparsely attended court – any peer who can will have headed back to his shire.

Branagh's *Henry V*, released four and half decades after Olivier's, has a very different approach to human relationships and kingly character than its famous predecessor, to be discussed in the next chapter. In the present context, the qualified medievalism of its costume and set designs should be noted. Olivier's courtiers and warriors advanced from doublet and hose to (medieval) tights and jerkins, and then to armour, with his own superbly elegant figure representing in the final wooing scenes an idealized male form corresponding both to the fashion of the 1480s and the conventional appearance of the *danseur noble* in classical ballet. Branagh and his companions wear jerkins, breeches, and boots, and in battle are definitely warriors for the working day. The English and French courts occupy simple halls, with little decoration: the French court was in fact the same set as the English, more brightly lit and repainted. There is a dark private room for the clergy to connive in, and Katherine has a light, airy chamber decorated with bird cages and a bed with filmy curtains. The inn scenes, including those in the flashbacks recalling happier days with Falstaff, are set in nondescript, drab timbered rooms. In this film, the self-conscious element is provided by Derek Jacobi's chorus, conceived as a 'timeless' war correspondent striding through the battlefield as occasion demands. His prologue is spoken 'behind the scenes' on the sound stage that holds the palace set, whose doors he flings open with 'kindly to hear – our PLAY!' before the screen is plunged into the obscurity from which Canterbury and York will be found conspiring. This relatively low-budget film (some $8 million) has no expansive establishing shots of the French or English courts, the tavern, or any of its other locations: the walls of Harfleur are impressive enough, but until the final travelling shot after the battle there is no impression of the whole of the field of Agincourt, and to some critics it has seemed to be scaled specifically for television rather than the cinema.[7] This is a distinctly intimate, un-epic view of its historical subject.

In *Chimes at Midnight* Orson Welles sets the chilly court of Henry Bolingbroke, staged in the gloomy, high-arched spaces of a monastery church, against the warm, hospitable world of Eastcheap, the 'Merrie England' that Falstaff embodies and that Hal, becoming Henry V, must forswear. The barn-like set for the tavern combines nooks and crannies – the latter scarcely able to accommodate Falstaff's bulk — with a large central space with galleries from which customers and assorted wenches can enjoy the sport going on below. (Compare the warm fireside of the tavern in Branagh's *Henry V*, far more convincing as a good place to be.) The post-synchronized dialogue and sound effects, the Spanish locations, and the fact that most of the sets resemble nothing commonly associated with medieval England, contribute here to the kind of estrangement found in most of Welles' other films, a reminder that every aspect of the work has been devised and constructed, from the world the actors move in to the sound of their voices and their spatial relationships.

This dimension of the Wellesian/Shakespearian universe will be discussed in the next chapter, within reference to his *Macbeth* (1948) and *Othello* (1952). For present purposes we should note only that in *Othello* and, to an extent, *Chimes at Midnight*, Welles sometimes seems to be achieving his artistic effects despite rather than through the patched-together surroundings he is able to provide for his actors. Inspirations such as the use of the walls of the fortress or the scene in the bath-house in *Othello*, supported by virtuoso camera placement and editing, prevail over a few awkward moments where the director was obliged to film the two sides of a conversation on different days or even in different locations. In *Macbeth* the studio-built set used for most of the action contributes to a film whose unity of effect is forceful, for all the shortcomings of performances and speech. In *Chimes* the battle of Shrewsbury was staged on a windy plain in Spain, but the ferocity of the combat, with armies battering each other to a muddy pulp, makes any incongruity of location a minor consideration. By contrast, Olivier's Bosworth Field, woefully undermanned and fought in a park near Madrid, disappoints because the sudden access to a real location that is inadequate breaks the unity of a film whose other settings are stylized.

History plays have been thought to call for recreations of the medieval world, with the notable exception of the Loncraine/McKellen *Richard III*, set in 1930s England with Richard and his faction as an alternative version of Sir Oswald Mosley and his British Union of Fascists. Mosley's career as a would-be leader of a fascist state ended in failure, imprisonment during the duration of the Second World War, and subsequently what might be called a notorious obscurity. Here Richard and his Blackshirts enjoy a temporary success story, in so far as he becomes king by a distortion of the democratic process – an uneasy fit with the politics of the play, supported only by the equivalent of Richard's deception of the Lord Mayor of London. The society represented, with the Victorian Gothic St Pancras station hotel standing in, aptly enough, for the royal palace, owes as much to the genre of 'heritage' film and television as to any specific historical circumstances. In contrast to the palace and the country house that suggest the home life of the house of Windsor, hard political reality is represented by the art deco monumentalism of locations that evoke the *Reichskanzlerei* in Berlin. Court behaviour is a more formal and decorous version of well-mannered society, and the new, brutal political order is marked by militarism, insignia indicating party membership (the boar), and the red–black–white colour scheme of Nazi banners. For all its bravura, the battle sequence is short-circuited by our sense of the distance between what really happened in the 1930s and the decisive victory of Richmond, aided now by the loyalist elements in the military and the Royal Air Force. (Lord Stanley is an air vice-marshal). The film's impact is undermined by the medium's pull towards completeness of period in design, so that what in the National Theatre stage production (1990) had been a stimulating analogy for action and characters in an Elizabethan version of an earlier generation's politics, now becomes incongruous. The revitalizing effect that such a shift can have in stage productions is harder to achieve in the conventions of absolute realism within which this and most other Shakespeare films have worked. In the theatre costume and setting are necessarily metonymic, with the part to be read for the whole, and the work of the imagination is already being performed consciously by the audience. However, in the conventionally realistic cinema the overriding impulse is to accept that access has been granted to the whole of the available 'reality', so that the sense of its being made is set aside and, as it were, the quotation marks I have just placed around the term have faded away.

Although television has had its way, often more than once, with all the available history plays, the cinema has so far been limited to *Henry V*, the Hal–Falstaff material, and *Richard III*. England, 'merrie' or otherwise, has been represented only by these or in the relocation of other plays to English period settings (Trevor Nunn's *Twelfth Night*, 1996, with Cornwall as Illyria) or to sardonic commentary on modern life (Edzard's *As You Like It*). Italy, by contrast, has been the subject of many scenic variations. Three films of *Romeo and Juliet* have either reconstructed their Verona in the studio (George Cukor in 1936 and Franco Zeffirelli in 1968) or found 'genuine' locations in one or more cities (Renato Castellani, 1954), while the real Venice has appeared in two versions of *Othello* (Oliver Parker, 1995 and Orson Welles, 1952) and one *Merchant of Venice* (Michael Radford, 2004). Here Belmont appears at first to be some distance from Venice itself, although in the scenes in which Bassanio and his companions set off to pay Antonio's debt and forestall the trial, the location seems to be close enough for a view of the ducal palace from across the Grand Canal. The Venetian scenes are predominantly dark, with handsome chiaroscuro effects in the interiors, whilst Belmont is a place of light, responding to the play's dichotomy of potential tragedy and somewhat fragile comedy. The final act's scene of explanation among the Christian husbands and their wives takes place in a salon flooded with bluish light, gradually invaded by the sounds of the dawn chorus and the coming of day – specified in the dialogue as two hours away (5.1.303). Before she and Bassanio leave for their bed, Portia stands with her back to a window, facing the camera and the rest of the company and figured as a source of light. Kenneth Branagh's *Much Ado About Nothing* ignores the play's location in the Sicilian city of Messina, shifting its ground north to a Tuscan villa and its estate, and choosing as its period a transitional stage between the eighteenth and nineteenth centuries. Any sense of urban life is absent, and Dogberry and the watch become the constabulary (one assumes) of the local village. Accused by some of encouraging its audiences to ignore the play's darker aspects by its location in a modified version of a favourite middle-class holiday destination known in Britain as 'Chiantishire', Branagh's film does create a world in which the action can be played out with minimal but credible support from its material surroundings.

Padua is represented in the 1929 Fairbanks/Pickford film of *The Taming of the Shrew* and in Zeffirelli's 1967 version. The earlier film has handsome sets by Laurence Irving and William Cameron Menzies, notable for the interiors of Baptista's and Petruchio's houses, the church and the square outside it, and a street shown in the opening sequence. Zeffirelli had his Padua built in Dino de Laurentiis's new studio in Rome, in the kind of studio realism that draws attention to its artifice, and framed the story with a credit sequence in which Petruchio, making his way towards Padua, is first seen as an image in a sepia tapestry that comes to life as the film begins. The director's visual taste, as Graham Holderness points out, is for 'historical realism, framed always by the pervasive influences of visual art' that results in a 'a colourful and chaotic genre painting which could be galvanised into vitality by the nervous mobility and fluidity of *cinéma-vérité* camerawork'.[8] The lavish and elegant sets for Verona in Cukor's MGM *Romeo and Juliet* locate the drama in an ideal Renaissance city, while Castellani achieves a picturesque equivalent of Italian neorealism using a number of Italian city locations and Zeffirelli suggests the dusty, boisterous, and hot-tempered life of young men with nothing much to do except look for trouble in the piazza – a colourful and romanticized equivalent of the street realism in such films as Federico Fellini's *I Vitelloni* (1953). The domestic interiors of Castellani's and Zeffirelli's Veronese households, prepared with similar regard for historical accuracy, seem desirable residences, with a degree of bourgeois comfort and good taste. The palatial interiors in Cukor's film seem made to pose in: grand, decorative but soulless, show-homes for a bleak if dignified pseudo-aristocratic residential development.

These Renaissance settings carry with them the responsibility (or advantage) of having to appeal to the audience's familiarity with the art of the *quattrocento*: Castellani and Zeffirelli appropriate it with an ease absent in Cukor's film, where MGM's production values largely prevail over the efforts of a director noted for the elegant facility of his work with literate scripts and subtle actors. The real Venice lends itself at a price to directors adept at filming 'period' subjects along its canals and in its palazzi, but *The Merchant of Venice* has to find its own Belmont and *Othello* calls for a substitute for Cyprus. Both Welles and

Oliver Parker use locations for the early Venetian scenes in *Othello*, and then move away, Welles to a variety of destinations, Parker to a lakeside castle. The latter carries conviction as a fortified town, but in the scene of arrival in Cyprus, and that where Othello threatens his tempter by the shore of a great lake (the latter part of 3.3), it does not succeed in conjuring up an impression of being near the sea. There is no storm to mark the arrival of Othello and his party, though one was planned in the shooting script, and it is a shame to lose the energy of elemental forces at this juncture and the sense of relief at being safe from them. (Zeffirelli's 1987 film of Verdi's *Otello* benefits from the composer's omission of the play's first act: it begins accordingly with a finely realized tempest to match the music.) Moreover, in a play in which the feelings of otherness are multiplied among Venetians, the Moor, the Cypriot populace, and the off-screen Turks, Parker fails to create an exotic identity for the castle that stands for Cyprus. 'Oriental' motifs in Charlie Mole's score help, but most of the sense of the exotic has to be generated in the performances, the costuming of Othello, and the set-dressing in the indoor scenes.

The recasting of Verona as Verona Beach in Baz Luhrmann's *William Shakespeare's Romeo+Juliet* (1996) fulfils the title's promise to combine respect for the author with radical revision of the work: the plus sign suggests high-speed modernization. Verona Beach appears to be in the USA, a version of Miami or Los Angeles, cities already comprehensively mythologized, but Luhrmann avoids the direct correlation of the play's rivalries with contemporary issues. This is not *West Side Story*: there is no hint of the musical's correlation of gang warfare with tensions between ethnic groups in a hard city, and no visible equivalent in Verona Beach of the tenements and vacant lots of 1950s New York. At the same time Luhrmann's gangs are not engaged in turf wars over criminal activity – drug-dealing, for example – that would align *Romeo+Juliet* with recent urban crime dramas, and the 'ancient grudge' is the pretext for a violent expression of what seems to be the exuberant defiance that goes with youth culture. It is arguable that the film's own lavishness of sights and sounds – especially its music, both within and outside the diegesis – correspond to and endorse the frenetic and gaudy rather than the contemplative and pacific elements in the society it creates.

Ancient Rome has been recreated with varying success, and the sets for Joseph L. Mankiewicz's 1953 Hollywood *Julius Caesar* gain from the plainness of their decoration and the choice of black-and-white photography, which confers a degree of distance and dignity. This distinguishes the film from the Technicolor epics then in vogue – part of the set for Brutus's orchard was inherited from *Quo Vadis* (1951) and stripped of its more elaborate features – and establishes the customs and ethics of Roman society as part of an austere classical heritage. The film's producer John Houseman describes black-and-white as being chosen because 'Caesar is a tragedy of personal and political conflict; it calls for intensity and intimacy rather than grandeur; for direct, violent confrontations that do not benefit from a lush, polychrome background'. Although he had worked with Orson Welles on the director's famous modern dress production in 1937, Houseman felt that 'the literal nature of cinema would make it difficult to find a satisfactory modern background'. Monochrome photography would also evoke the newsreels that dominated the reporting of the recent world war and its aftermath, and such events as the Nuremberg rallies or Mussolini 'ranting from his high balcony overlooking the wildly cheering crowd that would presently spit on his dead body as it hung by its feet outside a gas station'.[9]

A more radical version of Rome was devised by Julie Taymor for her postmodern *Titus*, a Cinecittà production combining archaic warrior rituals, Mussolini-period architecture, and an orgy reminiscent of Fellini's *Satyricon* (1969). 'I wanted to blend and collide time', writes the director, 'to create a singular period that juxtaposed elements of ancient barbaric ritual with familiar, contemporary attitude and style'. Costumes, designed by Milena Canonero, 'were conceived to express the nature of a character, the personality of people and of events rather than to maintain a specific time period'.[10] They range from senators with red-trimmed toga-like stoles over their white business suits to the New Look for the as-yet-inviolate Lavinia. Then there are the Goths: Tamora and her sons Chiron and Demetrius are all hair and fur in the early scenes, but once they have been absorbed into the Roman world they adopt more modern clothing – fetishistic fancy dress for Tamora in orgy mode and punk for her villainous sons. Although it may seem as though anything goes, this is, in effect, a tragic arena – literally in its opening and closing sequences – for a fragmented postmodern world, where authority is claimed by violence, challenged ineffectively by what is left of democratic institutions (the senate), and countered in the end only by the exaction of savage revenge.

The eclectic, modish Rome of Taymor's *Titus* seems detached from reality when compared to the state and city represented in *Coriolanus* (2011), produced and directed by Ralph Fiennes and starring him in the title role. Here, the play is transposed to the former Yugoslavia and filmed there with a multi-ethnic, multinational cast. The caption identifying 'a place calling itself Rome' (borrowed with due acknowledgement from the title of John Osborne's unproduced 1973 play) sets out the agenda. The crisis in Rome is an analogy for all situations where a society is being torn apart by internecine regional strife, and where a military regime seems inevitable. Fiennes revealed in an interview that the local significance was not the immediate reason for shooting in Serbia:

What happened was that I knew it would be hard to finance the film, but I wanted to maintain the scale of it. I wanted streets, the Parliament, the marketplace, and a location where I could shoot an urban battle sequence, with soldiers convincingly armed. In Belgrade there's a Serbian parliament building, a location that was an essential piece of casting . . . [that] gave us a sense of the place where power is exercised, or the place where those with power reside.

The 'battered, bruised, worn feeling' of the city also helped, and once he had 'fallen in love with Belgrade' as a potential location, the thought came soon afterwards that, "'Oh, my God, yes, the Balkan conflict plays into this," but we didn't make a film about that war'.[11]

Unlike the co-opting of the 1930s in Loncraine and McKellen's *Richard III*, there is no conflict with a known historical outcome like that of the Second World War to undermine the film's effect. It avoids specific reference to the region's civil war of the 1980s, but inevitably the film's action is haunted by those events, and the images of street-to-street fighting are all too familiar from reports of war zones across the world. Fiennes makes excellent use of the format of television news programmes, more thorough than the opening and concluding clips in Luhrmann's *Romeo+Juliet* and an economical means of advancing the plot and bringing events from one scene into the action of another as characters watch their television screens and react. In the opening sequence Aufidius, not yet identifiable, sits in a darkened room and sharpens the knife with which he will eventually kill his arch-enemy, whom he watches on a television news report.

Much of the filming uses cameras that are hand-held or manipulated on a dolly to produce an effect that is congruent with the 'actuality' shots. Rome itself has decaying tower blocks as well as ceremonial halls, and Coriolanus must show his scars to get the people's voices in a decidedly unpicturesque street market in one of the working-class neighbourhoods. The tribunes and Menenius are modern parliamentarians, and the senate is recognizably a modern European national assembly. Coriolanus's family home is a patrician villa. The combination of recognizable, realistic detail with an element of generalization – this could be a number of places we happen to be calling Rome – is powerful and direct. There is little to suggest the values of classical Rome, and the militarist stoicism of the hero and his mother lacks that specific background, but the distance between the patricians and the common people is vividly rendered from early in the film, with the violent suppression of the attempt to occupy the grain mills. The Volscians come from a neighbouring country but are dressed more like partisans than their opponents, whose city is tearing itself apart. Rome, an urban centre with major social problems, is ruled and defended by patricians of a kind not seen in Volscian territory. We are not told what the source of the Roman–Volscian conflict might be, but Antium is represented as more benign, with a relaxed street life, and Aufidius is greeted warmly as he passes through the streets.

The responsibility of creating a tragic universe has been accepted by some films of *Hamlet, Macbeth,* and *King Lear*: the Piranesi-like passages of Olivier's 1948 Elsinore, the dank, murky Scotland of Welles' *Macbeth* – discussed in detail in the next chapter–and the frozen Jutland locations of Peter Brook's *King Lear* (1971) make distinctive and forceful interpretative statements, an environment in which existential anxieties and criminal excesses will flourish. In conversation with Grigori Kozintsev and in an exchange of letters in which the directors discussed their approach to the play for their respective films, Brook said that 'he wanted to film *Lear* without any traces of history showing on the screen'. He explained that he and his colleagues 'tried to reach a simple picture, not by non-period, which is impossible, but by basing everything on shapes and objects that are dictated by climatic conditions'.[12] The worlds of Zeffirelli's and Branagh's *Hamlet* films (1990 and 1996, respectively) and Polanski's *Macbeth* (1971) are less self-evidently and pre-emptively dark, at least at the outset, although Zeffirelli begins with a view of a handsome medieval castle by the sea, then shows formidable warriors gathered in a courtyard before moving down into the shadowy burial vault to set up the tensions between Hamlet and his mother and stepfather. Branagh opens his *Hamlet* with a tense sequence in which guards patrolling outside a neoclassical palace (Blenheim) are frightened by a ghost, the statue of the old king, who looms at them out of the darkness beyond the gates. Inside, this Elsinore is spacious, brightly lit, and luxurious. In Polanski's *Macbeth* a 'neutral' and at times sunlit natural world, seen fitfully, is compromised and taken over by the forces of darkness. The first, startling, assertion of this is the opening sequence in which three witches bury a severed arm, its hand grasping a dagger. After chanting their spell, and confirming that they will meet on the heath to confront Macbeth, they fade into the sea mist that swirls around them, and we find that this is the aftermath of a battle, as a half-dead soldier is given the brutal *coup de grâce* with a ball and chain. Nevertheless, when Duncan and his entourage approach Dunsinane, seen on the horizon like a fairy-tale castle, it does seem to have a pleasant seat, with no hint of the dangers within.

Lists of genre definitions for the cinema do not commonly include tragedy, but the conventional (and by no means stable) generic labels for Shakespeare's plays are likely to lurk in the consciousness. At the very least, everyone knows that, in the words of the song 'That's Entertainment', *Hamlet* is a play 'where a ghost and a prince meet/ And everyone ends as mincemeat'. However, radical shifts in period or milieu may block some important elements of the play's ethical and spiritual world rather than making them available for examination. Thus, when in Michael Almereyda's *Hamlet* (2000) the kingdom becomes the 'Denmark Corporation', some elements of the family drama gain immediacy, but important prerogatives of royalty as depicted in the play lose credibility. Religion, moreover, has little place in this secular, corporate environment, although the ghost's references to the fires of purgatory remain, illustrated in the corner of Hamlet's apartment by a conflagration on a television screen. In his published script Almereyda insisted that such references to contemporary life as the ghost's disappearance into a Pepsi vending machine, or Hamlet's soliloquizing in a Blockbuster video store, are more than 'casual irony', and are 'another way to touch the core of Hamlet's anguish, to recognize the frailty of spiritual values in a material world, and to get a whiff of something rotten in Denmark on the threshold of our self-congratulatory new century'.[13] Spiritual values are represented most directly in the film by a video clip watched by Hamlet in which a Vietnamese monk outlines his concept of 'interbeing', but there is no framework of Christian belief to support such scenes as that in which Hamlet refrains from killing Claudius while he is at prayer. The director accepts that this is 'inevitably, an *attempt* at *Hamlet* – not so much a sketch but a collage, a patchwork of intuitions, images and ideas'.[14] As such it is undeniably effective, and is grounded (as his introduction to the script testifies) in an understanding of what he is *not* doing.

This summary survey of some of the settings devised by film-makers for Shakespearian adaptations suggests recurrent themes. One is the relationship, endlessly negotiable, between the pull towards realism in one kind of cinema and the visionary, expressionistic qualities of another. The middle ground on which they meet is the capacity of film to make fantasy convincing when it seems appropriate to do so. All the techniques of film have a dual potential, tending towards or away from the impression that the camera and the microphone have simply recorded what is 'there' or (the other end of this scale) that their access is as much a matter of artifice as the apparent reality that has been constructed for the film. These relative degrees of realism and fantasy can co-exist within one work: a film might move across from one to another at any point, so that dreams and visions might invade the world of characters living in the 'realist' world, and reality might leak into a work of fantasy. To take one example from the Shakespeare films cited above, Polanski's *Macbeth* makes this crossover, much as in *Rosemary's Baby* (1968) the same director allows arcane and hallucinatory representations of evil to invade a newly decorated middle-class apartment.

Starting from two notable examples of this 'tragic' darkness, and with the cinematic tropes associated with expressionism, the next chapter looks at the characters who inhabit these locations, focusing on examples of emotional relationships and states of mind that appear in part as conditioned by the societies depicted on screen, in part as the source of the material worlds the films have realized for them. These are 'figures in a landscape', an environment more fully realized and dominant than that established in most theatre productions, and conditioned by factors beyond the actors' own work.

People

Characterizations are created in the cinema by a number of means. Among these, the work of the actors themselves is the most important, but all the other elements of cinematic technique – including staging, design, costume, make-up, lighting, editing, and photography – are vital in the process. In discussing Paul Scofield's Lear or Welles' Othello, account has to be taken of the ways in which the actor's personal performance is part of the raw material of the film rather than a self-sufficient artistic whole, displayed to greater or lesser advantage. This chapter begins with discussion of two films released in the late 1940s, Orson Welles' *Macbeth* (1948) and Laurence Olivier's *Hamlet* (1948). Both feature their director in the title role, and are expressionist in the general sense of situating their action in an artificial décor and employing techniques of filming that play a major role in reflecting the protagonist's state of mind. In these tragedies, representing the inner turmoil of the principal character is high on the director's (and actor's) agenda.

In Welles' *Macbeth* the lowering studio sets, bounded inexorably by a cyclorama that confines the characters, admit little daylight, except in the twilight process shots that show Duncan approaching Dunsinane. James Naremore describes *Macbeth* as 'arguably the purest example of expressionism in American cinema', suggesting that here and in other films Welles' 'expressionist style and his penchant for tragedy enabled him to depict characters and emotions he was fascinated with, but which on the consciously moral and political level he found repugnant'.[1] The techniques of filming, like the settings, are those associated with the various forms of expressionist cinema, from the 'German Expressionism' commonly cited as a point of origin, through the horror films of the 1930s and 1940s to the atmospheric crime dramas constituting the genre of film noir. Welles leans towards the 'expressive emphasis and distortion' that John Willett identifies as one of the common traits of all varieties of expressionism, together with the 'concern with extreme despair, with human relationships at the point of highest tension' he finds in Scandinavian art and the theatre of Strindberg. Both films share elements of the tendency labelled 'Teutonic', described by Willett as 'darkness, introspection, concern with the mysterious and uncanny'.[2] As for film noir, although both directors make liberal use of chiaroscuro effects, Welles' film approximates more closely than Olivier's to a stylistic marker described by Janey Pace and Lowell Peterson in their seminal article on the genre: the 'constant opposition of light and dark', in which 'small areas of light seem on the verge of being completely overwhelmed by the darkness that now threatens them from all sides' (Figure 2.1).[3] The psychological dimension of this is identified by Foster Hirsch as an

Figure 2.1. *Macbeth* (Orson Welles, 1949): Macbeth (Welles) and Lady Macbeth (Jeanete Nolan, behind and to his left) in the banquet scene.

important element of the emphasis on subjective experience, which is also expressed in dream sequences: 'In moments of tension, *noir* dramas crawl with shadows. The image darkens to indicate sudden fear, to suggest that the characters are about to be attacked or to crack up'.[4] Welles comes closer than Olivier to establishing 'a visually unstable environment in which no character has a firm moral base from which he can confidently operate'.[5]

The production circumstances of the films differ widely. Olivier's is a handsome product of a prestigious British film company, lavishly funded by J. Arthur Rank. Its cast is dominated by seasoned Shakespearians, and its costumes and settings are the best that Denham Studios could afford. The music composed by William Walton is grand or lyrical by turns and always supportive of a sympathetic and dignified view of the action. *Hamlet* ran over its budget, its final cost being £573, 829. The production values of Welles' film, budgeted at $880,000 (less than half the cost of Olivier's) and drawing on the resources of Republic Pictures, a studio notable for 'B' Westerns, are less impressive, and his cast is, to say the least, uneven and in some cases grievously overparted.[6] Preceded by a stage production that served as preparation and rehearsal, and shot in three weeks, *Macbeth* is part of the legend – substantially true but also nurtured by its protagonist – of an actor and director of genius bringing in his pictures on a wing and a prayer. The music by Jacques Ibert, quirky, foreboding, and at times even sardonic, has none of the romantic confidence and rich sonority of William Walton's score. *Macbeth*, though, has a rough magic that Olivier's more polished *Hamlet* lacks. Michael Anderegg, in a study of Welles' Shakespearian films, contrasts the 'raw, gutsy, modern, and eccentric' Republic Pictures product, on its own terms 'commercially viable (at least in theory) because of its relatively low cost' with the tasteful and 'traditional' offering from Rank.[7]

As almost always with Welles, his film's journey from script to screen has a heroic quality, this time with the world's antagonism expressed by the call by the studio for re-editing (Welles cut some 21 minutes) and the re-recording of the soundtrack, and by the rivalry of Olivier's film in the bid for prestige and accolades. There were four Oscars for Olivier's film, but on its initial release only qualified *succès d'estime*, mainly from abroad, for Welles'.[8] Apart from their many other differences, the speaking of the dialogue marks the films' divergent approaches to Shakespeare. Olivier's cast is uniformly well-spoken, and, with the exception of Stanley Holloway's gravedigger, use the British received pronunciation of their time, while Welles' actors labour through the verbal fog produced by fitfully achieved pseudo-Scottish accents. Against Olivier's razor-sharp enunciation, Welles' thane seems to speak from a region beyond the play's action, a sonorous, grand and often petulant sound that is, of course, that of 'Orson Welles'. As Lady Macbeth, at least in the film's first movement while she is urging her husband to regicide, Jeanette Nolan harries him with a shrill, acidulous voice, her oddly elegant make-up and close-cut and modern-seeming costume suggestive of film noir's own *femmes fatales*. Nevertheless, 'the remarkable thing is the quantity of sheer power, melodramatic grandeur and intellectual feeling about the play that does come through', as Penelope Houston reflected after describing this 'film of crags and crones, shaggy warriors and ferocious incantations . . . fated by intractable circumstances'.[9] The power is that of a primitive rendering of the play, void almost completely of the poetic sensibility with which Shakespeare endows his heroic villain, and bringing the viewer (as Joseph McBride observes) into Macbeth's id rather than his superego: 'At its most effective, *Macbeth* resembles classic horror films . . . dramas which avoid nuance of character in order to more effectively present the clash of extreme emotions and free us into the world of nightmares'.[10] Welles' ruthless revisions to the text, including the division into separate sections and relocation of major soliloquies (notably the 'dagger' speech in 2.1), are sometimes ill-advised and, as Robert Garis puts it in *The Films of Orson Welles*, some of them 'can't have come from any considerable thinking about the play'.[11] Nevertheless, the film's visionary intensity carries the viewer through and past the obstacles these sometimes create. 'Fidelity' to a text may not be a valid criterion, but sometimes the original's craftsmanship has a validity that would have served the director better than his own decisions.

Elements of the horror genre are pervasive, beginning with the sinister, bubbling brew from which the witches extract a mass of clay and form it into a naked new-born babe in the opening moments. This could be the Thing from Scotland, but they address it as Macbeth, hailing it as Cawdor and 'king hereafter', placing a medal around its neck and a crown on its head. The horror-film effects are especially intensive in the sequence that moves rapidly from Duncan's arrival at Dunsinane. His entry into the courtyard and a religious ceremony led by the 'Holy Man' (a strange, equivocal figure invented by Welles) bracket the conversation between Macbeth and his wife: a corpse hangs from a gallows in the background and the head of Cawdor is already stuck on a high pole. Even as Duncan is making his way up to his bedchamber, Lady Macbeth is busy drugging the posset that will be handed to his guards.

Macbeth is absorbed immediately into a world of shadows, and as the film moves swiftly and inexorably towards the murder the camera and soundtrack share his disorientation. Faces are picked out – often barely distinguishable – in darkness, with Macbeth's swarthy features predominating. The camera shares his point of view as he sees a vision, not of the air-drawn dagger, but the clay figure moulded by the witches in their sinister rites at the opening of the film. After this has been glimpsed once, the screen moves in and out of focus as if replicating Macbeth's blurring, tortured sight, resolving itself after each miasmic vision into a sharper-focused medium shot of the actor. The shock effect of an inexplicable cry and the shriek of an unusually terrifying owl that startle Lady Macbeth, along with the off-screen screams of the murder victim, ensure that, as in a horror film, the spectator shares Macbeth's sensation at another inarticulate shriek – possibly 'Sleep no more!' – that 'every noise appals [him]' (2.3.39 and 56). When she rebukes him for failing to leave the daggers with the grooms, Lady Macbeth's rigidity of countenance, physical bearing, and even her make-up recall Judith Anderson as Mrs Danvers in Hitchcock's *Rebecca* (1939). When she returns, holding the daggers before her at arms' length, her automaton-like determination reinforces this effect. By contrast, Lady Macduff resembles the monster's victim in a horror film, a terrified and conventionally feminine figure with blond curls, anxious to discover from her husband what has happened, included in the general uproar and rushing-about of retainers and thanes after the crime is discovered. Macbeth is surprised in the act of killing the king's guards, and Banquo makes his suspicions undiplomatically clear to Macbeth with lines from a later scene in the play: 'Thou hast it now: King, Cawdor, Glamis, all/As the weird women promised ...' (3.1.1–9). As they prepare for bed, after brief scenes in which Macduff and Malcolm depart and the Holy Man takes some of Ross's lines, Macbeth speaks of his anxiety that he has 'filed his mind' for Banquo's issue, an implicit rebuke to Lady Macbeth for their lack of children, and draws a curtain that shuts her away from him. The witches are seen, and a spectral hand repeats the action from the opening sequence of crowning their clay child, an image that cross-fades to a back view of Macbeth, his face visible in a crude and distorting mirror as he places on his head a full-size version of the same crown.

Welles' compression of the play's scenes, the accumulation of images that instil a sense of terror, and the intensity and disorientation, make this a powerful and melodramatic sequence — or rather, sequence of sequences, for temporal continuity is unclear and because it is always dark we never quite grasp the spatial relationships of the passages and chambers, and even at times cannot tell whether the action takes place indoors or outdoors. This is the most successful sequence in the film, although the banquet (3.4) and the sleepwalking (5.1) are also powerful. In the scenes where they appear together the focus of attention is almost always on Macbeth rather than Lady Macbeth, and he even intervenes in her sleepwalking scene. This assertion of the protagonist's mentality as the centre and source of all we see and hear has the disadvantage of making some scenes outside the castle – such as the England scene – pale by contrast. Welles may open himself here, as elsewhere in his films, to accusations of hogging the screen, but this is a small price to pay for his extraordinary ability to think of his own role in terms of powerful cinematic images.

The designer Roger Furse described his task for *Hamlet* as the fulfilment of Olivier's vision of 'a dream-like, cavernous place as the setting for a drama which is centred in the shadowy regions of the hero's mind'.[12] This intention is asserted from the very beginning, when the title sequence is followed by an on-screen image of the lines intoned by Olivier as a disembodied voice of the film, 'So oft it chances in particular men', from 1.4 (in the second Quarto's version). The concluding assertion, 'This is the story of a man who could not make up his mind' is a gross simplification, as has often been pointed out, not only of the play but of the film itself, but the fact that the actor's voice is instantly recognizable may suggest that the funeral scene we see in the first overhead view of the castle's platform is that of the speaker, and that Hamlet's story will be related by and through himself. There are scenes in which the camera does adopt Hamlet's point of view, notably in the soliloquy

'To be or not to be' (3.1.58–92) where in a remarkable optical effect it seems to pass through the head of the prince, taking in a glimpse of his brain on the way to share his view of waves crashing on rocks below the platform where he sits. (The shot may have been suggested by the moment in the opening scene of Hitchcock's *Rebecca* where, as Maxim de Winter, Olivier gazes down from a cliff edge as if contemplating suicide.) In the queen's closet, however, the camera at one point adopts the ghost's point of view, panning from Hamlet to Gertrude with 'But look, amazement on thy mother sits' (3.4.102). At other times, beginning with its first exploration of the halls and staircases of the castle, it is an independent agent, conducting us from one scene to another. Although the interior geography of this Elsinore is not established with any great precision, it seems that with enough time and a proper guidebook we could find our way around. This does not have quite as much of the air of a well-organized state as Grigori Kozintsev achieves in his 1964 film, but its stylishly dressed courtiers and ornately equipped guards suggest a realm in which order can prevail – a far cry from the lack of any visible system, let alone household economy, in Welles' Scottish castle. Olivier's film is often tenebrous, but never at the expense of clarity. At the same time, the predominance of interiors further enforces our attention of the hero's situation, if only with the impression that Denmark may be a prison for him.

The effect of this on characterization is to reinforce a degree of formality. Claudius (Basil Sydney) and Gertrude (Eileen Herlie) are in costumes stylized to make them identifiably royal, he tending towards the 'bloat king' of his nephew's description, she conventionally glamorous. Hamlet himself, in black tights and a handsomely ornamented doublet, is athletic and dashing once he is armed with the information he needs – so much for the 'man who could not make up his mind'– and more than a match for the stolid Laertes (Terence Morgan), fussy Polonius (Felix Aylmer), and, more important, Jean Simmons as a waif-like Ophelia. There is no threat of the hero's limelight being stolen by Horatio (Norman Wooland), the epitome of unassertive and very 'English' good sense. Hamlet, whose soliloquy has been moved to follow rather than open the 'nunnery' scene (3.1.), overhears the plan to use an interview with Ophelia to investigate him, so that he is confrontational from the beginning of the encounter. When Hamlet has upbraided Ophelia and thrown her down violently on a flight of stone steps, he redeems himself somewhat with the gentlemanly gesture of returning to kiss her hair tenderly. Unfortunately, it is hard not to be aware of the actor-director's calculation in this as in other moments. Raymond Durgnat, who found Olivier's Shakespeare films 'hollow', reflected that 'their lack of conviction results ... from a scepticism that is not quite aware of itself'. The 'surface conventionality' in *Hamlet* was 'belied by something in Olivier's screen personality, something hard, stony, resentful, something that rebels, from within, against Hamlet's sensitivity because it see through it'.[13]

Burdened by the ghost's demands, but then motivated by the betrayal he experiences at the hands of Gertrude and Ophelia, this Hamlet has a simplified emotional trajectory to achieve. Because of the script's omissions, without Rosencrantz and Guildenstern to complicate his engagement with his coevals, or Fortinbras to take attention from him at the end, distractions are minimized, and he can focus on taking revenge on Claudius (his Freudian rival) and redeeming his mother. As Bernice Kliman observes, through the cuts and transpositions, and in the decisiveness with which he acts once he has conceived the play stratagem – the 'rogue and peasant slave' soliloquy at the end of 2.2 is cut – 'Olivier molds the play to serve his purpose of smoothing out Hamlet's progression towards serenity'.[14] This does not diminish the film's value as a forceful and eloquent version of the play. It does, however, reflect a conception not only of film-making but also of dramatic as well as cinematic characterization that differs markedly from that of Welles.

The two films represent the most intimate of relationships between their protagonists' state of mind and the surroundings created for them to move through, supported by cinematographic techniques that reinforce the sense of our being privy to their vision and experience of the world, to a lesser degree with Olivier and overwhelmingly with Welles. The insistent psychological symbolism of the latter's 1952 *Othello*, with shadows and bars that at times literally confine the hero and other characters, brings the director's expressionistic style into the daylight world of the Mediterranean. There are scenes where the blackness of Welles as Othello makes him a barely visible face in a dark screen, most notably when he approaches Desdemona's bed and his face, picked out in a key light, emerges in the absolute blackness of the screen and advances from right to left of frame. Earlier, huddled in a corner of a stairway to watch and hear Cassio seemingly boasting of his conquest of Desdemona (in the play's 4.1), Othello is a figure imprisoned by the deceit and his own imagination, with a correspondingly expressive confinement of the physical situation and framing of the shots. The film has opened with an assertion of patterns to come, like the statement of themes at the beginning of a symphony. At first the blackness of an indistinguishable shape fills the frame for a few moments before it is tilted away, light catching its contours and revealing it as the face of a body, Othello's, on a bier. Funeral processions cross the screen, one on the horizon, one at a steep angle closer to the camera. Desdemona's figure is white, covered with a filmy black veil. Her bier, unlike that of Othello, is preceded by a mitred bishop and a wooden cross. Suddenly a man is being dragged across the screen (still in silhouette) from right to left, and presently he is seen being hauled through a jeering crowd and then imprisoned in a small cage which is hoisted high against the walls of a fortress. Iago (Micheál MacLiammóir) peers through the cage's bars. A shot from his point of view looks down on the converging funeral processions. Darkness and light, confinement and the open air, and an ironic detachment even in deadly punishment are on display. As the film progresses Othello takes on the darkness, so that his shadow or his face emerging from shadows engulfs the innocence represented by Desdemona. Subjective montages are used at two crucial moments. When he swoons at the imagination of Cassio coupling with Desdemona, he seems to hear orgasmic gasps and see a mocking crowd on the battlements as he lies on the ground, while gulls wheel and cry overhead; when, after learning of Iago's treachery, he staggers towards the bed to take the dead Desdemona in his arms, we see giddying images of the ceiling vaults and bars of light and dark.

In Welles' *Othello*, as in the play, the social order is present alongside that of military rank, domestic tragedy framed by a recognizable world of domestic duty and affection. In Welles' *Macbeth* and in Olivier's *Hamlet*, social order is simplified to the point of abstraction. Royalty demands loyal service and treachery demands punishment, but beyond that there is little to indicate how the world works, especially in Welles' primitive Scotland. In his *Othello* Welles' symbolist filmmaking engages with a vividly rendered, real-seeming society. When Iago and Othello walk the ramparts of the fort, the open sky beyond them places them in the context of nature, and when they pass under the criss-crossed laths of a cattle pen their talk is framed by this symbolic commentary that seems to be 'found' rather than constructed. Welles give full value to the decency and passion of Emilia (Fay Compton) in her indignation and fear in the final sequence and to the banality and even comedy of Roderigo's envy of Cassio and Iago's manipulation of him in the service of his own spite.

Within this world, at first able to rise above its pettiness but eventually defeated by it, is Othello's apartness. He is a black man exuding charisma and dignity that prompt the white Venetians – with the exception of Desdemona's father – to entrust him with power and accept his marriage to the daughter of one of their grandees. Welles uses his grandiloquence and ability to dominate the screen and what is around him on it, always supported by his directorial ability to enlist the film's resources on his side, to better effect here than in his *Macbeth*. In *Othello* his character is vulnerable to the wiles of commonplace human emotions, rather than being prey to wickedness elicited from him by the ersatz horror-film supernaturalism of the witches and the influence of their accomplice in the castle, his wife.

In Oliver Parker's 1995 *Othello* the mundane, material world is more fully realized than in Welles' version, and symbolism is sparingly attached to a story told almost entirely within realist cinematic conventions, with the notable exception of a sequence in which Othello imagines Desdemona making love with Cassio. This, though, is an illustration of his erotic imaginings, not symbolic but within the range of psychological realism. The most determinedly symbolic action occurs when Iago (Kenneth Branagh) lets a chess piece fall into a well, anticipating the image of the burials at sea of Othello and Desdemona at the end of the film. Laurence Fishburne presents a comparatively low-key Othello, convincing in sensuality and quiet command and responsive to the subtle, persuasively confidential needling of Branagh's ensign, but hardly expansive or passionate. The film's sexual relationships will be discussed in Chapter 4; here, it is important to note the contrast with Welles' more compact, dynamic version – 95 minutes, as against Parker's 123. Parker achieves the momentum he aspired to in creating what he described as 'a sexy thriller', earning his extra half-hour of screen time, but there is little sense of tragedy brought about by elemental passions, rather than misfortune connived at by misapprehension on one side and cunning on another. The expression-istic mise-en-scène of Welles' film supports a sense of these qualities in the characters while the prosaic surroundings and style of Parker's film carry no effective psychological weight. Categories such as 'elemental passion' and 'tragedy', though, are culturally determined and relative to other performance conventions of a given era. They are also difficult to translate into acting for the screen, where intensity and subtlety are privileged. That Welles takes the risk in his two tragic characters has in itself a heroic quality, supported by his ability to bring settings and camerawork to bear on perceptions of personality and emotion.

Heroism is a more problematic attribute in the case of *King Lear*, where the title character, a wayward and tyrannical patriarch, has less immediate claim to victimhood and embodies greater contradictions than Othello. Paul Scofield, as the king in Brook's *King Lear*, has a formidable simplicity, consonant with his harsh subarctic realm. Here the consonance of environment with character is overpowering, an austere and hostile existence where it is surprising that anything other than hard hearts would be bred, and robes and furred gowns are indis-pensable. The first credits are superimposed as the camera pans across the faces of a crowd of silent, anxious men. In the first movement, from right to left, they are looking in different directions. The title is shown on a black background, and in a second pass, from left to right and viewed from a slightly higher angle, they are all looking towards the right of the frame as if waiting for some momentous event. A cut takes us to what is evidently a council chamber, and the camera faces the back of a pillar in the centre. A door slams, and the first sight of Lear is a tight low-angled close-up on his lined, severe face, framed by his beard and his grizzled hair. He utters the first word, 'Know', pausing so that the bleakness of its homophone 'no' hangs in the air for a moment. His face is isolated in the centre of an otherwise black screen.

As Lear addresses each of his three daughters in turn, they are handed an orb which they hold as they make their declarations of love. Goneril and Regan, with their husbands, are positioned closer to Lear's throne than Cordelia: Goneril speaks with solemnity, Regan smiles as she announces that her sister's professions 'come too short'. When Lear speaks to Cordelia, she is seen at a distance, seated alone against a wall. The orb is held in the foreground of the shot, and she comes towards it, as though approaching the task with some detachment, and the camera is closer on her as she replies than it was for her sisters. As Lear bids her mend her speech a little the camera looks towards his throne from behind her head, which almost completely obscures him until we cut to his face on 'Nothing will come of nothing, speak again'. He rises, revealing the massiveness of the fur coat whose collar reaches above his neck and bulges out at the back, making him look like a formidable wild beast. This is Scofield's Lear at his most commanding, seemingly impregnable as he vehemently disowns Cordelia. Kent and he face each other from the far right and left of an otherwise empty screen, in one of the many spatial arrangements – achieved by staging and the framing of shots – that denote relationships throughout the film. (For example, Lear and Goneril face each other in front of a blazing hearth when she confronts him about his knights' behaviour, and Albany and Goneril face each other in the same positions in their conversation after Lear's departure.)

Brook gives Goneril some cause for her grievance against Lear's followers, who seem indeed to have turned her house into 'a tavern or a brothel', pelting Oswald with food, and wrecking the hall when, after an ominous silence, Lear gives them the signal by overturning a table. Violence is never far from Lear's mind – he threatens Goneril with his riding crop – and there is no weakness and much danger in this formidable patriarch. At first sight Gloucester and his sons seem to be a harmonious family, with Edmund sharing some of his lines about illegitimacy (1.2.2–9) with Edgar as though this is a topic they can joke about. (The more sinister parts of the speech are reserved for a subsequent meditation.) Here there is little of the obvious potential for tragedy apparent in Lear's court. With the Fool, Lear has an intimacy not shared with others – they ride together in the king's creaking wooden coach – and Brook uses breaks in continuity during the exchange (in 1.4) that includes the breaking of the egg into two halves and the reference to Lear putting down his own breeches for his daughters to beat him. The effect is to convey subtly the disjunctions in time and attention in Lear's mind, but the camera is not taking his point of view, figuratively or literally. Similarly, lines from Kent's speeches in 1.4, when he gives an account of himself to Lear's 'What services canst do?' (31) are spoken as he disguises himself, the shots zooming in and fading to black at the end of each sentence. When Gloucester is blinded the screen goes abruptly to black, and after he pitches himself forward from the non-existent cliff the camera shows him from above, a pathetic figure sprawled on the sand.

In this re-creation of *King Lear*, character is fused with vision and perception, to the point where, when Brook creates his hallucinatory storm, there are flashes of white and black and a seemingly haphazard succession of camera angles and blurring of images that seem to be shared between Lear and the film itself. At times the screen becomes completely black or white. Sometimes the lens is fogged and smeared by rain, but looks objectively towards Lear, at others it represents his perceptions – for example, when he first sees Poor Tom. In the final scene, Lear lays Cordelia down on the beach, but he is not close to her corpse when we hear him say 'This feather stirs' and Lear seems to be alone when he speaks 'Never, never, never, never, never'. As Alexander Leggatt observes, at this point the 'fragmentation' of the film and of Lear's mind has set in:

On 'Look, her lips', Lear is pointing to the camera. Either there is no Cordelia, or we are watching from the perspective of a corpse. Where we do see her again is when once again we enter Lear's hallucinations. On 'What is't thou sayest?' she is standing beside him, then Kent stands in her place. She appears again on 'my poor fool is hang'd'.

The affirmation this may represent is, as Leggatt argues, qualified by the fact that 'there has been no strong Lear-Cordelia relationship in the rest of the film for these moments to draw on'.[15] These images, then, are not possessed solely by the king but also express what might be called the film's mentality. The word that would perhaps best characterize that would be alienation, not so much in the Brechtian sense of 'making strange' (*Verfremdung*) as the psychiatric register, indicating a distance from and fragmentation of reality. The madness and cruelty are shared by the camera, so that when Regan dashes her brains out on a rock after swaying to and fro in a trance, the film is complicit with the violence of the action. Madness is shared, as much as observed with unsparing and disturbing clarity, the black-and-white photography allowing no warmth of mood to mitigate the physical circumstances of the characters, from which there is no real escape. In his final moments, as Lear's face falls slowly out of the frame, the blankness of the screen that is left makes the film's ultimate statement of nihilism. Nothing has come of nothing, 'know' has indeed become 'no'.

Compared with Grigori Kozintsev's *King Lear* (1969), Brook's emerges as apolitical, a film with a world convincingly represented but endowed with the remoteness and fixity of a myth. Having established a bleak kingdom in which possessing fire and shelter are paramount for a play where (in his words) 'what counts from a psychological point of view is the contrast between the safe, enclosed places and the wild, unprotected places', Brook shows little or no interest in political and social process.[16] 'There's father against son' and the other apocalyptic signs found by Gloucester in the 'late eclipses of the sun and moon' are fully represented, but there is no indication of the wider implications for those outside the spheres of the king and his relatives by blood or marriage and the noble-men who owe him allegiance. There are none of the crowds of peasants whose well-being depends precariously on the king and his family, no band of 'naked wretches' to share (as they do in the Russian film) Poor Tom's hovel, and no signs of the aftermath of war such as Kozintsev's Edgar makes his way through after taking leave of the king. Tragedy in Brook's universe is final, and the gored state is not likely to be sustained for long, but in Kozintsev's there are men and women piecing together their belongings from the charred remnants of their houses: life will go on; a social order of some kind will be reasserted.

In the case of the English histories and the Roman plays, with the probable exception of *Titus Andronicus*, audiences will have some notion of the appearance not only of the Roman or medieval world, but also of the 'look' and personality of the principal characters, even if this is based on conventions of representation rather than hard icono-graphic or literary evidence. They are likely to have an idea of what happened next or at least that there was more to come – more history, other regimes, different people. The plays are effective even if we are not fully conversant with the events of the reigns from Richard II to Henry VI, or share the Elizabethan audience's sense of their signifi-cance in dynastic history. In the case of the king in *Henry V*, Olivier leaves us with the chorus's celebration of 'this star of England' and his achievement of 'the world's best garden', before returning to the 'gar-den' of the peaceful, quasi-pastoral view of Elizabethan London with which the film began. In the final moments of his version Branagh allows the chorus (Derek Jacobi) to reflect sadly on the disastrous reign of Henry VI, 'whose state so many had the managing/That they lost France, and made his England bleed' (Epilogue, 6; 7, 11–12). The future, stretching beyond the final scene of reconciliation and union, is available, even if relatively few of the film's spectators will know exactly what it held.

Although their leading characters are by no means free from mental strife, it is not the principal concern of films of the history plays – the two versions each to date of *Richard III* and *Henry V*, and *Chimes at Midnight* – and consequently they have not shared the expressionistic tendencies of Welles' *Macbeth* or Olivier's *Hamlet*, or the fragmenting techniques of Brook's *King Lear*. With exception of Welles' rendering of the court of Henry IV and the battle of Shrewsbury, and brief episodes in both *Richard III* films, darkness is reserved for plotting (the two churchmen in Branagh's *Henry V*) and visions for the ghosts and dreams that assail King Richard. (For his recovery from the ordeal of the night, Olivier borrows the famous line from the 1699 adaptation of the play by Colley Cibber: 'Richard's himself again'.)

In *Chimes at Midnight* Welles not only uses expressive lighting and (literal) chilliness of atmosphere to contrast Henry Bolingbroke's court with the tavern; he also stages the action in these scenes to convey the king's remoteness and domination of the rebellious nobles in the first court scene, and later his alienation from his son, who like them must approach his father, seated on a high dais and seen from a steep upward angle, from the floor of the monastery church that serves as the location. Welles' ability to fashion characterization from staging, lighting, and camerawork is once again in evidence. In a later scene (equivalent to 2 *Henry IV*, 4.3), when Prince Henry has taken the crown from his dying father's bedside, he is seen in an extreme long shot in a pool of light from a high window as the king approaches from the foreground: the effect is to raise him above the king, although in 'real' space the prince is not on a higher level. In the rejection of Falstaff, the newly crowned king turns towards his former companion and he is seen from a low angle, effectively Falstaff's *emotional* if not his physical point of view. When Falstaff makes his solitary way out of the precincts of the court, his receding figure is dwarfed by the contrast with the soaring pillars. *Chimes at Midnight* is remarkable for the systematic clarity of moments such as these, and for the paralleling of scenes that express the prince's mental and actual distancing of himself from Falstaff. When he leaves the tavern at the end of his first scene there, he speaks the soliloquy 'I know you all . . .' (1 *Henry IV*, 1.3.192) as if to himself but with Falstaff just behind him at the gate in the wooden fence, and then runs off towards the castle in a shot where the camera is placed at a high angle, with Falstaff below in the foreground. In an extreme long shot the prince turns back to answer Falstaff's shouted plea 'Do not thou, when thou art king, hang a thief' with 'No, thou shalt have the hanging of the thieves, and so become a rare hangman' (1.2.60–61; 65–7). A similar composition is used later when Prince Henry rides off to the council of war after the scene that has included the improvised comedy anticipating his interview with his father. It recurs at the end of the film, when Falstaff's outsized coffin is trundled away on a cart, this time with the hostess in the foreground of the shot. The set-up expresses the distance between Eastcheap and the court, with the long walls of the castle in the background and the fence that marks the limits of the tavern's territory in the foreground.

These are, of course, not the only means by which character and relationships are expressed, and *Chimes at Midnight* owes much to the individual performances of Keith Baxter as the prince, John Gielgud as his father, Margaret Rutherford as Mistress Quickly, and Norman Rodway as an exuberant Hotspur. Welles himself, especially in his scenes with Keith Baxter and with Alan Webb as Justice Shallow, engages more directly with his fellow-actors than in *Macbeth* or *Othello* – in the latter, his strongest relationship is with MacLiammóir as Iago, and there is little to suggest passion between him and Suzanne Cloutier as Desdemona. Nevertheless, there is a sign of Welles' idiosyncrasies (or limitations) as an actor even in the first scene of *Chimes at Midnight*, before the opening credits, with Falstaff and Shallow making their way through a snowy landscape to find the warmth of a fire in Shallow's house and reminiscing about the days they have seen. The give-and-take between the two actors is exemplary in itself, but Welles has to share his attention between Shallow and the camera, so that this is announced as the story not merely of Falstaff but of Welles-as-Falstaff, impressive and accomplished and at times intensely moving but insistent on collusion with his own camera. (It does, though, correspond to the character's intimacy with the theatre audience, achieved in the play through his soliloquies.)

Keith Baxter, in an interview that sheds light on many aspects of the filming process, relates how Welles identified strongly with the character and the significance of his eventual defeat, so that as work progressed the film became darker in tone.[17] When he creates his Battle of Shrewsbury, the result is relentless, grinding, and bloody, even though no blood is seen. Like the comic adventure among the trees when Falstaff and his cronies rob the travellers at Gad's Hill, it is a cinematic tour de force. The value of the battle scene is its contribution to a general characterization, that of the age itself, an invaluable supplement to the work of the actors in the main narrative. As much as the prince's rejection of Falstaff, and King Henry's victory in the triangle between himself, Falstaff, and his son, the battle is a sign of the decline and death of the 'Merrie England' that Welles considered his major theme.

The differences in setting between the two films of *Henry V* and the distancing effect of Olivier's more simply heroic king have already been noted (see p. 25). Branagh's *Henry V* is also notably different from Olivier's in the nature of the relationships it depicts. In the 1944 film, the intimacy between Henry and his former companions is referred to but not shown, whereas Branagh not only shows flashbacks of tavern life, but inserts one of them at the moment when Henry witnesses the hanging of Bardolph (Richard Briers) – itself an addition to Shakespeare's text, where the event is merely reported. (The episode was also included in the 1984 RSC stage production by Adrian Noble, in which Branagh played the king.) Olivier does not need to make much of the punishment of Bardolph, and his Pistol (Robert Newton) is a swaggering *commedia* figure who has overdosed on Christopher Marlowe, with none of the sinister quality that in the 1988 film underlies Robert Stephens' pickpurse, seen at his trade even among the dead on the battlefield. There, with the exception of the boy, all Henry's erstwhile Eastcheap cronies are dingy, tired, and unglamorous, managing to rise above the depression that besets Bardolph in his first scene and that is intensified by the news of Falstaff's death. As they and the other soldiers trudge through the mud on their way to possible annihilation at Agincourt, they contrast with the sprucely attired and confident herald Mountjoy (Christopher Ravenscroft), who is disconcerted to find himself confronted with the hanging body of Bardolph as he rides up to deliver his king's ultimatum.

In a film that, unlike Olivier's, is not dominated by bright heraldic colours and stylized costuming, Branagh individualizes the peers who support Henry – especially the formidable Exeter (Brian Blessed) — making sure that they, and the common soldiers, are identified during his rallying speech at Harfleur and are seen reacting with enthusiasm to his exhortations. Before this he has shown the scene (2.2) in which Henry confronts and condemns the friends who have betrayed him, omitted by Olivier in a script that depicted England as united behind its leader: Branagh's 'band of brothers' had to be established, could not be taken for granted. Unlike Olivier, Branagh makes the soldiers' anxiety in the face of the approaching French cavalry evident, and has them kissing the earth and crossing themselves before facing the 'fearful odds'. Except for Exeter and the veteran Sir Thomas Erpingham (Edward Jewesbury), most of the English peers are young men of or near Henry's age, another contrast with Olivier's mature entourage. The tactic is followed through before and after Agincourt, and Branagh takes full advantage of the opportunity to identify the boy (Christian Bale), seen among the Eastcheap irregulars, as one of those killed by the French in an action that is counter to the rules of engagement. Neither film includes the information that in response to the atrocity, reported in 4.7, Henry has commanded that French prisoners should be killed, but both make a point of his anger at it. Olivier rides off to take on the Constable – suitably in black armour – in single combat, and Branagh takes out his ire on the French herald. The culmination of this plot line in Branagh's film is the long tracking shot after the battle, in which Henry carries the boy across the battlefield and gently deposits his body on a cart. Accompanied by the soaring 'Non Nobis' composed for the film by Patrick Doyle, which becomes a full choral and symphonic rendering soon after Henry starts walking, this has been interpreted as a triumphal gesture contradicting the liberal message that few die well that die in a battle. It does, however, support Branagh's characterization of the king as a reluctant warrior. After his blood-curdling ultimatum to the citizens of Harfleur (1.3.84 etc., omitted by Olivier) he collapses in exhaustion, visibly relieved at not having to carry out his threats; his reaction to the hanging of Bardolph is stoical but clearly requires some effort; and he allows his men to hear his apprehension when he utters 'And how thou pleasest, God, dispose the day' (4.3.133) as they prepare for battle at Agincourt. During the battle anger at the vivid and bloody killing of York, shown in slow motion, prompts an extra impetus as Henry and his closest lieutenants renew their attack on foot. (York's death is elaborately described by Exeter in a 25-line speech in the play's 4.6.) In the final scene Burgundy's long speech conjuring up the ravages of war is illustrated with flashbacks recalling the personal losses of the young king – including the death of York – rather than the state of the French countryside.

Among the French, Branagh's king (Paul Scofield) is haunted, almost tragic, in contrast to the mildly crazed and ineffective monarch (Harcourt Williams) whose debility allows Olivier to imply that his country is being misled by vainglorious militarists: an important distinction between the French nation and its Vichy leadership in 1944. The most important of Branagh's French peers is the Dauphin (Michael Maloney), his aggression seemingly fired by hatred rather than the casual, foppish arrogance displayed by Max Adrian in Olivier's film. As I have noted, Branagh establishes Katherine's personal world as one of light and gaiety: this is contrasted with the court when she opens the door of her room and encounters her grim-faced father and his peers striding down a dark corridor towards the council chamber.

Branagh's *Henry V* deploys many of the cinema's available techniques to establish and articulate character, but in several scenes it is the actor's performance that is privileged. Such moments include Judi Dench as Mistress Quickly describing the death of Falstaff, illustrated by cutting away to what is being described, but dependent for its effect on her performance, as the camera moves slowly in towards her; the moment when the French king, seen in profile, raises his face from his hands and announces 'Tis certain he hath passed the river Somme' (3.5.1); and the wooing scene. Branagh allows his actors full scope, staging these moments simply and editing many scenes with a minimum of cuts. The same principle has been applied subsequently in his other Shakespeare films, and is supported by his predilection for long takes, often with the camera following the actors through a good deal of complicated physical action.

The environments created in Branagh's films of *Much Ado About Nothing* and *As You Like It* have been discussed in Chapter 1. In both cases a location has been adapted to provide the principal setting for the action, the idyllic rural Tuscan estate contributing to the sense of well-being and (to put it simply) holiday humour that made the first of these so successful. The *Japonaiserie* of *As You Like It* is more problematic. Silvius, Phoebe, and William are played by British Asian actors, but the other characters are European, and considerable ingenuity was needed to account for Corin's presence as an exiled Christian priest. (Consequently Touchstone and Jacques are mistaken in treating him as a 'hedge-priest' in the equivalent of the play's 'Oliver Martext' scene, 3.3.) The text's 'holy man' is a Buddhist monk, and we see his conversion of the usurper, but he plays no part in the festive ending. The most significant effect of the film's setting on characterization is in its treatment of the usurping and exiled dukes, both played by Brian Blessed in respectively sinister and benign modes. (After Frederick has banished his niece and been defied by his daughter, however, there is an indication of the regret that is to come.) Here the association of one brother with dance and music and the other with the martial arts provides a convenient means of accounting for their divergent mentalities, though this necessarily ignores the co-existence of aesthetic finesse and swordsmanship in the Japanese culture that is invoked.

In *Love's Labour's Lost* (2000), recast in imitation of a 1930s musical comedy, with numbers by Irving Berlin and others, Branagh used impressive, self-evidently artificial sound-stage sets for the 'little academe' (an Oxbridge college quad with a luxuriously appointed library), the canal-side approach to Navarre, and the parkland where the Princess and her ladies practise archery. Within this setting some of the characters approximate to comic clichés: Costard (Nathan Lane) as a vaudeville comedian in a loud check suit; Sir Nathaniel (Richard Briers) as a vicar from a P.G. Wodehouse story; Jaquenetta (Stefania Rocca) as a starlet from a 1950s Italian film, and so on. The actor's work on their roles was done with considerable regard for the realities behind the stereotypes, with Geraldine McEwan's Holofernia (*sic*) based in part on the appearance and reported mannerisms of the Shakespearian scholar M.C. Bradbrook. Don Armado (Timothy Spall) has a Salvador Dali moustache, a grotesque accent, a fantastic military uniform, and an impressive repertoire of extravagant poses and gestures. The King of Navarre (Branagh) and the Princess of France (Alicia Silverstone) and their respective entourages were given a more restrained treatment, although for the 'dream' musical number suggesting Astaire and Rogers ('Heaven' from *Top Hat*) they appear in the appropriate top hat and tails and ball gowns, and for 'There may be Trouble Ahead', a steamy homage to Bob Fosse, the men strip down to undervests and black trousers while the women are in leotards and fishnets. The consequences of these choices for characterization, although not inappropriate for what is in many respects Shakespeare's most mannered comedy, were that some (though by no means all) aspects of the character relationships were simplified.

Branagh truncates the pageant of the Nine Worthies, which is seen only in brief moments; omits the men's masquerade as Russians (replaced by the 'Fosse' number); and in general cuts the text radically to accommodate the musical numbers. The framing of the whole action with the build-up to the Second World War, the Occupation of France, and the celebration of VE day were more problematic. The musical comedy characterizations and incidents of the main body of the action are uneasily reconciled with a historical time and place that have too many serious, indeed tragic connotations. Whereas in *Much Ado About Nothing* and (to a lesser extent) *As You Like It* Branagh provided a free arena for the actors, here they worked to pleasing effect but within a stylized mise-en-scène that pre-empted some decisions. In *Much Ado* each major role (except for Michael Keaton's Dogberry) was invested successfully with a strong sense of psychological realism that negotiated between acknowledged dramatic function and the need to create a convincing character in the manner of modern screen acting. *Love's Labour's Lost* called for this kind of realism to be reconciled with two levels of stylization – 1930s musical comedy, plus that devised by Shakespeare.

Michael Radford's *The Merchant of Venice* (2004) and Trevor Nunn's *Twelfth Night* (1996), having established a more-or-less convincing milieu, leave the actors to their work. Both rely for their central roles on players with theatrical experience of Shakespeare, and neither effects any radical intervention of mise-en-scène, though (as has been noted in Chapter 1) Radford characterizes Belmont and Venice as respectively light and dark places, which affects the presentation of Portia on the one hand and Shylock and Antonio on the other. Al Pacino, who had showcased his ambitions as a Shakespearian actor in his semi-documentary *Looking for Richard* (1996), plays Shylock effectively in the sardonic/pathetic mode favoured since Henry Irving's performance at the end of the nineteenth century, and Antonio (Jeremy Irons) loves Bassanio with some suggestion of (probably closeted) sexual desire, and kisses him on the mouth before he leaves for Belmont. Jessica is clearly upset at the news of her father's defeat and her unlooked-for access of wealth. Both she and Antonio are left as outsiders at the end. He gazes out of the window of the salon where the revelations have taken place, and she looks out over the lagoon as the sun rises. She fingers a turquoise ring, presumably that given to Shylock by Leah when he was a bachelor and exchanged for a monkey in Genoa – and since somehow redeemed. Back in Venice, Shylock is shunned by his co-religionists, and stands in the rain and darkness outside the synagogue doors, which are firmly shut against him. Radford has to deal with the racism of the jokes about Morocco, which is done partly by endowing him with an absurd sense of entitlement (more genial than that of the arrogant and fantastic Aragon) and an entourage of black-robed compatriots. Portia's 'Let all of his complexion choose me so' (2.7.79) after Morocco's departure is cut: it has no place in a film that must not allow its heroine to be compromised by any tinge of racism.

   This is in line with the strategy announced in the opening sequence. This is 'Venice – 1546'. We are told that Jews are forced to live in a gated quarter of the city, the Ghetto, and to wear distinctive red hats. A mob throws a Jew from the Rialto, taunting him as a 'usurer', to the approval of a tonsured priest who arrives on the scene in a gondola equipped with a wooden cross. A title card informs us that 'The sophisticated Venetians would turn a blind eye to [anti-Semitism], but for the religious fanatics, who hated the Jews, it was another matter'. Shylock is among the small group of red-hatted Jews who witness the assault, and Antonio spits on his 'Jewish gaberdine' as he passes him. We subsequently see Antonio in church, being blessed by the priest who egged on the mob. This would seem to qualify the claim that 'sophisticated' Venetians ignore anti-Semitism, or at least jeopardize the Christian merchant's claim to sophistication. Identifying the priest as a 'fanatic' also invites us to exonerate the majority of Christians who are not active in their prejudices. When Bassanio accosts Shylock to ask him to meet Antonio, the Jew is buying a pound of flesh in a street market. The scene begins with a shot of a carcass being butchered, and the choice of setting is ambiguous: the cutting and weighing are treated with attention that makes the transaction seem more than an example of Shylock's housekeeping. Nothing explicit, though, is done to make him appear merely bloodthirsty in temperament, here or in the subsequent action when he has to steel himself to make an incision in Antonio. Belmont, as well as being freed from the taint of racism, does not have to bear the burden of the draconian stipulation of the will of Portia's father that candidates for her hand must swear never to marry if they fail the test of the caskets. In the court, after Bassanio and Lorenzo have declared themselves ready to give up their wives to free their friend, Shylock does not exclaim 'These be the Christian husbands' (4.1.292), but perhaps the point does not need making. Radford establishes the parallel between the bond and Belmont when he cuts directly from the signing of the document in Shylock's shadowy office to the island villa, where Morocco is kissing Portia's hand. The cumulative effect – or at least, intention – of these touches is that of many costume dramas, subtly modernizing the mentality of the play's world but dressing and setting it meticulously 'in period'.

Freedom from a sense of historical period, or at least the illusion of it, is an advantage in versions of plays less rooted than *The Merchant of Venice* in the mundane world of getting and spending. In Derek Jarman's *Tempest* the multiple periods of costuming (noted above, p. 21) suggest a hierarchy of social identities but do not to fix characters and their relationships in it. Prospero, in his knee breeches, open waistcoat, and scarves, has a Byronic air as well as a touch of Robespierre. Miranda's crinoline of feathers and her low-cut bodice suggest a ball gown that has either been dismantled or is not yet complete, and at one point she makes her way downstairs in a parody of balletic steps and gestures. The elaborate confection she wears during the performance of 'Stormy Weather' that effectively replaces the play's masque, resembles an eighteenth-century theatrical costume that has been put together from odds and ends of fabric and ornament found in markets and fished out of a designer's hoard of materials.

The eclecticism of the costuming complements the dream-like quality of much that is seen and heard, which begins with Prospero asleep 'dreaming' the storm and murmuring lines from the play's first scene over stock footage of a sailing ship in a heavy storm, shown through a blue filter. In the final moments of the film after the release of Ariel, Prospero, his eyes closed, speaks 'Our revels now are ended' (4.1) rather than the epilogue, ending with the word 'sleep'. Although it is referred to much later, when she asks her father to explain why he has raised the storm, the tempest itself is not mentioned by Miranda in what would normally be the first part of the action. She seems to have been disturbed in her sleep, and goes to seek her father, but her anxieties are all related directly to Caliban, whom she passes as she creeps, candle in hand, through the room where he sits by a fire, eating raw eggs. Prospero's 'Be collected, no more amazement' (1.2.13) responds to her alarm at this encounter and the sound of Caliban's mocking laughter. The following line-and-a-half (1.2.14–15) come in the next scene, when she is back in her bed and Prospero is comforting her. The closeness of father and daughter and the specifically sexual threat of Caliban are made clear. Nevertheless, details in Toyah Willcox's performance suggest adolescent fearlessness and even a childish delight in the situation. She puts her tongue out in mocking defiance of Caliban, and is perfectly capable of routing him when he spies on her bathing.

Ariel (Karl Johnson) is dressed in white overalls until the final scenes, when he appears as a master of ceremonies in a white tuxedo. He has an enigmatic, somewhat combative attitude towards the master who, if worse comes to worst, can still pin him in an oak tree or (in this version) behind the glass of a mirror. Ariel disappears at will, and does not always come immediately at Prospero's bidding, and the sardonic clarity of Johnson's speech, like that of his quietly-spoken master, suggests a degree of social if not magical authority. Ferdinand and Miranda also speak with 'received pronunciation', as do the other characters, although Stefano adopts a painfully affected upper-class accent. By contrast, Jack Birkett as Caliban speaks with his own Yorkshire accent, which allows him to savour and exploit the vehemence of his language. The overall effect is of a well-spoken but not self-consciously eloquent film. Heathcote Williams was for Jarman 'an ideal Prospero [who] performs sympathetic magic, destroys the poetry and finds the meaning'.

I've rarely heard lines spoken with such clarity – 'and my zenith doth depend upon a most auspicious star'. These words are spoken softly, not bawled across the footlights. How Shakespeare would have loved the cinema![18]

Prospero speaks to the 'ministers' he controls with the same quiet authority, and addresses Miranda in tones of quiet explanation, so that the effect is startling when he commands her not to speak on Ferdinand's behalf or reproves his treacherous brother and his allies. Even then, sharpness of speech is not accompanied by a notable increase in volume. This is effectively a chamber production of the script, the loudness reserved for the cackling of Caliban, the drunken whooping of Trinculo and Stefano, and the howling of the unseen hunting dogs that harass them. (Their physical torture is administered by two female dwarfs, like those in Velazquez' painting *Las Meñinas*.)

Rather than devise on-screen magic tricks beyond simple superimpositions or jump cuts to effect Ariel's appearances and appearances — there is no flying — Jarman instead creates an atmosphere of magical foreboding, with eerie sounds, atmospheric lighting, and shots of Prospero at work in his study with books, geometrical instruments, his magic staff, and a good many candles. The candlelight chiaroscuro effects are often handsome, and – especially when naked male bodies are available — anticipate his *Caravaggio* (1986). Apart from these moments, the tensions between Ariel and Prospero, and the crowd of happy sailors who entertain the lovers and welcome Elizabeth Welch as she sings 'Stormy Weather', there is less in *The Tempest* to reflect Jarman's sexual and social politics than in such determinedly queer films as *Sebastiane* (1976), *The Angelic Conversation* (1985), and *Edward II* (1991) (Figure 2.2). The defeat of Caliban's comic lasciviousness lends

Figure 2.2. *The Tempest* (Derek Jarman, 1979): Elizabeth Welch sings 'Stormy Weather'.

the film an air of innocence. Jarman wrote that he composed the film simply in 'masters, mid-shots and close-ups', and that 'the camera hardly ever goes on a wander'. This was deliberate, 'as I've noticed that if one deals with unconventional subject-matter, experimental camera-work can push a film over into incoherence'. In *The Tempest*, he observed, 'we paint pictures, frame each static shot and allow the play to unfold in them as within a proscenium arch'.[19] Only the ineffective blue-filtered exteriors, with courtiers and clowns among the Northumbrian sand dunes of Bamborough, and Ferdinand emerging naked from the icy waves, break the otherwise consistently maintained painterly and magical aesthetic of the film.

Taymor's *Tempest* is full of elaborate special effects, beginning with a spectacular realization of the storm, but it lacks the intimacy of Jarman's. However, more of the original text is heard throughout, and the play's ordering of the action is followed more closely. The scenes with the shipwrecked courtiers, the weakest element of Jarman's *Tempest*, both visually and in the acting, are given full effect: in their black doublets, like so many shiny beetles, they bring the murderous intrigue of Milan and Naples to the 'innocent' but disorienting Hawaiian island landscape of thick woodlands, volcanic rocks, and tempestuous sea. Whereas Jarman's court figures were all clownish, here they are credible reminders of the machinations that removed Prospera from the Dukedom that had been willed to her, branded her as a witch – lines for this being added to her narration – and exiled her. Neither director presents the masque, though Jarman uses lines from it in two scenes where Miranda is alone: in one of them she stands on a rocking horse, reciting Juno's 'Honour, riches, marriage blessing' (4.1.107 etc.) as though charmed by the idea. Taymor, convinced that the theatrical mode would be unintelligible to her audience and not anxious to pursue the celebration of marriage and sexuality, replaces the entertainment with a vision of the sky filled with animated celestial diagrams, compared by one critic to 'a trip to the planetarium'.[20]

Taymor retains Shakespeare's construction of the play's long second scene, which is fragmented by Jarman. This allows full scope for Helen Mirren's outstanding performance, which combines bitterness at her treatment, maternal affection for (and anxiety on behalf of) her daughter, and complex relationships with both Ariel (Ben Whishaw) and Caliban (Djimon Homisou). The former is an androgynous spirit – lacking the genitalia that in a Jarman film would be fully displayed – who continually fades in and out of view in water and among trees, visible at times in multiple images at different points on the screen and making his first appearance as a high plume of water rising from a semi-circular pool in Prospera's cell. As he describes the storm he is seen literally 'flaming amazement' around the foundering ship. This triumph of blue-screen and digital technology tends to place him at a remove from his master. (The masculine noun is used throughout, though at times she is addressed as 'ma'am' as if she were royalty or a senior police officer, both roles associated with Mirren.) On occasion he is outspoken, as when he shouts 'my liberty!' in response to her 'How now, moody?/What is't thou canst demand?' (1.2.244–6), but most of the time he does her bidding with good grace. The contrast between this pale wraith-like being and Caliban is emphasized. The latter is recognizably an African male – Homisou was born in Benin – his powerful physique encrusted with elaborate scars and protrusions of hardened skin and muscle, and a white patch running across one side of his face. His movements, derived from the Japanese dance discipline Butoh, have an eloquence that corresponds to his expressive use of the language he has learned. 'This island's mine, by Sycorax my mother' is not easy for Prospera to hear: she seems shaken by its force. At the end of the film he and Prospera stare at each other, their conflict unresolved, as he does not declare he will 'sue for grace hereafter'. She is now clad in the gown and tightly laced bodice that have been fetched from her cell, abandoning the trousers and skirted jacket she has worn hitherto. After the final act of conjuring in which she created a ring of fire within which the courtiers would be lodged until she appeared to them, her magic staff was cast into the sea, shattering on the rocks below her. Unlike Jarman's Prospero, who is unlikely to make the journey back to Milan, even after his magic has been forsworn, Prospera now assumes the honours and burden of her dukedom. There is no reflection that 'every third thought shall be [her] grave' (5.1.314), and she will no doubt get on with running the dukedom.

The post-colonial dimension of the play is made vividly and uncomfortably present by Taymor, but is wholly absent in Jarman's film, where although Caliban is described in the opening credits as 'a savage and deformed slave' he is really nothing of the kind. Jack Birkett is dark-skinned with a shaved head and disconcerting, staring eyes – the actor is in fact blind – but there is little that would register as more than alarming eccentricity. The planned revolt of Caliban is more threatening with Taymor, not only because of the intensity of Caliban himself but because it is supported by Alfred Molina's ability as Stefano to shift from geniality to hard-faced cruelty. Ferdinand and Miranda are a sweet pair of modern teenagers in love – he even croons 'O mistress mine' to her – as against the more adventurous couple played by Toyah Willcox and David Meyer for Jarman. Taymor's greatest advantage remains Mirren, whose speaking of the verse is sinewy, subtle, and passionate and, on occasion, sardonic. Unfortunately, the epilogue is handed over to a singer (Beth Gibbons) and intoned with many tedious repetitions over the end credits, themselves shown over images of books being drowned and falling from top to bottom of the screen. Like the 'penny arcade' sequences in *Titus* and some similar episodes earlier in her *Tempest*, the effect is that of a director commenting on her film: here it is also an usurpation of Prospero's role in mediating between the story and the audience. The director has the last words – and images.

For all their strong elements of fantasy and romance, both Taymor's and Jarman's films engage with *The Tempest* as being on one level a family drama. The tensions between personal and familial relationships and the larger political systems of obligation and duty are common to the plays and films discussed so far. In some changes of historical period, the exploration of these issues is blocked rather than fostered by the new setting: without a world in which the exercise of patriarchal authority is credible, the questioning of it or its presentation as an obstruction to the desire of lovers becomes problematic. The next chapter examines more closely some presentations of a range of amatory relationships, from the taming of shrews in Renaissance Italy to the love between men in ancient Rome.

Gender Matters in Comedy

Since the early 1970s the analysis of representations of gender conventions and sexuality has been a vital and energizing element of film studies. With varying degrees of engagement with psychoanalytical theories, the ways in which the camera directs and controls the view of bodies, specifically those of women, have been debated in response to a seminal article by Laura Mulvey, whose central proposition – usually referred in terms of her concept of the 'male gaze' – has been the basis of searching analyses of individual films and whole genres.[1] At the same time, another strand of feminist criticism has attended as much to the narratives as to the 'ways of seeing' in films. Alongside the feminist interpretation of Shakespearian and other early modern drama, these developments have informed some of the most valuable commentary on Shakespearian films. Because romantic love of one kind or another is a dominant factor in many film comedies, this chapter focuses on two aspects of gender at play. Stanley Cavell's claim, in *Pursuits of Happiness* (1981), for a connection between Shakespearian comedy and 'comedies of remarriage' of the 1930s has been noted in the Introduction (p. 13). These were films in which the advent of sound empowered heroines styled by Maria DiBattista as 'Fast-Talking Dames', whose high-speed articulacy is interpreted by her as a challenge to men, making comedy 'a dramatic and certainly literate alternative to the distinctly American film genre concerned with masculine codes: the Western'.[2] Given this cinematic pedigree – and the challenge it constitutes – how have the Shakespearian works fared in the medium that, by Cavell's reckoning, has profited by their example?

Comic Patriarchy, Masculine Assumptions

The fact that the two feature films of *The Taming of the Shrew* both cast Katherine and Petruchio with major stars – Mary Pickford and Douglas Fairbanks in 1929, Elizabeth Taylor and Richard Burton in 1967 – ensured that the emphasis would be on the pairs of actors whose mutual involvement stood in a direct relationship with that of the characters. In 1967 the off-screen marriage seemed to fulfil an dream; Taylor and Burton had been the subject of gossip-column scandal ever since the making of *Cleopatra* (1963). Whereas Pickford and Fairbanks were moving towards their divorce, Taylor and Burton, married in 1964, were for the time being a newly respectable married pair. Earlier in 1966 they had appeared as the mutually destructive couple George and Martha in the screen adaptation of Edward Albee's play *Who's Afraid of Virginia Woolf?*

Pickford, although idolized as 'America's Sweetheart' and famous for playing lovable and spirited young girls, was nobody's fool on-screen or off. As Jeanine Basinger puts it, she 'managed to be likeable and unthreatening yet also a character who was all about will, something audiences clearly responded to in her.'[3] Even in films with a strong dose of sentiment, independence of mind and intolerance of injustice were recurring elements in the Pickford persona. Fairbanks, celebrated until the mid-1920s principally for his comedy roles as a peppy incarnation of upwardly mobile, likeable American young manhood, notable for physical daring that enabled him to overcome adversity with a smile, seemed the perfect partner for her in real life, if not on the screen. (*The Taming of the Shrew* was their first and last film together.) Basinger sums up the public perception of their marriage:

The public loved them both individually, and to have them together was beyond a fan's wildest dreams of star heaven. From the beginning their devoted public dubbed them 'Doug and Mary', 'Mary and Doug' – just two down-to-earth, lovable people the fans felt they knew on a first-name basis . . . In the public's mind, who else would either of them ever possibly want to marry? They deserved each other and belonged with each other.[4]

By 1929 Pickford had decided that the 'little girl' roles were no longer for her, and Fairbanks was close to the end of a career that had shifted after *The Mark of Zorro* (1920) into historical romances, and roles in which the values he stood for as a juvenile lead took on a new dimension. His swashbuckling always has an edge of good humour, and engenders a delight in his prowess and the defeat of adversaries which transfers the violence to a realm of masculine sportsmanship. Gaylyn Studlar has characterized Fairbanks's appeal as a confirmation of 'the childish type of man, as the ideal symbolic merging of a dynamic masculinity associated with modernity and an anachronistic male individualism associated with the "primitive" American past and cultural nostalgia.'[5] The costume roles extended this mixture of the modern and primitive to the medieval England of *Robin Hood* (1922), the Arabian Nights world of *The Thief of Baghdad* (1924), and now to Renaissance Padua. Pickford and Fairbanks together incarnated a version of the American Dream, but the celebrity of Taylor and Burton seemed to reflect a more cynical, self-indulgent glamour, rather than the idealized homeliness of the Hollywood house, Pickfair, that Mary and Doug built. Unfortunately, the 1929 *Shrew* marked the turning point in the Pickford–Fairbanks marriage. The stress of working within the restrictions required by sound recording seems to have exacerbated tensions already present. Fairbanks's uncharacteristically unprofessional behaviour contributed to the film going over budget by $75,000 (reaching a total of $578,191, 56) and box office was disappointing, despite *Variety*'s assurance that this was 'a money picture, easily, for it's worth 75¢ for anyone to see Mary Pickford and Douglas Fairbanks do this stuff in a vastly extravagant burlesque of Bill Shakespeare's best laugh.'[6]

Other considerations apart, the differences in chemistry between the pairs of leading actors, and between them and their audiences, make for divergent approaches to the play. Neither film addresses with any critical acumen the patriarchal assumptions underlying the plot: that fathers can dispose of their daughters in marriage, making one sister's betrothal conditional on finding a match for the other; and that in principle women should be subordinated to their partner. Nevertheless, acceptance of the social order is not absolute in either case. In Zeffirelli's tirelessly rumbustious film, Petruchio begins as a lout and Katherine as a violent termagant, but they achieve stillness amid the fuss and frantic laughter of Padua. For all the overdone eccentricities of the supporting characters and the florid detail of the *mise en scène*, Zeffirelli's film pursues a consistent line in romanticizing the relationship between the principals. The moments when Katherine is seen and admired by Petruchio are marked carefully, and the distinctive quality of the actress's eyes becomes a counter to the masculine gaze on his part and that of the camera.

The turning point comes at Petruchio's house. Zeffirelli has a sequence that parallels that in the 1929 film in some respects, but the outcome is different. After a scene in their bedroom where she invites him to join her on the bed, then brains him with a warming pan, Burton as Petruchio flings the bedding around before going onto the gallery overlooking the hall and announcing to his servants that 'this is the way to kill a wife with kindness'. Katherine is shown sobbing into her pillow, but presently a thought seems to strike her and she smiles. The score's 'love' theme suggests what this might be, and in the morning Petruchio is astonished to find her supervising the servants as they clean the chandelier. Perhaps the smile was because she realized that she could 'kill' his arrogance with a display of housewifery?

In the final scene the sight of children playing with a dog seems to suggest something to her, a hint of the maternal instinct that in this society can (or ought to) be fulfilled only in marriage. From her arrival leading the errant wives back to the room, the scene is staged and shot in a more stable, less frantic mode than many of the other episodes. During her speech there is no background hubbub and on 'True obedience' she looks directly at Petruchio. Zeffirelli reports in his autobiography that after the 'submission' speech 'I saw [Burton] wipe away a tear. "All right, my girl, I wish you'd put that into practice." She looked him straight in the eye. "Of course, I can't say it in words like that, but my heart is there."'[7] Katherine and Petruchio have won the wager by a demonstration of true feeling, and done so in the face of conventional attitudes that Bianca and her father espouse but which (in Bianca's case) are clearly a cover for a determination to have her own way. Petruchio for his part has been jolted out of his swaggering, carousing manner, but after he has spoken his final lines to the other men, he turns to find that Katherine has disappeared, and he has to pursue her through the crowd of guests. Barbara Hodgdon, in a persuasive reading of the two films, suggests that 'Kate/Taylor's desire for Petruchio/Burton, and for children, has apparently transferred to all women; and Burton's newly eroticized body must fight through this unruly mob to make his exit, much as Burton and Taylor were plagued by intrusive Roman *paparazzi* wherever they went.'[8] Even without this possible evocation of contemporary stardom, the effect is once again to distinguish the couple from the Paduan crowd.

The 1929 film has a different agenda, conferring victory subtly but more directly on Pickford's crafty Katherine, notwithstanding her humiliation at the wedding and the ill treatment she has received on the road to Petruchio's house. Both Katherine and Petruchio wield whips, and in their first encounter she keeps him at bay with hers, standing at the top of a high staircase that allows her to begin with an advantage. The wooing takes its course, and the wedding follows, with Petruchio's display of indecorous dress and behaviour (he eats an apple noisily during the ceremony) and his assertion of male privilege to be master of 'what is [his] own', his goods and chattels (etc.) and 'buckler [her] against a million' (3.3.101–11). Once they have reached his house and she has been denied the food she craves, an episode follows that has no equivalent in the play and that foregrounds Katherine/Pickford's skill in manipulating her man with winsome but effectively dominating behaviour.

After preventing her from having any dinner, Petruchio escorts Katherine upstairs to their bridal chamber, ushering her in at the door with a show of uxorious pride. But he then sits down to a game of patience, neglecting her. Having starved her of food, it seems he is going to deprive her of the sexual satisfaction that (whether or not she wants it) should be her right. Frustrated, she goes into an adjoining room where a nightdress and negligée are laid out ready for her. He goes downstairs to eat the meal he denied her, feeding scraps to a large hound, Troilus. We see her standing in front of the dressing table in her bedraggled dress, which is then transformed in a dissolve into the wedding-night finery. She sneaks out onto the landing and overhears him boasting to his dog about his plan to disrupt their night. This is her opportunity to beat him at his own game. Petruchio returns to the bedroom and makes as much noise as he can, throwing a stool across the room, then sitting down and singing nonsensically at the top of his voice. She at first feigns sleep, but then sits up and applauds his singing. He opens a window to let in a blast of cold wind and she calmly opens another, pretending to enjoy the fresh air. When he insists that the moon is the sun she at first contradicts him, then in a close-up we see her realize that this is a tactical error, and she accepts his claim for whichever celestial body he chooses to call it. (The episode from 4.6 is thus folded into the new scene.) Petruchio pretends to find a spot on the bedclothes and pulls them off, but she betters his example by heaving the whole mattress onto the floor, making herself comfortable there and inviting him coyly to join her. After he pulls a pillow from behind her head, they have a tug-of-war over possession of it until the struggle becomes a contest in pushing one another. Exasperated when a violent shove sends her back onto the mattress, she picks up a stool and throws it, hitting him on the head. He staggers round, dazed, muttering 'I that have heard lions roar', and she takes him under her arm and leads him to sit on the mattress. She sees a whip on the floor – they both brought whips into the room when they first arrived there – registers it with a sidelong glance to camera, and surreptitiously picks it up and throws it on the fire as she nurses her wounded would-be tyrant. (As he has a whip with him in the final scene, this one must be hers.)

What was planned as his taming of her has become her victory over him, though he may not realize it. At the same time, casting the whip into the fire is an abandonment of the strategy by which she has sought to control him. The implication is that she now has better means at her disposal. The quasi-maternal moment has an edge to it that carries over into the very next shot, the final feast. Unlike Zeffirelli's staging, this is a private occasion, with only a few guests seated at a table in a spacious loggia. There is no wager between the men, and the dialogue opens directly with Katherine's line, 'Thy husband is thy lord, thy life, thy keeper' (5.2.151). Pickford's 'submission' is qualified by a wink. Within the scene this is directed towards Bianca, who acknowledges it, but the angle of the close-up on Katherine ensures that it is also aimed at the cinema audience. The moment of complicity is a reminder that this is 'Mary' as well as Katherine. Petruchio, basking in the apparent confirmation of male supremacy but with his head bandaged as a result of the stool she threw at him, smiles in approval, oblivious to the pyrrhic nature of his victory, and Baptista initiates a chorus encouraging the guests to drink to their wives 'and the wives yet to be'. Petruchio may be seated at the head of the table, but his wife stands beside him, implicitly the power behind the chair. There are no comments from the assembled company and no references to children being a likely outcome of the marriage: the final image is about the mastery women desire – to invoke the wisdom of Chaucer's Wife of Bath – and the fact that it can be attained without men realizing it. In this respect the film from 1929, which had opened with a shot of a Punch-and-Judy show and its crude image of violent male domination, is more radical in its final scene than its successor from 1967.

Branagh's *Much Ado About Nothing* (1993) begins with an idyllic scene that establishes Beatrice as a source of poetic reason. The lyrics of 'Sigh no more, ladies . . .' are spoken by a warm, knowing female voice as they are spelled out against a black background, which then fades to a watercolour of a villa in its hillside setting. This fades in turn to the view of the villa that Leonato (Richard Briers) is painting. The camera pans across the group of family, labourers, and household staff relaxing happily at a picnic after their not-too-demanding toil. The words are being spoken by Beatrice (Emma Thompson) as she sits in a tree, a book in one hand and a grape in the other. Suddenly a messenger arrives with the news that Don Pedro is on his way, accompanied by Claudio and Benedick. There is a foretaste of the 'merry war' between Beatrice and Benedick, and Hero's interest in Claudio is indicated. The guests are seen, riding towards the villa. A phalanx of riders thunders towards the camera: a series of crescendos in the accompanying music underlines the moment when each of them rises over the crest of a hill in slow motion, raising their arms and cheering.

After this parody of self-satisfied machismo, in another slow motion shot their hosts rush down from the hillside. A montage of frenzied preparations follows, and both parties bathe and change their clothes. The women shriek with anticipation as they shower and dress, and Beatrice and Hero look down from a high window as the 'cavalry' approaches. As they arrive at the villa, one of Don Pedro's men plunges from horseback into the waters of the open-air washhouse where many of them strip naked and cavort. After final adjustments to their dress – with a shot that shows Beatrice with a look of determined anticipation and another in which Margaret powders her bosom – household and guests meet in the inner courtyard. Seen from above, they are in two V-formations, with Pedro and Leonato heading their respective groups. The music that has accompanied all this rises to a climax and then, like the conclusion of an overture, ends on a triumphant note.

As well as characterizing some of the leading figures deftly, this tongue-in-cheek homage to *The Magnificent Seven* sets up the contrast between the masculine realm of Don Pedro and his comrades-in-arms and the predominantly feminine atmosphere of the villa. The stereotypes are clear: women shriek and primp, men josh each other and splash around as though they were in a Tuscan locker room. At the same time, these commonplace attributes are qualified: Beatrice is already seen to be a force to be reckoned with and Leonato paints (showing sensitivity), and although he is clearly in command of his situation, he has trouble getting his boots on. Don Pedro (Denzel Washington) exudes quiet authority as he and his newly washed cohort stride through the garden, while Don John (Keanu Reeves) already wears the scowl he can never banish from his face. There is also, in the formal precision of the final overhead shot, a quasi-theatrical image of principals and a supporting cast that reinforces the sense of comic organization, and it is soon apparent that, for their friends, Benedick and Beatrice are a familiar and keenly anticipated comic turn. The conventional delineation of male and female spheres, which Branagh adopted from the 1988 stage production in which he had been directed by Judi Dench, helps to naturalize the terms of the subsequent conversations between Benedick, Pedro, and Claudio (Robert Sean Leonard) that set up the wooing by proxy. When Don John is later seen being given a massage by his henchman Conrade (Richard Clifford), he is naked, at least from the waist upwards, and in the softly glowing light there is a suggestion of the homosocial – if not homosexual – world he inhabits. When Benedick, now convinced that Beatrice is in love with him, is seen trying on scarves before a mirror, the taunting by Leonato, Antonio, Pedro, and Claudio marks his transformation into a lover as an adoption of 'effeminate' behaviour. This complements the scorn he shows in his soliloquy that begins his overhearing scene (the play's 2.3) for the change in Claudio from a soldier to a lover. The watch (formed from the villa's servants) may be considered a parody of the military discipline and masculine solidarity of Pedro's party, though any such connection is obscured by Michael Keaton's performance of Dogberry as the village psychopath, physically abusing his 'partner' Verges at any opportunity.

For a modern audience the strong identification of the guests with military solidarity and chivalric codes of honour explains – though it cannot excuse – the subsequent slander of Hero and its consequences. Branagh does his best to account for Claudio's behaviour by having him witness Margaret masquerading as Hero, though it may be thought that nothing will completely exonerate him. Although the event is still described as 'speaking out of a chamber window', the supposed Hero is seen enjoying energetic sexual intercourse with Borachio.[9] Both Hero and Claudio are handsome juvenile leads, idealized conventionally by the photography but (especially in her case) with little to say for themselves. By way of contrast, the glamour with which Beatrice is presented is always qualified by Emma Thompson's expressive looks of anxiety, scorn, or – after she and Benedick have accepted their love for each other – affection. The wedding scene is made as violent and distressing as possible: Claudio flings Hero to the ground, and her father also attacks her physically and has to be restrained. Nevertheless, this is where the film shifts the narrative no closer to darkness than its idyllic mise-en-scène and pre-emptive optimism will allow. Establishing the sexual and social mores of the society depicted so that they correspond to those assumed in the plot while seeming credible – or at least acceptable – to modern audiences is never easy, even in a production set (albeit vaguely) in a version of the past, but Branagh does not have to deal with the kind of problem identified by Anthony Lane in his *New Yorker* review of Joss Whedon's stylish contemporary production. There a prologue that shows Benedick gathering up his clothes and stealing away from Beatrice's bedroom as she sleeps provides a credible modern backstory, but, as Lane points out, the conduct 'scars the moral landscape in which the play takes root', making the film 'float free, away from social contracts of any import, towards the fantastic'.[10]

The centre of Branagh's film, as of Whedon's, remains the bringing together of Beatrice and Benedick. After the tricks played on them by their friends, the contrasting soliloquies of the two reluctant lovers give a powerful impression of sincere attachment finally acknowledged. The crucial scene, which shows the principals at their very best, is that of the reluctant lovers' mutual admission of affection, and Beatrice's command 'Kill Claudio', which is rendered with fine intensity by Thompson and received with proportionate dismay by Branagh. This takes place before the altar in the little chapel where the wedding should have been solemnized, a private space that concentrates the seriousness and emotional force of the exchange. Beatrice, standing with her back to the altar, exclaims 'Oh that I were a man!'

and defines the challenge as 'a man's office', her fierceness underlining the frustration of the restriction dictated by conventional gender roles. Benedick accepts the serious consequences of his position as a man for the first time: until now, male identity has been a matter of conviviality and humour. The effect is of course inscribed in the play itself, and Whedon's actors, Alexis Denisof and Amy Acker, achieve a comparable intensity and clarity. Through the performances of Branagh and Thompson in this sequence the 1993 film takes on its own responsibilities more fully than in its lenient treatment of Claudio. Branagh makes the discovery of the deception, the confrontation between the two 'old men' and Pedro and Claudio, and the scene in which Benedick carries out his promise to challenge his friend appropriately uncomfortable. After Claudio's penance at Hero's tomb and the restoration to him of the woman that was lost, the final festivity is allowed its full value. In a single continuous take the camera follows dancing couples through the villa's inner courtyard and out into the garden, rising high above the rejoicing crowds to end with a view across the valley towards the gentle hills and the sky. Don John has been dragged back, and his punishment promised but postponed. Don Pedro does not join in the dance, a decision made on the day by director and actor that matches Benedick's 'Prince thou art sad, get thee a wife, get thee a wife' (5.4.121–2) and adds a moment (but no more than that) of melancholy to the holiday humour that prevails. Although this concluding production number is not to everyone's taste, the dance and song, and the ever-widening travelling shot with the camera rising to a giddy vantage point above the villa and the whole valley beyond, provide an expansiveness that Whedon's film lacks, given the prevalence of medium shots and close-ups and the confines of the house and garden, which preclude such cinematic gestures of release.

The traditional familial model, with distinctions between masculine and feminine spheres and a patriarchal construct of marriage, that underlies *Much Ado About Nothing* is present in other comedies, with similar threats to its stability and variations on the difficulty of reconciling youthful desire with social imperatives. *A Midsummer Night's Dream*, beginning with the assertion by Egeus of his rights over his daughter Hermia, ends by granting happiness to four couples, three of them mortal and one supernatural. (In 4.1, as though anxious to dispose of a dramatic device that has served its purpose, Shakespeare has Theseus off-handedly overrule Egeus when the sleeping lovers are discovered in the forest.) The play also encompasses the tragic end, rendered as mirth, of the legendary mortal pair Pyramus and Thisbe. In Michael Hoffmann's 1999 film, a sixth couple is added, that of Bottom and his wife – a feature that was planned in Max Reinhardt's 1935 film but did not make the final cut.[11] To these pairings should be added the coupling of Bottom and Titania, though the consummation of their affair is made explicit only in Hoffmann's and Noble's versions. Reinhardt is more discreet, but he achieves an overall effect of mystical eroticism more powerful than that signalled in Hoffmann's elaborately detailed fairy realm, and his First Fairy (Nini Theilade) becomes a dancing surrogate for this dimension of his somewhat asexual Titania (Anita Louise).

Hoffmann's Oberon (Rupert Everett) is sulkily sexy, but there is little chemistry between him and Titania (Michelle Pfeiffer), for whom Bottom (Kevin Kline) is clearly a superior choice, especially as his ass's ears are more of a fetishistic decoration than a bestial transformation, and he has become a cuddly but implicitly well-endowed bedtime toy. David Denby, reviewing the film in the *New Yorker*, described Kline's 'rounded, glutinous voice from the back of his mouth which is the essence of asshood – self-satisfied, almost gurgling' as he is 'caught between disbelief and obscene relish of [Titania's] folly.'[12] Hoffmann has written about Bottom and Titania in terms of the late twentieth-century Hollywood's concern with 'relationships' and personal development: Bottom's home life is loveless, and if in the forest he 'glimpsed the possibility that he was truly lovable, it might give the film the emotional spine [the director] wanted'. As for Titania, Hoffmann 'saw her as a woman who wanted to love simply, unconditionally, in a way the politics of her relationship with Oberon made impossible'.[13] Reinhardt had made Oberon (Victor Jory) a sinister dominator of the forest, but without suggesting any physical designs on the fairy queen, whose attendants are almost all of them children and who seems more interested in cherishing Bottom (James Cagney) than bedding him. Anxiety about the Fairy Queen's love life was not on the German director's agenda, and Bottom's shrewish wife would have been a comic grace note, not a reason for him to seek counselling.

In Peter Hall's film Judi Dench as Titania – naked except for strategically applied leaves – makes it clear with her first words to the transformed Bottom that she finds him irresistibly attractive, and she is unequivocal about having her love 'to *bed* – and to arise' (3.1.153). Such is Dench's mastery of the language that she can infuse such lines as 'The moon methinks looks with a wat'ry eye,/And when she weeps,/weeps every little flower,/Lamenting some enforcèd chastity' (179–81) with a frank but at the same time tender desire to proceed with his liberation. In their second scene together (4.1) she nestles against the already sleeping ass with similar exquisitely modulated erotic feeling – 'O how I love thee! How I dote on thee!' (42) – but when she wakes, after a moment of revulsion and some tears, she clearly feels the same way towards Oberon. Their hands clasp in the air in shots intercut with delicate kisses and contented embracing on her part. (Ian Richardson, as Oberon, smiles happily but is less active in expressing his desires.) However, the first prize for explicit eroticism among the fairies has to go to Adrian Noble's film. Alex Jennings, doubling Oberon and Theseus, is restrained and formal, but nevertheless makes his desires clear. This plays effectively opposite the high-class, murmuring eroticism of Lindsay Duncan's Titania and – in a less overt fashion – her Hippolyta, who clearly looks forward as much as Theseus to their wedding night. As Titania she encounters Bottom (Desmond Barritt) with unequivocally erotic delight, lying down and stretching up a leg to massage his groin with 'Thou art as wise as thou art beautiful' (3.2.140). She takes him to her bower, an inverted umbrella, its interior upholstered in red. As it floats off across a lagoon, the new lovers are silhouetted against the giant image of the full moon. When Bottom awakes after his enchanted evening, it is clear that the magic augmented his physique in more than ears and facial hair: he pulls back the waistband of his trousers on 'methought I had' (4.1.102) and registers disappointment when he discovers that he is no longer equipped as generously as he had been. In Hall's film the gesture on 'methought I had . . .' refers simply to the ass's ears, and in Hoffmann's, Bottom finds a ring left with him by the Fairy Queen. After gesturing towards the missing ears, he glances down, then holds out his flat palm as if pushing away the very idea of what else he might have had.

These variations on sex and marriage among the fairies might be supposed to be accompanied by a corresponding range of treatment for the mortal lovers. Apart from their speech and costume, young Athenian couples in the later films are distinguished from those of

Reinhardt by greater frankness about what might have been going on between them in the woods. All end their night in the forest the worse for wear, although the most bedraggled are Hoffmann's. His decision to make much of mud and the new-fangled bicycle also entails a good deal of sprawling in mire, which results in some near-nudity for the women and tactfully depicted (genitalia kept out of the frame) nudity for the young men. When the lovers are discovered by the hunting party they are lying naked on the green hillside outside the forest, with their clothes beside them, freshly laundered and pressed. When Theseus asks them to stand up (4.1.138) there is a moment of embarrassment and they manage to find enough linen to cover their private parts, for all the world like a quartet of Adams and Eves newly expelled from their Paradise. These mortals have been transformed into a frank and charmingly erotic group portrait. The fairy kingdom in the film is, as Celia R. Daileader puts it, 'quintessentially quasi-nude, with the visually compelling difference that fairy attire tends to be translucent and fairy skin dusted with glitter – that is, the categories of "clothed" and "nude" are harder to distinguish'.[14] Once in the woods, anything goes, and the mortals get more than they bargained for or cared to admit they desired, but although Hoffmann has, in the opening titles, set his film so firmly in a period when bicycles are a sign of the emancipation of women, he nevertheless has to have Theseus threaten Hermia with death as well as the nunnery if she does not obey her father. The use of Italian opera in Hoffmann's film, witty in itself and sustained throughout, suggests an imaginative realm corresponding to the love tragedies and chivalric romances evoked in the character types and situations of 'Pyramus and Thisbe'. However, this extension of the period setting reinforces the anachronism of the sentence passed on Hermia. Noble's production, established as the dream of a little boy who is first seen in a bedroom furnished with vintage toys, helps to detach this assertion of patriarchal oppression from any contemporary reality. Nor does the logic of the scene pose a problem for Reinhardt with his half-classical, half-Elizabethan (and partly Rococo) Athens, or Hall with the eclectic mixture of modern and Elizabethan dress in an English country house identified defiantly on its first appearance as 'Athens'.

As for Hippolyta's identity as an Amazon whom Theseus has wooed with his sword, both Reinhardt and Hall contrive more or less appropriate attire for her first appearance. Reinhardt had planned to show the defeat of the Amazons, but this was not included: instead the opening scene shows her arrival, not entirely pleased by her situation, in a 'classical' costume wound about with a snake. The next time we see her she appears to have cheered up, and is dressed in a farthingale, and the scene has shifted to a terrace of the palace.[15] Hall's Hippolyta (Barbara Jefford) is in a leather minidress and boots, ready for the part of a (James) Bond Woman. For Hoffmann and Noble, the emphasis is on her indignation at the sentence passed on Hermia. Noble has Theseus and Hippolyta spied on through a keyhole by his voyeuristic little boy as they anticipate the erotic fulfilment of their marriage. After Theseus' insistence to Hermia that he cannot extenuate the 'harsh Athenian law' she slaps him on the cheek before stalking off, and he hurries after her with a bewildered 'What cheer, my love?' (1.1.122). She seemed content with his assurance that he would be wedding her 'in another key', but the relationship has taken a step backward.

'Manhood', as defined by readiness to defend the honour of women, is mocked by Puck when he adopts the voices of Lysander and Demetrius and gets them lost in the fog: 'Follow my voice; we'll try no manhood here' (3.2.413). The conventionally masculine qualities of valour and chivalry are shadowed in the decisions that must be made by the amateur actors. Is Pyramus a lover or a tyrant? Is Thisbe by any chance a 'wandering knight'? (No such luck, Flute.) How 'condoling' is a lover's voice? That ladies will be frightened by a lion, whether or not it is a hanging matter, suggests another gender cliché, given full effect in the performance when Snug reassures the 'ladies ... whose gentle hearts do fear/The smallest monstrous mouse that creeps on floor' (5.1.217–18). Thisbe, although played in comic drag in all the films, is a notable example of feminine valour, the equal of her lover in resolve as well as eloquence. As well as replaying the anxieties of the past night in the mode of 'tragical mirth', this also resonates with the behaviour of Hermia and Helena. They have shown courage and initiative in leaving the city, and throughout the central action of the forest scenes, although bewildered by being lost in the wood and betrayed or frustrated in love, they are not especially timorous. (Hermia is alarmed after a nightmare that is in fact the only real dream in the play or the films, but she sets off in pursuit of her lover with renewed determination.) When Demetrius accuses Helena of 'impeaching' her 'modesty' by risking herself with a man in the forest at night (2.1.214–19), she puts up a spirited and reasoned defence which he responds to by running off like a cad. Gender roles are being undermined, even when they sustain common decency. All the films make the most of this, as they do of Bottom's pretensions as an alpha male, anxious to show his friends by singing that he is not afraid of being left alone in the woods, and ready to accept as his due the blandishments lavished on him by the fairies. Hoffmann undermines Bottom's pretensions by introducing him as a dandyish poseur in the little town (see Figure 3.1). (His first appearance is even heralded by a shot of a donkey pulling a cart.) To the amusement of his fellow citizens, after he has shown off his powers of declamation his dapper white suit is drenched in red wine by street urchins, and later he has to sneak away from his glowering wife to go to rehearsal. Reinhardt, having discarded the planned episodes with Bottom's spouse, creates a cosy, candlelit atmosphere for the mechanicals' discussion of their production (the play's 1.2), and Noble places the scene in a village hall. In Peter Hall's film the setting is a stable yard, self-evidently a 'found' location in the vicinity of the great house. They appear to have sneaked around the back of the mansion. This is more private than Hoffmann's scene in the *piazza*, but fails to establish an environment that the workmen own, distinct both from the palace and the woods. In a comedy where transactions in gender and power and adjustments in amatory relationships are the chief business to be transacted among the fairies and the upper crust characters, the lifestyle of the male working class – not so rich and famous – needs to be grounded in a sense of homosocial comfort: soon, in rehearsing and playing the tragedy of Pyramus and Thisbe, they will make their own comic foray into more exotic and hazardous territory.

Figure 3.1. *A Midsummer Night's Dream* (Michael Hoffmann, 1999): Bottom (Kevin Kline) shows off his talents in the *piazza*.

Cross-Dressing for Comedy

In the film adaptations of *As You like It* and *Twelfth Night*, in which a young woman disguises herself as a boy, the medium calls for a more thorough disguise than the theatre, if only because of the camera's ability (and need) to get close to faces. On stage, except in extreme circumstances, the dialogue and the responses of the other actors bear much of the responsibility for convincing an audience that Ganymede or Cesario are boys. In a prologue to his *Twelfth Night*, accompanied by a newly written verse narration (insisted on by the producers after test screenings), Nunn has Viola (Imogen Stubbs) performing as a man with her twin brother for a ship's concert. His luggage, washed ashore after the wreck, includes the wherewithal (including a false moustache) to repeat the impersonation.[16] Elisabeth Bergner in Paul Czinner's *As You like It* (1936) makes few concessions to credibility, and seems to have arranged for beauty treatments and hairdressing appointments in the forest. Coupled with the archness of her physical and vocal performance her Ganymede is scarcely credible, even when 'he' is impersonating Rosalind. Perhaps his enforced rustic upbringing has kept Orlando (Laurence Olivier) from meeting any saucy lackeys until now: unfortunately his comment that Ganymede's 'accent is something finer than [he] could purchase in so removed a dwelling' (3.2.331–2) and her claim to have been taught by 'an old religious uncle' who was 'inland bred' seem to apply to her strong German pronunciation. There is much skittishness and soulful glancing on her part, and a generally bemused response on his, and there is never any threat of a closer approach that would give the game away. Her jerkin, shorts, tights, and ankle boots do nothing to disguise her femininity. In Edzard's *As You Like It* (1992) Emma Croft is convincingly disguised in her woollen watch cap (hiding most of her hair), hooded sweatshirt, and jeans. Her insistence that, though 'caparisoned like a man', she does not 'have a doublet and hose in [her] disposition' (3.2.190–3) is allowed to stand.

Bryce Dallas Howard, in Branagh's film, does not speak the line: her breeches, boots, cap, and tweed jacket are believable forest apparel for the reasonably prosperous young countryman of the nineteenth century, though she does not wear a 'curtle axe' or carry a boar spear. Celia (Romola Garai) declares that she will adopt 'poor and mean attire' and 'with a kind of umber smirch [her] face' (1.3.110–11), but wears a passably fashionable dress throughout and does not alter her complexion. (For the wedding, both appear in kimonos with their hair dressed in a suitably 'Japanese' manner.) More important than the sartorial details, though, is the sense of adventure. Howard broaches the idea of dressing like 'a man' in a half-whisper, mouthing the word as though impressed by her daring, and Garai as Celia responds in kind. The balance between the two personalities is developed as the story unfolds. Celia's impatience with Rosalind's volubility and anxiety about her 'simply misusing' their sex in her 'love prate', and her reluctance to speak the lines that will 'marry' Ganymede to Orlando (in 4.1) are grounded in an understanding of what is at stake. The sense that women's rights as well as desires should be attended to is also served in the treatment of Audrey (Janet McTeer), who stands no nonsense from Touchstone (Alfred Molina). She slaps him both times he refers to her as a slut (3.3.33 and 35) and he realizes he will get nowhere with her unless he offers to marry her. Confirming her admiration for his manly fortitude, she looks on approvingly as he sends the hapless William packing.

Both Edzard and Branagh allow for a moment in the scene of 'marriage' by Celia when Ganymede and Orlando come close to an embrace, or even a kiss, and Edzard has the couple almost kiss in 4.1, with Orlando's 'I would kiss before I spoke' (68). Rosalind kisses him on the lips, much to his surprise – he involuntarily raises his hand to wipe his mouth – on 'I do take thee, Orlando, for my husband' (130–1). Patricia Lennox points out that until now the 'relatively unimaginative Orlando' has been fascinated by Ganymede 'as a kind of very smart kid brother'. Now, as 'he looks at Ganymede and puts the finger back in his mouth as if rechecking its pleasant taste', we have arrived at 'the moment where the erotic enters the film', and 'it is this awareness of adult sexuality that begins the loss of Arden's freedom'.[17] In Branagh's film Orlando (David Oyelowo) holds Rosalind in a tight embrace with 'I would kiss before I spoke', and a few lines later she has her eyes closed in anticipation and finds it hard not to complete the kiss that seems imminent with, 'Why then, can one desire too much of a good thing?' (115–16) before she asks Celia to marry them. He pulls away, as if realizing that they are in deep waters. None of the films suggest more than a frisson of this kind – *Shakespeare in Love* goes much further (but not all the way) in gender-bending. Edzard omits the epilogue, but both Czinner and Branagh feature it. In 1936 Bergner appears in her wedding dress on 'our' side of the gates (now bearing the word 'Epilogue') behind which the rustic revelry can be seen to continue. With 'my way is to conjure you' a dissolve returns her to her doublet and hose until she says 'and I charge you, O men ...'. The parenthetical reference to the men's feelings about women – 'as I perceive by your simpering none of you hates them' – is omitted. With 'that the play may please' she curtsies, and the epilogue lacks the references to beards, bad breath, and displeasing complexions. Branagh takes the breaking with illusion a stage further. After the first of the end credits, we suddenly see a shot of the woods, and Rosalind strides towards us speaking the first lines of the epilogue. As she comes level with it, the camera swings round to reveal the film unit's base. Howard walks past the technicians and their equipment and a wardrobe assistant takes her jacket as Howard is handed a coffee cup. She continues towards the parked trailers, and delivers the final lines from the step of her dressing room. At one point the director can be glimpsed scuttling out of the shot behind her, hunched over his portable monitor, and when the door of her dressing room has closed after 'bid me farewell' his voice is heard off-screen calling 'a-a-and cut'. The whole of the speech is spoken, and Howard's 'O men' is drawn out slightly with a touch of comic reproach, though she steps back into character as Ganymede with, 'If I were a woman'.

Branagh's treatment of the epilogue may be no more than a charming grace note, but the sudden reference to the filmmaking process, a reminder of the audience's pleasurable suspension of disbelief and the means used to support it, is of a different order from Czinner's trick photography. This celebrates Bergner herself and also reminds audiences of the 1930s of the androgynous appeal common to many of the actress's favourite roles. An important dimension of the 1936 film, no longer immediately accessible, is its participation in the cult of its female star, who had been a significant contributor to the discourses of sexual ambiguity in Weimar Germany. One admirer had described her in 1928 as 'the most charming and complete edition of the femme-enfant ... a ghost, a spirit of the air, a Puck, an Ariel, who unsettles and preoccupies a great, earnest hard-working city [Berlin], who confuses the minds and even the senses of people – and not only those of the young and the men'.[18] What we see in this epilogue is one of the iconic figures of twentieth-century androgyny, whose power extended beyond this relatively conservative film.

In Trevor Nunn's *Twelfth Night* (1996) cross-dressing takes its place among other disguising stratagems, including Malvolio's adoption of what is shown to be his secret erotic persona. Nunn suggests a general, if suppressed, erotic atmosphere in Illyria, with disguise as a common theme in more than one relationship. As for definitions of manliness, the nineteenth-century setting conveniently allows for Orsino's court to be characterized as a male, military preserve, while Olivia's is a more comfortable country household, not dissimilar to Branagh's villa in *Much Ado* and supplied with an appropriate complement of servants. The director was anxious to avoid 'the page-boy Viola' he had often seen, 'cherubic with long, girly hair, padded doublet, codpiece, decorated pantaloons, heeled shoes and still enjoying the femininity of lace cuffs and ruffs'. Nunn insists that 'such a Cesario . . . would be costing Viola very little' and 'not liberating her from the over-protective view of women that has enveloped her'.[19] After she arrives in Illyria Viola (Imogen Stubbs) prepares to be a man, having her curls cut off, binding her breasts tightly, and buttoning her brother's (presumably, spare) tunic with difficulty. After a moment when she pulls out the waistband and glances down, she stuffs a piece of cloth into her breeches. The thin moustache seen on shipboard now comes in handy, and for the time being she is convincing as a well-favoured youth. Her disguise withstands such moments of intimacy as that when Orsino holds her close to him and touches her lips with his finger on 'Diana's lip/Is not more rubious' (1.4.30–1); the 'near miss' during their first encounter when she faces Olivia across the frame in a tight two-shot; or her being obliged to sponge Orsino's back as he sits in his bathtub. (She carefully averts her eyes from a frontal view.) In the recognition scene, when she is brought face to face with her brother, the contrast between the two may suggest – if the viewer is disposed to cavil – that only distress or myopia can have caused Antonio to mistake the one for the other, but by this point the differences hardly matter. Sebastian peels off her moustache, confirming the end of her disguising, and in the dance that concludes the film she is in a ball gown. Cuts to the dialogue sidestep the awkwardness of Orsino's insistence that she shall be called Cesario 'while [she is] a man', until she is seen in 'other habits' and he does not declare that she will be his 'mistress and his fancy's queen' (5.1.374–5). Viola, for her part, has dissembled well, despite being tested by a series of manly activities, including fencing, smoking cigars, playing billiards, and riding without a side saddle. At fighting she is an unwilling but spirited adversary and more than a match for Sir Andrew, an accomplishment prepared for by an earlier scene in a fencing school. There is no question here of the comedy of the scene (3.4) playing, as the original text arguably suggests, on a woman's timorousness or lack of ability to defend herself.

Malvolio's adoption of yellow stockings and knee breeches at what he assumes to be Olivia's behest is supported by a brief scene during the night of noisy revelry where he is shown in his room, dressed in this dandified attire and enjoying a glass of wine as he reads a magazine entitled *L'Amour*. His erotic reveries clearly connect sexual pleasure with luxury, and also (in contrast to the military milieu of Orsino) a degree of effeminacy. When he discovers the letter, Malvolio embraces a nude female statue, pressing his face against its midriff, as though the Victorian soft porn of his magazine is about to become a more tangible reality. Olivia, for her part, overhears the song 'O mistress mine' as she lies in bed, and the revels in the kitchen are intercut with part of Viola's discussion with Orsino of women's ability to love (2.4). In another deft juxtaposition Nunn splices together the scene in which Sebastian has been accosted by Olivia – she already has him down on the sofa with her – and concludes he must be either dreaming or mad (4.3.15), with that in which the imprisoned Malvolio insists that he is sane ('Believe me, I am not [mad], I tell thee true', 4.2.106), thus juxtaposing the play's most important amatory disguises. However, one of the other significant and potentially erotic relationships is less fully explored. Antonio's love for Sebastian and his preparedness to sacrifice himself for the young man take their place alongside the other love relationships – including that of Maria and Toby – but without emphasis on any possible erotic element. He does not profess to 'adore' his friend after they first part company (2.1.41), and when he later tells his friend that he is lodging 'at the Elephant' he does not add 'There you shall have me' (3.3.43) a line whose gay potential has been underlined in more than one stage production. Nunn does nothing, though, to satisfy any desire we may have to see Antonio taken care of at the end of the film. He has been freed from his manacles, but like Malvolio he is alone when he leaves the gates of Olivia's house.

None of these versions of the cross-dressing comedies captures the pleasurably disturbing ambiguity that has been identified (and debated) in their Elizabethan counterparts, the frisson of the comely boy player shifting in and out of farthingale and doublet and hose, a potential treat for gazes of any gender. The transformation of Nunn's Viola is not nearly as erotic as the undressing of 'Thomas Kent' in a bedroom scene in *Shakespeare in Love* (1999), and it is difficult to recapture the erotic appeal of Bergner's outfit now that it corresponds to everyday fashion. Edzard's disguising of Rosalind as Ganymede in urban casual wear, though, is so convincing as to shift the emphasis to something more disturbing than Orlando's inability to see through a disguise: what is it about this boy that has the effect a girl ought to be having on him? The next stage of this speculation is not embarked on, and Orlando does not wonder (the text won't let him, but the subtext might) whether he has discovered he really fancies young men. In Edzard's film the question hangs, unasked, in the air. One wishes Derek Jarman or Sally Potter (director of *Orlando* (1992), after the novel by Virginia Woolf) had adapted one of these comedies. The result might have been an edgier version of the legitimately playful goings-on in Arden and Illyria.

Eros *in Tragedy*

No one can ever have mistaken *Romeo and Juliet* for anything but a tragedy. The play is advertised on the title pages of its earliest texts as 'an excellent conceited tragedy' (Q1) and 'the most excellent and lamentable tragedy' (Q2), and one of its major sources is a poem, *Romeus and Juliet*, identified as a 'tragical history'. Shakespeare's prologue promises the 'fearful passage' of the 'death-marked loves' of its title characters. A reminder of the prologue's promise comes before Romeo and his friends go to Capulet's feast, a moment of foreboding that anticipates 'some consequence yet hanging in the stars' (1.4.107). Nevertheless, up to the deaths of Mercutio and Tybalt and banishment of Romeo in the first scene of the third act, it has the makings of a comedy, with the lovers not yet 'star-cross'd' and busy with familiar strategies (willing accomplices, rope ladders) to bypass the opposition of their parents and families. If we leave the stars out of the matter, the crossing of the lovers' purposes can be identified with three more mundane factors: the 'ancient grudge' (never defined) between the Capulets and Montagues; the insistence by Juliet's father that she must marry the manifestly eligible Paris; and the testosterone-fuelled energy that permeates Verona's streets – 'For now', as the temperamentally pacific Benvolio warns Mercutio, 'these hot days, is the mad blood stirring' (3.1.4). The code of honour, emphasized in comic mode by the rival families' servants in the opening scene, requires any man wearing a sword – the defining emblem of 'gentle' status – to answer a word with a blow, and the deadliest insult is to call one's adversary a 'boy' or to accuse him of lying.

The films respond with different degrees of emphasis to the underlying assumptions of patriarchy and the identification of masculinity with a predisposition to violence, both of which are put in question by the play. The 1936 MGM production, which casts very mature actors as Benvolio, Mercutio, and Tybalt (necessary to complement a Romeo, Leslie Howard, in his mid-thirties), seems staid to generations that, since the success of *West Side Story* (on stage in 1957, on film in 1960), expect to see teenagers fighting and loving. It also removes most of the dialogue's sexual references, so that the bawdiness of the opening scene is missing; Mercutio (John Barrymore) stops short in his 'Queen Mab' aria before the lines about what Mab does for maids when they lie on their backs (1.4.91–4); and we do not hear him 'conjuring' the absent Romeo by the body parts of Rosaline (2.1). A surprising exception is made for Mercutio's explanation to the Nurse (Edna May Oliver) that 'the bawdy hand of the dial is even now upon the prick of noon' (2.3.104–5), which she responds to with an appreciative leer followed by a blow from her fan.

Both Castellani (1954) and Zeffirelli (1968), with much younger actors, achieve a stronger effect of hot blood rising, in the lovers themselves and in the rival gangs. Zeffirelli's treatment of the 'balcony scene' (2.1) features the bosom of Juliet (Olivia Hussey) with a frankly exploitative low-angle medium shot as she leans against the balustrade, and in the bedroom the upper part of her body is shown from the front. 'What satisfaction canst thou have tonight?' is spoken with a suggestion that, like any teenager in the 1960s, she would know what might be intended by his 'O wilt thou leave me so unsatisfied?' (2.1.167–8), though she is glad that Romeo is effectively proposing marriage. Zeffirelli has the lovers keep apart, until Romeo manages to clamber up a tree to be in kissing distance, when a dissolve to a view of the trees suggests that they make the most of their opportunity without (as used to be said) going all the way on their first date. The voyeurism here is charming in itself, and the bedroom scene is a relatively restrained affair compared to that in Luhrmann's film. There, the balcony scene has included a good deal of comic business, with Romeo setting off the security lights and stumbling among the furniture of the Capulets' swimming pool. The pool is important because a great deal of caressing goes on in it, accompanied by lyrical slow motion shots and appropriate music. (One of the images of the lovers seen in flashback as they lie dead will be from the underwater sequence.) In Luhrmann's equivalent of 3.5, Romeo (Leonardo di Caprio) climbs into Juliet's bedroom after he has been patched up following his spectacular fight with Tybalt, and they spend the night together, their awakening being filmed with tasteful eroticism: they are seen only from the waist up as they lie in bed and he manages to drape a sheet across his lap as he struggles into his undershorts. Both Zeffirelli and Luhrmann, although undoubtedly conscious of the need not to receive a censor's certificate that would cut out much of their 'youth' audience in the major markets, still enjoy greater freedom than Cukor in Hollywood in 1936, who had to reshoot his very decorous bedroom scene in response to the anxieties (and potential refusal of a certificate) by the Breen Office. At no point should Leslie Howard have been seen to lie (or have been lying) on the same bed as Norma Shearer.[1] Lurhmann's death scene has Juliet wake just before the poison has completely overpowered Romeo, a practice that dates back to David Garrick's performances in the mid-eighteenth century.[2] The death-in-love is underlined by the soundtrack, with Leontyne Price singing Isolde's 'Liebestod' – the 'love in death' – from the final scene of Wagner's *Tristan und Isolde* as the camera gazes down on the delicately interlaced bodies on their bier, surrounded by hundreds of candles. The last of the images intercut with this is of the white sheet Romeo had playfully pulled over them before he left her bedroom (in 3.5), which fades to a white screen and thence to the white of a hospital sheet in which one of the bodies (Romeo's?) has been wrapped before being loaded into an ambulance. The cumulative effect is one of a youthful eroticism that is innocent.

As for the young men of the two factions, in Zeffirelli's case the obsessive sexual wordplay of Mercutio (John McEnery) is augmented wherever possible by physical business, so that even when, lying in a fountain, he taunts Tybalt with the 'fiddlestick' that will settle his account he raises his sword from below the water in an unmistakably phallic gesture. At the end of the 'Queen Mab' speech, Mercutio has run away from his companions and stands alone in a small piazza. It is clear that the thought of Mab's erotic powers disturbs him, and Romeo goes to calm him down. They face each other from either side of the screen in a close-up suggesting the intimacy of their relationship, which is reinforced with a similar moment as Mercutio lies dying. At the end of the fight between Tybalt (Michael York) and Romeo (Leonard Whiting) the adversaries, now stripped to their shirts and rolling in the dust before Tybalt falls against Romeo's sword, lie together in a bloody parody of an embrace.

The leading uniformly attractive young men of both factions are eroticized, by their short tunics and figure-hugging tights and prominent codpieces, notably when the Capulets, led by Tybalt, move in on Mercutio and Benvolio to demand satisfaction for the insult of Romeo's presence at the feast, as a wide low-angle shot presents a careful arrangement of gracefully rounded buttocks and elegant legs (Figure 4.1). Like the camera placements in the bedroom scene (3.5) this has been cited as an example of the director's sexual preferences.[3] Even if we set aside this interpretation in personal terms, the erotic appeal of the film's youths is one of its most striking features. Zeffirelli recalls in his autobiography that Whiting 'was beautiful in that Renaissance page-boy way that was revived during the 1960s'.[4] In this respect casting served the director's desire to appeal to contemporary tastes while satisfying the demand for historical authenticity. Lady Capulet (Natasha Parry) clearly prefers the company (and possibly the favours) of Tybalt to that of her fussy husband, clearly her senior by at least a decade. During the feast she is given one of Capulet's lines to rebuke him, and she speaks 'You are a princox, go' (1.5.5) to the young

Figure 4.1. *Romeo and Juliet* (Franco Zeffirelli, 1968): Romeo (Leonard Whiting) is confronted by Tybalt (Michael York) and the Capulets.

man with a look of appreciation. She then turns on her husband with 'For shame, I'll make you quiet' (87).

The same suggestion of an affair between Gloria (i.e., Lady) Capulet (Diane Venora) and her kinsman is present in Luhrmann's film, though when she appears at the ball in fancy dress as Cleopatra, she is for the time being a comic parody of rampant sexiness, complementing the gross Caesar presented by her husband. There is more than a hint of the mafia boss about Capulet senior, and conspicuous consumption is clearly high on his agenda and that of his wife, but the political significance of their standing in Verona Beach is not explained or explored. Juliet's father is, credibly, 'the great rich Capulet', and that is sufficient for present purposes. It is implied that the disguises express their true personality, and the emphasis is on the embarrassment they cause to their daughter, who is present while her mother is made up and dressed for the party in a scene enlivened by speeded-up motion and other comic devices. The agenda here is clearly the generation gap: to Juliet (Claire Danes), dressed as an angel, they are tasteless, and Dave Paris, clumsily outfitted as an astronaut, is personable but vapid. Romeo is costumed as a knight in shining armour and obviously on her side against the grotesque, self-regarding 'mature' world. Mercutio (Harold Perrineau) goes to the ball in a miniskirt, high heels, and a skimpy top, but his regard for Romeo does not seem to have an erotic dimension of the kind suggested strongly by Zeffirelli. The drag appears to be more a parodic disguise than an expression of his 'real' nature. As Luhrmann has explained, 'wherever Mercutio is, there is a party' and he is 'flamboyant but angry' in his relationship with the world he has to inhabit.[5] In these scenes, *Romeo+Juliet* conforms most closely to the aesthetic of the director's 'Red Curtain' trilogy, identified by Pam Cook in her study of his films as 'a self-contained theatrical world in which stereotyped characters are deliberately devoid of psychological depth'.[6]

Luhrmann's young hotheads, introduced in a spectacularly fiery but almost bloodless fight in a filling station, identify themselves through differences in clothing – Hawaiian shirts for all the Montague men except Romeo, stylized bulletproof vests and tight black trousers for the Capulets. Tybalt and his ally 'Abra' (a new character, his name perhaps derived from that of the play's Montague servant Abram) and their acolytes have slicked-back hair, darker skin tones, and sharply cut facial hair, with a strong suggestion of the machismo associated with Latino culture. Luhrmann contrives to turn gunplay into sword-play, not merely by labelling the firearms with appropriate trademarks ('Longsword', etc.) but by staging and filming combats as if they were a mixture of spaghetti western shoot-out and duelling. There is much twirling and juggling with pistols, and the confrontation between Mercutio and Tybalt is prepared for in terms of an invented etiquette. It soon degenerates into a bloody hand-to-hand struggle, and Romeo gives chase to his friend's murderer by car, shooting him after a spec-tacular crash. Romeo, taunted with unmanly behaviour in refusing to accept Tybalt's challenge, has been transformed by rage into the hyper-masculine hero of an action movie.

As for the female sphere, both Zeffirelli and Luhrmann give scope to Capulet's anger at being defied by his daughter, though in the 1996 film the violence is visited as much on his wife – he strikes her down viciously when she tries to mediate. The mother's refusal to support Juliet is perhaps motivated partly by this, and Diane Venora seems shaken as she makes her way unsteadily from the scene of the con-frontation. Zeffirelli's Juliet is initially in thrall to her coldly elegant mother but is supported by a warmly sympathetic and down-to-earth nurse (Pat Heywood). Luhrmann's Lady Capulet is a trophy wife who employs a nurse (Miriam Margolyes) who is a downmarket version of herself. In Luhrmann's collage of images from all parts of the twen-tieth century and evocation of a range of film genres and styles, his strategy falls down with the nurse: from the beginning it is clear that if Juliet is going to grow up she will have to put this manic fusspot to one side. There can be no real pathos in the nurse's 'betrayal' of her young charge, only the defeat of a patently self-serving woman who, unlike Pat Heywood in Zeffirelli's version, could never be a credible or appropriate maternal figure. Castellani marks the intimacy between the nurse (Flora Robson) and Juliet (Susan Shentall) meticulously in terms of body language and kisses, and creates a household that includes a distinctive female realm: Juliet is busy with embroidery and other women are working on a tapestry or mending linen when the nurse brings news of the planned meeting with Romeo. For all this attention to a domestic world inhabited and supervised by women, productions of *Romeo and Juliet* invariably figure as a counterpoint to (but not an effective defiance of) the dominance of male privilege, whether expressed in the fathers' rights to control their households or the young men's assertion of their masculinity through quarrelling. Passion lends the lovers only a limited power.

The values of a patriarchal society are central to *Hamlet*, albeit with emphasis on loyalties and betrayals within the family rather than the obstructions they may put in the way of lovers. The conflict in the royal family is paralleled by anxiety of Polonius, supported by Laertes, to protect the honour of their own as personified by Ophelia from the threat of Hamlet's overtures to her and – at the worst – the danger that she will 'ope' her 'chaste treasure' to his 'unmastered importunity'. (1.3.31–2). Ophelia's reaction to her brother's lecture on this awkward topic, and her spirited response that he should take care of his own virtue, and not preach abstinence to her while 'like a puffed and reckless libertine/Himself the primrose path of dalliance treads/And recks not his own rede' (49–51), have been inflected variously, according to the nature of the brother–sister relationship. Jean Simmons in Olivier's 1948 film administers a sweet rebuke to her brother, and bids him farewell with a chaste kiss on the cheek; Marianne Faithfull and Michael Pennington, in Tony Richardson's *Hamlet* (1969), enjoy an intimacy that borders on the erotic; and in Branagh's 1996 film Kate Winslet kisses Laertes on the lips but puts no real passion into the gesture. (Zeffirelli omits the warning about Ophelia's 'chaste treasure', and the kiss exchanged between brother and sister has no passion – his film is more concerned with goings-on between Hamlet and his mother.) After Laertes' departure, Simmons takes her father's admonitions with modest grace, though she does glimpse Hamlet at the end of a long enfilade of arches – one of several deep-focus shots in the film – and hesitates before following Polonius. Branagh sets the second half of the scene, from 'And these few precepts . . . look thou character', in the chapel of the palace, and Winslet is cornered in a confessional by Richard Briers' stern Polonius. When he asks what is between her and the prince, a flashback showing her in bed with Hamlet indicates that her protestations are untruthful, and her final 'I shall obey, my lord' (136) is patently reluctant. Bill Murray, in Almereyda's version (2000), is an obsessive controller of his children, and although Julia Stiles projects stony indifference and disapproval throughout she submits to being fitted with a hidden microphone before going to return his 'remembrances' to Hamlet. She shows so little emotion in her scene with Laertes that it is hard to tell what she thinks of his anxiety – she probably considers it beneath her contempt. It may be that in this respect Almereyda has reached the limits of what will be credible when the play's period is shifted so far: it is hard to credit acquiescence to such strict paternal rule in an urban teenager from 2000.

The trials of the Polonius family intertwine with those of the Danish royalty, and although Ophelia is a victim of Polonius' desire to serve his monarch as well as control his children – he also keeps track of his son's behaviour in Paris – he is of course mistaken in his belief that love-melancholy has been the cause of Hamlet's 'madness'. Gertrude is frank in suggesting to the King that 'his father's death and our o'er-hasty marriage' (2.1.57) are more likely to be at the root of the problem. The royal marriage, accepted as expedient by the court's 'better wisdoms' but considered adulterous by Hamlet and the ghost of his father, has been characterized with varying degrees of emphasis on the erotic appeal of Claudius as well as the depth of Gertrude's regard for him. The first glimpse of Olivier's Claudius is a close-up in profile in which he is draining a goblet of wine. This is superimposed over an image of the royal bed of Denmark. The curtained canopy has been interpreted as strongly suggestive of a vagina, but even without this implication, Claudius is introduced with quite enough phallic symbols: raised trumpets, the firing of a cannon, and the sword of state held erect behind his throne. Gertrude (Eileen Herlie) gives every sign of finding her new husband attractive, although her demeanour towards her son hints at something more than maternal affection. There is indeed a Freudian complication in Hamlet's relationship with his mother, first signalled when she kisses him on the mouth after urging him not to return to Wittenberg – Claudius interrupts with 'Madam, come' as though he thinks this is rather too intimate – and followed through later on the royal bed of Denmark (Figure 4.2). Olivier was frank about the line to be taken when he approached actresses who might be cast as Gertrude. To one candidate he wrote:

There is between many a wife and son an over-developed affection, that is commonly known as the 'Oedipus complex'. I think it is probably true to say that in most families that exists, either on the mother or the son's part . . . this not quite passion, but more than love, can be found . . . She must, in other words, be the most wonderfully glamorous mummy to Hamlet. Glamorous and mummy. *Very* difficult; very hard to find, and almost impossible to cast in

Figure 4.2. *Hamlet* (Laurence Olivier, 1948): the Queen (Eileen Herlie) entreats Hamlet to stay in Elsinore, while the King (Basil Sydney) looks on – she is about to give her son a lingering kiss on the mouth.

a film in view of the difficult situation wrought by their either being too old for the part or too young to me.[7]

The 'impossible' solution was Herlie, some twelve years Olivier's junior, who gallantly agreed to being photographed unflatteringly, but remains a more likely partner for Hamlet than for Claudius. However, Basil Sydney's behaviour, including his stance and his commanding voice, emphasizes the King's virile authority. Olivier thus supports the hostile view of Claudius (the 'bloat king' given to excessive drinking) and Gertrude (posting to incestuous sheets with indecent haste), allowing most of the blame to lodge with the usurper rather than the imperial jointress of his warlike state. Richardson, who has Ophelia lie in a hammock for the 'nunnery scene', with a strong suggestion that Hamlet and she have shared it more than once, shows the royal couple breakfasting in bed as they receive Rosencrantz and Guildenstern.

The ages of Mel Gibson (born 1956) and Glenn Close (born 1947), as Hamlet and Gertrude in Zeffirelli's 1990 *Hamlet*, again make the queen a better match for the prince than the clear-eyed but distinctly maidenly young Ophelia of Helena Bonham-Carter (born 1966). In the first scene, set in the family vault, the exchange of looks sets up a tension between son, mother, and stepfather (Alan Bates) that is followed through in the moments when Gertrude caresses her son and – tellingly – when he watches her beadily as she kisses her husband. In the first court scene she is intent wholly on her admirable, sexy new husband (the casting of Bates helps a lot). In the revision of the play's script that breaks off the lines from 1.2 before the discussion of Hamlet's plans for Wittenberg, she is ready to go hunting with the king and hurries down to meet him, embraces him passionately then turns with a meaningful look towards the door of Hamlet's study, a flight of steps above. The royal pair visit Hamlet in his den, and Gertrude is able to laugh at his punning response on being too much in the sun. The king leaves, and Gertrude's plea with her son to stay at home becomes an intimate scene between them. Having received a more positive response than his behaviour has so far promised, she is light-hearted as she rushes off to join her husband again and ride off for the day's sport. Hamlet watches this with stony-faced distaste – Gibson's strongest suit as an actor – from the window of his study. In general, as Robert Hapgood has observed, Zeffirelli uses overhearing to simplify the hero's progress through the film: nothing really takes him by surprise.[8] In the queen's bedroom Hamlet pushes his mother onto the bed and is violent in his reproaches as he forces her to compare the miniatures of his father and Claudius. With 'Nay but to live/In the rank sweat of an enseamèd bed' (3.4.82–3) he has turned her onto her back and underlines the rhythm of his lines with what can only be pelvic thrusts as he lies on top of her. With 'O speak to me no more' (84) she kisses him on the mouth to stop his rant. As Patrick J. Cook observes, with what one assumes to be a double meaning, 'if the bedroom scene is the film's climax [this sequence] becomes a climax within the climax'.[9] It is hardly surprising that the ghost should intervene at this point, and Hamlet sees him over Gertrude's shoulder as he appears in the doorway. In the final scene, after he has received his death wound, Hamlet manages to lean close to the dead queen, taking her hand and pausing for a few moments with it against his cheek as he speaks 'Wretched queen, adieu'. It is the last gesture of filial affection and completes the pattern of intimacy between them that is one of the film's main preoccupations: this has been the story of a man who could not make up his mind about his mother.

As befits their elegant court, Branagh's Claudius and Gertrude are far more restrained than Zeffirelli's, and are fully dressed and preparing for the day's duties when Hamlet's 'friends' arrive in their suite. In the queen's closet – here, as so often, her bedroom – Branagh does fling her on the bed, but there is little to suggest a sexual dimension to their relationship. The director has been reproached for consciously (or is it subconsciously?) suppressing this aspect of the play, though surely this is an interpretation of the text rather than an established fact: the reader and viewer have to make up their own mind on this.[10] Matters are complicated by the fact that Hamlet looks more like the trim, blond-haired Claudius (Derek Jacobi) than his formidable and well-built father (Brian Blessed). In any case, except for some public exchange of endearments and a lusty approach to their wedding bed shown in flashback to illustrate the ghost's account, indecorum is not part of the royal couple's lifestyle. Another flashback to show the growing intimacy between Gertrude and her brother-in-law, during a game of indoor quoits, seems relatively decorous. In the corporate world of 2000 Almereyda's Claudius (Kyle MacLachlan) and Queen (Diane Venora) can hug and kiss in public with greater freedom, but go no further until they are alone. The juxtapositions of recorded images in which the film abounds include Hamlet's cut from her anxious face during his video in the 'play' scene to that of the near lookalike actress in the clip from a porn film that Hamlet has inserted to show his contempt for her sexuality. In a scene in the 'royal' bedroom, Gertrude and Claudius are in the preliminaries of sex – she wraps her legs round him and is unbuttoning his shirt from behind – when they receive a phone call from their spies. However, this is no more shocking in itself than any mildly erotic episode between grown-ups in the late twentieth-century cinema. Hamlet really does need to 'get over it' with regard to his mother having a sex life. This is about as far as Freud can take us in the film: Ethan Hawke, as the withdrawn (or cool) prince, shows no overtly erotic interest in his mother – or indeed in anyone, including Ophelia.

In the most radical treatment of that relationship, Branagh includes flashbacks that show the prince in bed with Ophelia and, in what seems to be a post-coital musical moment, side by side with her at a piano. As has already been noted, an immediate consequence of the first of these interpolated scenes is to make it clear that Ophelia is lying when she tells her father that nothing more than 'tenders of his love' have passed between them (1.4.99), but the seriousness of the involvement informs subsequent developments and, of course, her descent into madness. The violence of Hamlet's treatment of her when he realizes she has betrayed him in the 'nunnery' scene (3.1.91–160), when he drags her around the mirrored wall of the great hall before pushing her against the two-way mirror concealing the King and Polonius, raises the emotional temperature to a degree not achieved in Olivier's or Zeffirelli's versions. (Zeffirelli weakens the scene by transposing lines to augment Hamlet's exchanges with Ophelia during the play.) The effect on the gender-political balance sheet is difficult to assess: the on-screen love scenes and the violent rejection – ended with a passionate kiss – make this dimension of the story as problematic as the question of Hamlet's feelings towards his mother. Olivier clears the field for the Freudian business by the contempt his Hamlet shows for Ophelia after he perceives she has betrayed him. Nothing happens between them that can compare with the erotic urgency and violence displayed in Gertrude's bedroom.

The other significant personal relationship in the play – that between Hamlet and Horatio – has received relatively muted treatment. Norman Wooland, Horatio to Olivier's Hamlet, never gets further than a handshake or a friendly touch on the shoulder until the final scene, where he kisses Hamlet's forehead before 'Goodnight, sweet prince'. Almereyda's Horatio (Karl Geary) has a significant other in the shape of Marcella, and is no more emotionally outgoing than any of the other disaffected young people in the film. Branagh, in the commentary to the 2007 DVD release of his *Hamlet*, explains that he wanted to avoid 'the big hug' in the characters' first meeting, but to show 'princely' restraint, saving greater intimacy until later. Even then, the closeness is not expressed in physical gestures, and in the final sequence he was anxious to avoid the cliché (as he saw it) of Hamlet dying in his friend's arms: Nicholas Farrell speaks his farewell from a distance of some feet. In the overall balance of the narrative, it is probably just as well that directors have kept the Horatio/Hamlet story as an undercurrent of manly friendship and understanding, allowing Horatio's sympathetic but detached observations their full value. A sexual dimension to the relationship would not in itself contradict that, and might even enrich it, but it would probably be a distraction. It is to Horatio that Hamlet can confide his apprehensions before the fencing match, but also his arrival at a philosophical resolution expressed in 'The readiness is all' (5.2.168). A play whose hero had been lectured by his stepfather/uncle on 'unmanly grief' (1.2.94) has reached a point where he can acknowledge the uneasiness 'here about my heart' but then set it aside as 'such a kind of gain-giving as would trouble a woman'. (5.2.158–61) Manliness, defined in terms of courage, steadfastness, and readiness to do the right thing – once that has been identified – are given grounding in Horatio's identity as a figure from Wittenberg, where thinking about the moral significance of action is prized. By the end of the story, the ghost's simpler definition of manly accomplishments – smiting sledded Polacks, defeating Old Fortinbras in single combat and being unable to conceive that his queen could be attracted to anyone else – has been superseded by a more sophisticated understanding of what it is to be a man. Horatio is 'not passion's slave' and is consequently worn in Hamlet's 'heart of heart' (3.2.70–1). In the final scene he is prepared to drink poison, declaring himself 'more an antique Roman than a Dane', but Hamlet snatches the cup from him. In staying alive to tell Hamlet's story, Horatio will be fulfilling a duty and at the same time living up to the stoicism that has made him a sympathetic observer of a prince who has been passion's slave on more than one occasion. Olivier omits the lines and the action, keeping the focus firmly on Hamlet, but forgoing the opportunity to make Horatio more than a stolid, dependable sounding-board: the earlier tribute to him had been delivered and received with a restraint that is more 1940s British than antique Roman.

Virility of a traditional Roman kind, and the concomitant association with stoicism, are very much in evidence in Joseph L. Mankie-wicz's *Julius Caesar* (1953), though there is an intriguing distinction between the more austere, intellectually as well as emotionally intense relationship of Brutus and Cassius (James Mason and John Gielgud) and the glamour of Marlon Brando's Antony. Encountered at first when he is stripped (so far as modesty permits) for the race and the

Figure 4.3. *Julius Caesar* (Joseph L. Mankeiwicz, 1953): Caesar (Louis Calhern) tells Antony (Marlon Brando) to touch Calphurnia (Greer Garson) during the race.

object of quiet admiration on Calphurnia's part – she has a moment of annoyance when Caesar refers to her being barren – Antony has the physique of an athlete (Figure 4.3). As Jack Jorgens points out, Louis Calhern 'portrays Caesar's weaknesses more than his strengths', and he suggests that Mankiewicz draws on the 'fear, vulnerability and softness to the core' that the actor had depicted in the vicious and corrupt lawyer Emerich in *The Asphalt Jungle* (1950), making a contrast between these qualities and the power Caesar wields.[11] The film has three male love stories: Caesar and Brutus; Caesar and Antony; and Brutus and Cassius. As in the play, the relationship of Caesar and Calphurnia (Greer Garson), like that between Brutus and Portia (Deborah Kerr), is less fully developed, although the dignity and intelligence of the Roman matrons is given its fullest value. Portia's 'voluntary wound' to prove her constancy under pain, and the report of her suicide confirm her as an exemplary figure of Roman virtue, but Mankiewicz also contrives a moment conferring tragic dignity on

Calphurnia after she has left Caesar and his friends preparing to go to the Senate, registering her private anticipation of what she believes must be to come.

Male bonding, with much stronger sexual overtones, has long been a feature of stage productions of *Coriolanus*. In Ralph Fiennes' 2011 feature film Tullus Aufidius and Caius Martius share, as one might expect, the same values, and their single combat is given an appropriately erotic dimension. As in Luhrmann's *Romeo+Juliet*, a way is found of reconciling the use of firearms with the need for prolonged one-to-one contention. When Aufidius and Caius Martius fight in Corioles, after a long struggle they grapple together on the ground in a close embrace, until the blast from a mortar shell throws them apart and their officers rescue them. In the final scene, when Coriolanus, goaded as a 'boy of tears' and denounced as a traitor, is attacked by Aufidius' men, the fight ends in another embrace, as Aufidius delivers the death blow with the knife we saw him sharpening at the beginning of the film. He holds the back of the Roman's head, then cradles him in his arms as he lowers the body to the ground. Here the embrace is almost fatherly on Aufidius' part, rather than that of a lover. The ascendancy of Coriolanus among the Volscians has been shown by the desire of young soldiers to have their heads shaved in imitation of the new general, making them a band of brothers. This fascistic masculine personality cult has aroused Aufidius' envy and rekindled his desire for revenge.

Among the Romans Volumnia (Vanessa Redgrave) represents a proud reversal of traditional gender roles. She has achieved an intimacy with her son that his wife Virgilia (Jessica Chastain) will never achieve: it is Volumnia who sits at his bedside to dress Coriolanus' wounds, and when he is being persuaded to return to the market place to apologize for refusing to show his scars to the citizens, Virgilia remains behind a glass door in an outer office. However, Chastain does not allow Virgilia to be merely a cipher. Her eloquent features are in their own way as strong a point of reference for judging the ethics of war as Redgrave's steely countenance.

Young Caius is being trained by his grandmother and Menenius to take his place in the military elite. They follow the battle at Corioles on television news reports, learning that Caius Martius 'is himself alone/ To answer all the city' (1.5.23–4) as the events unfold. The exchanges between Menenius, Volumnia, and Virgilia when news arrives of Martius' triumphant return take place as they are leaving the villa to welcome the returning hero. Menenius speaks 'every gash was an enemy's grave' (2.1.152) to little Martius, who is wearing a uniform like that of his grandmother. As Martius enters the ceremonial hall Volumnia's grimly satisfied face is seen as if from his point of view, at first slightly blurred, then coming into focus before the shot that reveals the whole of the party on the dais. Her chilling 'These are the ushers of Martius. Before him he carries noise, and behind him he leaves tears' (2.1.155–6), is spoken softly to herself as her son approaches the podium. When Martius kisses Virgilia he remarks that she is weeping to 'see [him] triumph': 'Ah, my dear,/Such eyes the widows in Corioles wear,/And mothers that lack sons' (174–6). In the previous scene the retreating Aufidius had paused by the side of a car in which a slaughtered civilian mother and son lay. This prompted his vow to settle accounts, and the image is strong enough to cast a shadow over Coriolanus' glib remark about widows, mothers, and sons.

The pared-down dialogue and unhurried pace of the scene in which the women come to plead with Coriolanus render it all the more powerful. Chastain's Virgilia is especially powerful in her confrontation with Coriolanus, and the kiss between husband and wife is long and passionate – 'a kiss/As long as my exile, sweet as my revenge!' (5.3.44–5). Fiennes allows full scope to Redgrave, whose Volumnia moves here from pride and arrogance to despair and then stony-faced anger. Her speeches are softly spoken and intense, and she kneels before him, placing her hands on his knees. She does not raise her voice until she exclaims 'This fellow had a Volscian to his mother' (5.3.179). (He does not 'hold her by the hand, silent' as the play's stage direction indicates, but faces her, and then kneels to her.) Until this scene her wholeheartedly militaristic spirit distinguishes her from the business-suited politicians, marking her as a member of a caste to whom democratic politics are an irrelevance. When she comes to plead with her son, she wears a black dress, in striking contrast to the uniform of the triumphal scene. The last shot of Volumnia is a close-up as she stands, once again in uniform, and salutes in response to 'Behold, our patroness' after her son and Cominius have signed the fatal peace treaty: she knows what the consequences will be.

For all its grotesque horrors, or perhaps paradoxically because of them, Taymor's *Titus* (1999) is less disturbing than Fiennes' *Coriolanus*. The postmodern bricolage of ancient, modern, and simply fantastic modes of dress and behaviour allows for analogies with the modern world but effectively pre-empts the possibility of any searching social or political analysis. This society is organized on principles so self-evidently deranged that only a completely new start will have any effect. In the sentimental conclusion, the boy who began the film as a destructive brat seized from his suburban kitchen by a strange figure identifiable as the 'clown' picks up the baby engendered by Tamora and Aaron and walks slowly towards a landscape illuminated by the rising sun.

There is formidable masculine power in the image of the Roman soldiers in the arena at the beginning of the film, advancing automata-like, full-size equivalents of one of the martial toys played with in the prologue. This is Rome at its most ancient. When Titus (Anthony Hopkins) and his warrior sons wash away their battlefield grime, they become a tableau of nude statuary sitting under cascading water in an underground chamber. Once the exercise of Titus' 'cruel, irreligious piety' begins, and he shows his inflexible belief in extreme patriarchal power – offering his daughter Lavinia to the emperor out of a sense of patriotic duty – the inhuman rigidity of his ethical code is made patent. Ultimately, the barbarous behaviour of his enemies is avenged in the final 'honour killing' of Lavinia, but the effect is to make this satisfaction all the more appalling. These attitudes, though, do furnish an appropriate basis for the developing revenge tragedy. Jessica Lange's Tamora ('lovely queen of Goths') is more than a match for the hysterical ninny Saturninus (Alan Cumming), and a monster worthy of being Titus' nemesis, but her cruelty is apolitical and fantastic. Lavinia (Laura Fraser) moves convincingly from prize fiancée to ravaged victim and then to instrument of revenge, and the violence done to her and to the nurse (Geraldine McEwan), who is skewered with a billiard cue by Aaron, is appallingly misogynistic. Taymor's 'penny arcade' sequences express the play's horrors in an allegorical mode, commenting on them rather than being integral to the action itself. Savage violence, especially against women, is wrong, just as much when it is sanctioned by a code of honour embedded in the state as when it is merely the indulgence of vicious desire.

Even allowing for the conventions of the early 1950s filmmaking, Welles' *Othello* evinces little erotic power in the relations between Othello and Desdemona. The strongest bond is that between the hero and Iago. Although she is spirited in her defiance of her father and in the energy with which she urges Othello to pardon Cassio, Suzanne Cloutier projects a degree of affection but no passion towards Othello. In a brief scene on the eve of their departure from Venice, Desdemona is lying in bed, and Othello leans down to kiss her, unequivocally initiating love-making (though fully clothed) with 'I have but an hour of love to spend with thee. We must obey the time' (1.3.298–300: omitting 'of worldly matter and direction'). When the couple retire to bed on the night of their arrival in Cyprus their lighted window, high in a tower, is seen from below in separate shots by both Iago and Roderigo, the camera adopting their points of view. Within the chamber Othello closes the shutter across this window, before moving towards the bed, and as he leans over the recumbent Desdemona with 'If it were now to die . . .' he and his shadow seem to engulf her, a fairly explicit metaphor for sexual possession. This is one of the few scenes in which they are alone together without there being some matter of dispute or suspicion to (literally) darken them. In the murder, after the face of Othello has emerged from the darkness that he will deepen by extinguishing candles in front of an altar and a small devotional image of the virgin and child, there is a shot in which his black face appears as a vertical alongside the horizontal form of Desdemona. The murder itself is accomplished by smothering her with a white veil, a close-up image of horror full on to camera that is a startling change in the dominant darkness of the scene. Effectively, she has been blanked out, and the image is a reversal of that formed in the very first moments of the film by the face of the dead Othello.

As for Iago, his apartness and isolation are constantly emphasized, and although his soliloquies have been cut there are enough meaningful looks to establish his mingled jealousy and malice. When Othello embraces Desdemona on the ramparts, enveloping her in his cloak, Iago looks on, and his expression seems to reflect the envy that MacLiammóir and Welles agreed would be at the centre of the characterization. The director carried out fully the intention recorded in MacLiammóir's account of the making of the film: 'Monotony [in the playing of Iago] may perhaps be avoided by remembering the underlying sickness of the mind, the immemorial hatred of life, the secret isolation of impotence under the soldier's muscles, the flabby solitude gnawing at the groin, the eye's untiring calculation'. Welles' design, endorsed by MacLiammóir, was for 'the growing depend-ence of Othello on Iago's presence, the merging of the two men into one murderous image like a pattern of loving shadows welded'.[12] The combination of impotence (however construed) and male bonding is powerful, and it is arguable that inclusion of Iago's explanations of his motivation in the soliloquies would have compromised the effect of this interpretation. The beginning of the 'temptation' scene (3.3) is played in two long travelling shots as Iago paces alongside Othello on the ramparts. When they go indoors to an armoury after Iago has warned Othello to 'look to [his] wife', the ensign busies himself with pieces of armour while Othello gazes into a small mirror whose convex surface distorts his image, with that of Iago at his side. Later, when he has brushed aside the handkerchief she offers to bind his brows with, Desdemona is seen in the same mirror, a tiny figure in the background. Although Welles has moments of tenderness, except for an extraordinary sequence (4.2.46–63) in which Othello runs his hand down her dress from her breasts to her genitals, the camera does the work of fetishizing Cloutier's body, particularly her hair, that confirms the passivity and 'to-be-looked-at-ness' of the woman.[13]

In the decade following Welles' *Othello*, major changes in racial pol-itics had brought about corresponding shifts in perceptions of the play. One would never guess this from the pedestrian film made in 1965 from the National Theatre's 1964 stage production, with Olivier in the title role, which conveys no sense of sexual intimacy between Othello and Desdemona, and seems to have been made with no particular consciousness of its racial politics. What was generally acclaimed as a powerful theatre performance by Olivier registers as exaggerated and mannered on camera, making Frank Finlay's Iago far more cred-ible and effective than the Moor. Olivier's elaborate and meticulously burnished make-up, studied 'black' body language and laboriously articulated and deepened voice seem like a caricature. By the 1960s the cinema's depictions of sex had also become more explicit though not invariably subtler, but Stuart Burge's film, trammelled by its aim of reproducing the theatre production's action on an expanded version of the stage set, makes no room for the kind of intimate scenes audiences might expect.

Oliver Parker's *Othello* (1995) is another matter altogether. The ethnic dimension is complicated to an extent by casting Bianca with an actress of colour, and Parker omits most of the grosser racial slurs from the dialogue. As Othello, Laurence Fishburne presents an exotic image of his character, emphasized by the scars and tattoos on his body and head and his 'moorish' costume in many of the scenes (including, importantly, the murder of Desdemona). He has a quiet dignity that contrasts with Welles grandiloquent and overbearing figure or the studied posturing of Olivier. In comparison with Welles' stylized cinematic version and Burge's staid copy of a theatrical original, a much greater sense of intimacy among all the characters is achieved in this *Othello*, where long dialogue scenes run their course without the fragmentation of Welles' film. Desdemona (Irène Jacob) is frank in her physical endearments: in a flashback showing the wooing of her by Othello we see her looking tenderly at his scars, and when he arrives in Cyprus she kisses him lovingly in public. Later she dances invitingly before him at dinner. It is clear that this is their first night of love-making, and he speaks 'The purchase made, the fruits are to ensue./That profit's yet to come 'tween me and you' (2.3.9–10) privately, as they prepare for bed. We see them both undressing, and she slips naked into bed behind the diaphanous curtains. A montage of intertwined limbs includes a shot of her hand grasping the sheets as – implicitly – she reaches orgasm, and of his hand covering hers. The strawberry-marked handkerchief lies near the clasped hands. A corresponding image occurs later, when Othello imagines an even more graphic scene of Cassio making love to Desdemona. This develops the less explicit but none the less erotic depiction on Parker's part of the married couple's first love-making. Now we see Desdemona imagined by Othello in an even more provocative disposition, with her breasts clearly in view, and a brief montage seen later during Othello's fit is even more explicit, with close-ups of tongues and lips and the suggestion of caresses centred on the thighs of the lovers.

Parker's desire to make a 'sexy thriller' is evident elsewhere in the film. Intercut with the bedchamber scenes of the bridal night is the dialogue in which Iago persuades Roderigo (Michael Maloney) to attack Cassio (Nathaniel Parker). This takes place underneath a cart, which is shaken by the anonymous pair energetically coupling on top of it. Iago grabs Roderigo's groin with 'lechery by this hand' (2.3.248). Maloney's Roderigo is not the comic stooge of Welles' film, and there is no slapstick. He is passionate and dangerous, and when in the final movement of the play he confronts Iago with his belief he has been duped, the threat is genuine and violent. Unlike MacLiammóir's dapper, cynical Iago, Kenneth Branagh's ensign is disarmingly sensible and his bonhomie is convincing. He has the advantage of the soliloquies, spoken direct to camera and creating an appropriately uneasy sense of connivance on the spectator's part. However, this complicity is a consequence of the realism of Parker's direction, and neither Iago nor Othello are the quasi-mythical figures created by Welles.

Parker has little interest in symbolism, except for a few touches noted already (Iago 'drowning' a chess piece is the most notable), but he has described his approach to the script in terms of light and darkness and the elements:

The passions are tidal, deep and uncontrollable as the ocean . . . Light and dark fight it out on the screen. We descend from the bright Cyprus sky to the pitch black bedroom where Othello blows out the final candle before he murders his wife.[14]

In fact, the dark scenes are not as near to 'pitch black' as those in Welles' *Othello*, where the contrasts are rendered starker by the monochrome medium. The dominant indoor lighting effect with Parker is one of warm candlelight, with a colour palette that favours the browns, ochres, and beige of many of the costumes and the warm skin tones of Desdemona and also of Othello, whose colouration is much lighter than that of Welles. The major contribution to thematic unity is that of the many scenes of intimate behaviour and the repeated instances of sexual activity. Irène Jacob as Desdemona, although less passive in demeanour than Suzanne Cloutier, is dressed (in some scenes, undressed), lit, and photographed so as to emphasize her physical beauty, but it seems clear that she reciprocates the male gaze of Othello. Nevertheless, the economy of looking and imagining in the film may amount to a racist view of the action and the characters, implicit even if it is unconscious on the part of the director. The play is, in Ania Loomba's phrase, 'both a fantasy of interracial love and tolerance, and a nightmare of racial hatred and male violence'.[15] *Othello* is to be handled with care in the cinema, where who looks at whom and how we share it can intensify a problematic situation.

At the centre of the general sense of intimacy and expressions of emotional commitment is Iago. The very warmth and camaraderie of his apparent relationships with Roderigo and Cassio is expressed with hearty embraces. On most of these occasions he looks over the other person's shoulder towards the camera, as if to confirm that this is a strategic display of affection. But when he swears loyalty to Othello with 'I am your own forever' there is no such irony: the emotion is sincere, even as it is deadly. In one situation, what we see of Iago's private life seems to suggests a perverse background to his voyeuristic absorption in the lives he destroys. Emilia (Anna Patrick) brings the handkerchief to their bedroom, where he is lying face down (and clothed) on the bed. She lies down beside him and caresses him when she says that she has 'a thing' for him, but he shows no interest in her until she tells him what it is. Then he lies on top of her, before turning her over roughly and pushing up her skirts. The handkerchief is seen in slow motion as he tosses it into the air, and the screen fades quickly to black. It is not clear whether he is about to sodomize her – neither the director nor the camera operator, asked about the scene, think this was the intention – but the brutality of the gesture is manifest.[16] This does not, however, limit the relationship to one of dominance and reluctant subjection. Patrick is forceful in her appraisal of men – 'Let husbands know/Their wives have sense like them' (5.1.91–2) – but reserves her contempt for Iago until the final scenes give grounds for it: until then, there is a rueful affection in her behaviour towards him. After Othello's violent accusation of whoredom, both she and Iago comfort Desdemona (4.2), and Iago's embrace of her mistress seems to bring the three into an almost familial group. In the final scene, Emilia drags herself to the end of the bed and lies down beside the body of Desdemona, Othello joins them to kiss Desdemona after he has stabbed himself (with a knife passed to him surreptitiously by Cassio), and Iago, hauled by Lodovico to 'look on the tragic loading of this bed', crawls onto it. Montano opens a shutter, and the tableau is lit by the rising sun, the shot being held for a few moments. In the final sequence a boat bearing the bodies of Othello and Desdemona is rowed out to sea, which shimmers with the golden light of the sun. The two bodies, shrouded and tied together, are cast overboard, and in an underwater shot they are seen sinking beneath the waves.

The theme of sexual jealousy makes the presentation of at least one erotic relationship inevitable in any performance of *Othello*, with varying degrees of graphic and explicit depiction. *Macbeth* lends itself to similar treatment, although Welles located the sources of tragedy elsewhere, downplaying this dimension (or subtext) once the initial impulse of Jeanette Nolan's vampish energy in the first scenes has marshalled Macbeth the way he was going. In George Schaefer's 1960 film – shown on television in the USA but only in cinemas in the United Kingdom – the staid performance of Maurice Evans and the stately tragedy queen of Judith Anderson suggest a marital relationship that may never have been exactly lively. Roman Polanski's *Macbeth* (1971), a project that had its origins in his state of mind after the brutal murder in 1969 of his pregnant wife Sharon Tate by followers of the psychopathic cult leader Charles Manson, also develops elements of the director's previous films. Virginia Wright Wexman observes that 'the motifs of brutality and witchcraft suited [Polanski's] state, and, most importantly the theme of sexual enslavement could be integrated into the portrayal of the hero without doing too much violence to the original text'.[17] Polanski describes a basic element of his approach, the casting of Macbeth and Lady Macbeth as 'young and good-looking – not, as in most stage productions, middle-aged and doom-laden', and recalls the advice of the critic Kenneth Tynan (then literary manager of the National Theatre), who collaborated with him on the script: 'They don't know they're involved in a tragedy; they think they're on the verge of a triumph predicted by the witches'. In Tynan's view 'their tragedy was that in trying to fulfil the witches' prophecy, they uncovered a dark side of their own natures, the existence of which they'd never suspected'.[18] In some respects *Macbeth* seems like a follow-up to *Rosemary's Baby* (1968), in which the young, upwardly mobile couple also discover a 'dark side'. The film's hauntings linger, and the scene of love-making in the newly rented apartment seems to be the source or at least the decisive element leading to what follows, in what one hopes against hope is a fantasy rather than a tragedy.

Macbeth takes sexuality and violence a stage further, with scenes of brutality that include state-sanctioned violence (carnage on the battlefield, bear-baiting, the execution of Cawdor) as well as the murders of

Duncan and his grooms, Banquo and the Macduff family. The beheading of Macbeth, rendered with almost comic realism and followed by a shot that seems to be the point-of-view of his severed head, is not to be the end of the cycle: as the film ends, Donalbain is on his way to consult the witches. At the centre of the play's politics – promoted from a role less significant in most productions – Ross figures as a turncoat, whose treacherous support for Malcolm and Macduff is motivated by disappointment that Macbeth has not rewarded him adequately. Malcolm is deprived of his speech promising peace and the settling of accounts, and there is no room for Macduff's assurance that 'The time is free' (5.11.21) – the message seems to be that it never can be.

Polanski writes that the slaughter of Lady Macduff and her children was based on his childhood experience of 'how the SS officer had searched our room in the [Kraków] ghetto, swishing his riding crop to and fro, toying with my teddy bear, nonchalantly emptying out the hatbox full of forbidden bread'.[19] Tynan recalls another dimension of the scene, revealed when he queried the director's estimate of the amount of blood that would be shed by a small boy stabbed in the back: '"You didn't see my house in California last summer", he said, bleakly, "I know about bleeding"'. Tynan notes that this was the only reference the director made to the murders since they started work.[20] In preparing the script it was decided to omit almost all references to religion except such lines as Banquo's 'In the great hand of God I stand' (2.3.126) and Polanski insisted that the witches should be 'real old women who live in a real place and mix real potions', rather than 'metaphysical . . . abstract spirits of evil'.[21] The general effect, as Wexman observes, is to depict history as 'a nightmare filled with chaotic and little understood horrors'.[22] In this case, though, the 'nightmare' is political and psychological reality, palpable and inescapable.

In the world Polanski creates, sexuality is no less compromised than any other activity or passion. Lady Macbeth (Francesca Annis), first seen as a fairy-tale princess on the ramparts of her castle, is 'thinking' her summons of the 'spirits that attend on mortal thoughts' in voice-over even as she gazes out towards her approaching husband. When he arrives, he sweeps her up into his arms and carries her upstairs from the courtyard. In the next shot she helps him take off his sword belt and the chain that signifies his elevation as Thane of Cawdor, and as he lies down, she kisses him passionately on the mouth: the chain, which she is still holding, connects the erotic moment with the achievement of power. However, as the film progresses, there are no scenes of sexual intimacy between the couple. After the appearance of Banquo's ghost and the disruption of the feast, she sits on the opposite side of a table from her husband, but when he holds out his hand to her she does not clasp it and instead takes up the flaming lamp that is between them. In bed, they lie side by side, she facing upwards and not engaging with him as he tells her that he has 'strange things . . . in mind'. In her sleepwalking scene she is naked, and eventually after she has fallen to her death, she has become a pitiful rag doll sprawled on the stones of the courtyard. Polanski's charting of the erasure – one might almost say, exorcism – of the erotic may bear out Janet Adelman's claim that Shakespeare's play 'becomes . . . a representation of primitive fears about male identity and autonomy itself, about those looming female presences who threaten to control one's actions and one's mind, to constitute one's very self, even at a distance'.[23] From her voice-over thoughts willing her husband into her power, to the crumpled corpse lying in the courtyard, Francesca Annis's Lady Macbeth is just such a presence.

For what might be expected in a *Playboy*-financed production this *Macbeth* is notably short on erotic content – at least of a straightforward kind. In its place are scenes in which bodies, human and animal, are invaded, disfigured, and dismembered by weapons. Macbeth pulls back a sheet to stab Duncan frenziedly, and later he has a vision – in a daylight dream after ordering the murder of Banquo and his Fleance – that the son, now in armour, sits aside him and pulls back a coverlet to reveal his naked breast and pierce his throat with an arrow-headed dagger while the father holds Macbeth down. Before the banquet we have seen a bear being baited, and presently its bloody carcase and that of one of the dogs assailing it are dragged down a corridor. A servant steps into the frame to wipe up the trail of blood, a gesture that is repeated later when Macbeth, confronted by the ghost, lets his goblet of wine fall. This ghost changes its shape alarmingly, from the first appearance as a pale but substantial figure to its last approach, naked to the waist and carrying a falcon on its wrist as Macbeth cowers against the pillar to which the bear had been chained.

The slaughter of Banquo is a prolonged and bloody struggle, as is the final combat between Macbeth and Macduff. The image of the SS officer in the attack on Macduff's wife and children has already been mentioned: at the beginning of the scene Lady Macduff is bathing her naked son, an arresting image of the vulnerable body, and as well as the brutal stabbing of this child the scene includes the horrific and prolonged gang rape of a female servant (seen at the end of the sequence, but heard off-screen throughout) and the image of the other 'pretty chickens' as blood-boltered corpses in their nursery cradles. A crowd of naked witches prepare the hallucinogenic draught that gives Macbeth his surreal prophetic vision, which includes a shot (repeated fleetingly when Macduff reveals he was 'not of woman born') in which a knife slices open an abdomen and a naked newborn babe is removed from it. The convincing images of the damage done to human flesh and blood complement and are part of a language of disturbing visions, of which the air-drawn dagger is the least effective. Violence seems to have taken over from sex in the imagination both of the film and of Macbeth, while the presence of Ross as a plausible traitor and Donalbain as a potential schemer against Malcolm suggests that the tragic protagonist has merely entered a previously unacknowledged world in which sights and deeds of this kind are a commonplace of political life. In 1974 *Chinatown*, the director's great homage to film noir, paradoxically shot in sumptuous colour, tells a story of incest, cruelty, and the politics of greed in 1930s Los Angeles. Its themes can be read back into *Macbeth*, much as the terrifying visions of *Repulsion* (1965) and *Rosemary's Baby* anticipate elements of the Shakespearian film. In its movements from sexuality to violence, and from both to politics, Polanski's work anticipates the theme of the next chapter, the getting and maintaining of power.

5

Power Plays – Politics in the Shakespeare Films

If we examine the treatment of politics in a number of films – not primarily the politics *of* the films, the work they do in their own society, but rather the ways in which the political process has been represented *in* them – we soon discover that the two are of course not entirely separable. Any consideration of the films of *Henry V* makes this clear: what place does a vivid call to arms in a foreign campaign of doubtful legitimacy have in our own world? Is any scepticism built into the play transferred effectively to the screen? Do audiences – especially those in England – need to be shielded from any temptation to cry 'God for Harry, England and Saint George'? But the distinction remains an important one. Previous chapters have referred to the political action of Mankiewicz's *Julius Caesar*, Fiennes's *Coriolanus*, and Taymor's *Titus* in relation to choices made in setting and characterization, but here the focus is on more specific elements of the political process in a number of versions of the tragedies and the historical plays. I have suggested the ways in which Polanski's *Macbeth* can be identified as a political work, and it can be argued that the absence of the gods (or God) from Brook's *King Lear* is in itself – in terms of the politics *of* Shakespeare production – a statement with cultural-political significance. Brook's work, influenced by the writing of Jan Kott, carries with it the force of the Polish critic's vision of a godless universe, a historical machine:

[T]he history of the Renaissance is just a grand staircase, from the top of which ever new kings fall into the abyss. There exists only the Grand Mechanism. But the Grand Mechanism is not cruel. There is another side to it: it is a tragic farce'.[1]

Kott's alignment of Shakespeare with absurdism in the chapter 'King Lear or Endgame', carries this idea into the heart of the tragedy. After Gloucester's imagined fall from the cliff 'all that remains at the end of this gigantic pantomime is the earth – empty and bleeding'.[2]

The political dimensions of some of the comedies have also been touched on, but they call for more consideration in this context. Shakespeare's audience would arguably have been impressed, indeed disturbed, by the spectacle of usurpation in *Macbeth* or *King Lear* or the problems of royal succession and the danger of a foreign power filling the vacant throne left at the end of *Hamlet*, but a modern audience is less likely to feel as personally concerned, unless by some means an analogy is made with their own political world. In the comedies, the displacement of a good duke by his brother in *As You Like It* or *The Tempest*, serving as the lever that starts the action, might be treated with some degree of seriousness (Branagh's *As You Like It*) or as a matter of fairy-tale-like convenience (Czinner's). Julie Taymor takes pains to fill out the backstory of *The Tempest* not merely because the medium calls for such explicitness in visual and textual terms, but because her female Prospera calls for (or is occasioned by) a desire to make a feminist point: whereas Prospero was exiled in a simple act of usurpation, Prospera has also been stigmatized as a witch, with her occult studies as a pretext. In Taymor's film, moreover, Gonzalo's thoughts about the 'plantation' of the island as an ideal commonwealth, and the conspiracy of the courtiers against Alonso, are given their full value. In his *Tempest* Derek Jarman pays little attention to either theme or, as I have suggested, the postcolonial dimension of the play. Branagh's *Much Ado* does nothing to fill in the background of the 'ended action' from which Don Pedro and his followers have returned, or the treachery of his half brother Don John, beyond the play's scanty references to them. However, the period setting and military organization of the men make it probable that some battle or other has been won. In Joss Whedon's 2013 film of the comedy, in modern dress and performed in a luxurious house in Los Angeles, it is not made clear what the 'action' in question might be, and the implication has to be that either it was a complex takeover bid or – conceivably – some criminal activity, though this seems unlikely. In any case, after the first scenes, it matters very little. The principals are articulate people in more than comfortable circumstances and with relationships that include a sense of honour and allegiance to those in power – of whatever kind it may be. In his *Twelfth Night*, Trevor Nunn feels obliged to establish Orsino as a military commander with a squad of cavalry at his disposal, and to make vivid the threat to Antonio that they represent: this enlivens the exposition of the scenes corresponding to the play's 1.2 (Viola's arrival in Illyria), 2.1 (Antonio's temporary parting with Sebastian), and the end of 3.4 (the arrest of Antonio). The contribution of these to the gender issues of the film – Viola's having to accommodate herself to a masculine milieu – is more important than any sense they may give of Illyrian politics. They also aid Orsino in what can be the thankless task for an actor of establishing himself as more than a Prince Charming who has run off the rails: he does at least have a daytime job more comprehensible to a modern audience than that of being a Duke (a handy general term for a prince of power) and a self-absorbed bachelor.

It can be argued that in these comedies the demands of the filmic conventions adopted, those of the mainstream commercial cinema, have called for a greater degree of specific detail than would be the case with most theatre productions. (Though directors might well choose to opt for such emphases for their own artistic and political reasons.) The politics of Venice are more significant in themselves. In *The Merchant of Venice* the characterization of the racial and religious policies of the state can no longer be left to a casual assumption that anti-Semitism, however reprehensible, is 'normal', a minor failing among eloquent and otherwise sympathetic characters. It was suggested in Chapter Two that Michael Radford's attempt to begin by distinguishing between unenlightened Venetians and a more sophisticated majority is not really successful. The play has no reference to the Ghetto, which Radford plainly needs, but represents powerfully the differences between Christians and Jews. This is both visceral and practical – Shylock hates Antonio because 'he is a Christian' (a clause omitted by Radford) but all the more because his interest-free lending 'brings down/The rate of usance here with us in Venice' (1.3.37–8) – and the resolution of the legal action is as much to do with the reinforcement of the city's terms of trade as humane ethics. Even under arrest and threatened with the forfeiture of his pound of flesh, Antonio insists that failure to honour the bond will 'much impeach the justice of the state,/Since that the trade and profit of the city/Consisteth of all nations' (3.3.29–31). Beyond this, the workings of the

Venetian state, a matter of some interest to Shakespeare's audiences, are hardly even alluded to. For the purposes of the play it is a great and wealthy maritime trading city exotic enough to be an appropriate counter to the more romantic atmosphere of Belmont, where a dead father's will has a force comparable to that of a merchant's bond.

There is little to be said of the politics depicted in most of the *Hamlet* films – the business world of Almereyda's version, and the vague medievalism of Olivier's and Zeffirelli's. Almereyda's Claudius has a corporation to run, which is enough to indicate that he has responsibilities beyond his family, and by inference the politics of the 'Denmark Corporation' are those associated with capitalism. In that respect, the opposition of Hamlet and the defiantly un-business-like clothing, pursuits, and attitudes of the younger people have a counter-cultural edge (Figure 5.1). Douglas Lanier has pointed to elements of film noir, although these should be distinguished from psychological expressionism of the kind identified above (pp. 36–38), with Olivier's film. His list focuses appropriately on the political and societal dimensions of the 'Manhattan 2000' setting:

the film's brooding atmosphere; its use of the city as a character; its images of an oppressive urban world of blue-lit neon, chrome and asphalt; its emphasis on systematic corruption, surveillance, and violence behind a façade of benign

Figure 5.1. *Hamlet* (Michael Almereyda, 2000): Hamlet (Ethan Hawke). soliloquizes in the video store.

normality; and its characterisation of the protagonist as a fallen innocent who struggles against his own impotence, alienation, and complicity with the system he resists.[3]

This is persuasive, though one might question the claim that this Hamlet is 'a fallen innocent' in the spiritual sense present in Olivier's characterization of Hamlet or Welles' of Macbeth: this is a secular, materialistic world without any such dimension, though even here imagining one's mother as a porn star may well qualify as a falling from grace.

Back in the (vaguely) medieval era, and without Fortinbras, Olivier's Elsinore is an isolated, intensely focused environment, and the characterization of Claudius as a man of power is made more personal and, as has already been noted, erotic. Zeffirelli also omits Fortinbras, although he makes surveillance – in the simpler medieval mode of characters watching each other – a pervasive element of life in Elsinore. Hamlet sees Laertes taking his leave of Ophelia, watches as Polonius and the king set up his encounter with her, and later is able to see Rosencrantz and Guildenstern go to make their report to the king. Beyond this, though, there is nothing to suggest how the state functions when it is not protecting the king or enjoying itself at banquets and festivities like the players' performance. The massed warriors in the yard between the keep and the family vault in the opening sequence indicate merely that this is a well-defended regime.

In Branagh's film every room in the palace seems to have at least one concealed door, and being alone, even in his study, is no easy feat for 'the observed of all observers'. The Norwegian elements of the plot, and the impression of a regime under threat from external as well as internal forces, are important aspects of this 'full text' version. However, the specific treatment of Fortinbras creates some difficulties. At the end of more than four hours of viewing, it would have been weak to have him simply arrive and, after politely saluting the English ambassadors with a 'warlike noise', enter to find himself presented with the throne of Denmark and responsible for funeral arrangements for the entire Danish royal family. Consequently, he invades Elsinore, easily dispatching its few defending guards and sending his shock troops crashing in through the windows, and takes his place on the throne with a smouldering arrogance that only Rufus Sewell can provide. At intervals throughout the film he has been glimpsed as a hothead whom his uncle (John Mills) can scarcely hold back. When

Hamlet leaves for England, the army that he sees on the horizon is a formidable force, marching past in impressive numbers. This is the point at which Branagh, needing a strong conclusion to the film's first part, delivers the soliloquy 'How all occasions do inform against me' (in the Second Quarto ending of 4.4) as a declamation that grows in volume and vehemence as the camera pulls back gradually, a shot resembling Olivier's 'Once more unto the breach' in *Henry V*.

The suggestion of a mid-European regime has placed the film's events within the broad range of late nineteenth-century history without drawing specific parallels. In Branagh's Elsinore, Claudius and Gertrude both attend to matters of state – they are signing decrees when Polonius brings Ophelia's letter (and Ophelia) to them – and the king has attendants who are more than merely set-dressing or convenient message-bearers. Richard Briers' Polonius is a formidable prime minister, who emerges from what must be a regular encounter with a prostitute to give instructions to Reynaldo (Gérard Depardieu), who appears to be his pimp as well as his private man of affairs. Although Polonius' fussiness may annoy Gertrude, he is by no means the senile fool Hamlet makes him out to be. His severity with his daughter has been noted already, and he is no less imperative in his instructions to Gertrude before her private encounter with Hamlet. He and his son and daughter stand at the side of the royal dais in the first court scene, in military uniforms that indicate that all of them, including Ophelia, have a rank in this 'warlike state'. All the male courtiers are in uniform. During the first part of Laertes' leave-taking (1.3) Hamlet is seen in the distant background, inspecting a corps of cadets, and the same group appears at other points in the action. Only Horatio, Rosencrantz, Guildenstern, and Gertrude among the principal characters are never seen in uniform. Beyond the court, the civilian population of Denmark consists of Laertes' followers, the sailors who bring Hamlet's letters, the two gravediggers and the priest officiating reluctantly at Ophelia's interment, and the small group of the Danish bourgeoisie who watch the proceedings of the first court scene from a bridge across the grand hall.

Although analogies with late nineteenth-century royal or imperial houses may provide a credible background for the film's events, they do not necessarily bring *Hamlet* closer to the preoccupations of present-day audiences. Surveillance, whether by the use of secret doors or (as with Almereyda's film) electronic means, and the plight of an individual combating a plausible but villainous ruler, have their equivalents in every society, but we never see how the kings in Olivier's or Zeffirelli's films govern their state or how they achieved power – apart from by killing their brother and convincing the 'better wisdoms' of the council that they are the natural choice as his successor in the royal bed as well as on the throne. Grigori Kozintsev's king is shown controlling the conference of counsellors, and his opening speech is divided between the courtyard – where a soldier reads the first lines as a proclamation to a silent crowd of peasants – the lobby of the court and finally the inner sanctum of the council chamber. Hamlet's first soliloquy is thought by him in voice-over, but not, as in Olivier's case, when he is alone: Innokenti Smoktunovski makes his way, tight-lipped, through milling courtiers, who smile and nod to him as he walks towards the open air. The image of an intellectual forced into an internal exile, and of a smiling tyrant who can control all levels of society, resonates with the circumstances of the Soviet film-maker and lends the film's political world an authenticity that the English-language counterparts cannot achieve. The Russian *Hamlet* evokes a system in which the disappearance through murder or exile of inconvenient rivals for power had been all too common.

With Olivier's film of *Henry V*, even without the dedication to the troops involved in the Normandy landings (added before the release in the autumn of 1944) comparisons with current events were straightforward, although the national identity of the enemy might have caused some confusion. The means by which the problem was finessed in characterizing the French king and the Dauphin have been mentioned in Chapter 2 (p. 54).[4] So far as politics within the film are concerned, Olivier is careful to circumvent the speciousness of the grounds for Henry's campaign by making the Bishop of Ely (Robert Helpmann) a comic figure. Henry cuts through the elaborations of the justification, with its convoluted genealogical points, to insist on a straight answer to his question 'May I with right and conscience make this claim?' (1.2.96). Unlike Branagh, Olivier does not emphasize the anxiety of this mature, decisive ruler to satisfy his conscience before going to war or to prove himself worthy of his office. There is no hint of any insecurity in the claim that there should be 'No king of England, if not king of France' (2.2.189), and there has been no emphasis on the clerics' influencing policies for their own ends. Once arrived in France, Olivier's Henry does not threaten the citizens of Harfleur with punishments that would have seemed like the worst stories of Nazi atrocities ('the fleshed soldier . . . mowing like grass/Your fresh fair virgins and your flowering infants' 5.3.88–91), and he is able to deal thoughtfully with the questions of his soldiers on the eve of battle and answer suavely the direct question of Catherine in the wooing scene: 'Is it possible dat I should love de *ennemi* of France?' (5.2.162).

Olivier's command in this scene is otherwise largely unchallenged by a less confrontational Catherine, whereas Branagh has to face the more searching scrutiny of Emma Thompson, but neither film includes the more forthright analogy between ravishing countries and deflowering women that Burgundy indulges in with the bawdy 'frankness of [his] mirth' that prompts Henry to remark that in his 'blindness [he] cannot see many a fair French city for one fair French maid that stands in [his] way' and the French king to reply that he is seeing the cities 'perspectively, the cities turned into a maid – for they are all girdled with maiden walls that war hath never entered' (5.2.293–8). Neither director can be reproached for omitting a passage that would try the patience of all but the most determined moviegoer – or theatre spectator for that matter – but the cut is consistent with the general policy by which both films moderate the male aggression latent – and sometimes patent – in their story.[5] Branagh's inclusion of the pessimistic concluding lines of the epilogue, a gesture hardly appropriate to the time and place of Olivier's film, is also of a piece with the later film's emphasis on the growth of the king, his sustaining of a heavy responsibility, and his relationship with his peers and allies.

The connection of Branagh's film with contemporary events has occasioned much discussion, in which it has been interpreted as an apologia for war in general and (in some cases) specifically the conflict of Britain with Argentina in 1982 over possession of the Falkland Islands and even the activities of troops in Northern Ireland. Branagh himself made it known that he had consulted the Prince of Wales – patron of his theatre company – about his role, a move that was interpreted as politically naïve, but the question is surely one of the film's resonance rather than (as with Olivier) any political or propagandistic intention. The 1944 film is effective largely because, like the best war films made in Britain during the conflict, it is frank in its patriotism but avoids vaingloriousness, and appeals to a sense of calmly resolute leadership found in such films as Noël Coward's *In Which We Serve* (1941). The reception of the film on both sides of the Atlantic reflected its subtleties as well as the social and political imperatives that surrounded it. The most striking response is probably that of James Agee, an American critic and essayist who testified to the appeal of the experience without surrendering a degree of critical distance:

I am not a Tory, a monarchist, a Catholic, a medievalist, an Englishman, or, despite all the good that it engenders, a lover of war: but the beauty and power of this traditional exercise was such that, watching it, I wished I was, thought I was, and was proud of it. I was persuaded, and in part still am, that every time and place has since been in decline, save one, in which one Englishman used language better than anyone has before or since, or ever shall; and that nearly the best that our time can say for itself is that some of us are still capable of paying homage to the fact.[6]

In Britain most of the reviews were favourable, though none as fulsome as this. More than one critic regretted the omission of the scene (2.2) in which Henry deals with the treacherous peers – compared to 'Fifth Columnists' – and the left-wing documentarist Edgar Anstey commented on the 'Hitlerian' rationale for the invasion of France. But the dominant tone was celebratory: Helen Fletcher in the *Sunday Graphic* (26 November 1944), under the headline 'An English Film That Will Thrill England', welcomed an event that would 'Give Shakespeare back to the groundlings'.[7]

Branagh's film, differently inflected and consciously responsive to at least some of the spirit of its own age, tells the story of a sensitive and thinking leader shouldering his burden reluctantly but with fortitude and seeing – or suffering – it through to a well-nigh miraculous conclusion. In this it is more sentimental than Olivier's, although it allows more space to the politics within its narrative. Olivier's bright, colourful film was released when morale needed boosting, as the war in Europe moved towards a close but England was attacked with the new unmanned rocket bombs and the Pacific campaign continued. It is questionable whether in 1988 Branagh's film encouraged anyone to think invasion of another country was justifiable in itself: Agincourt was then, not now. But its premise – war is terrible but sometimes necessary and is a proving ground for (masculine) virtues – is conservative. For some critics, this has been acceptable enough: as Emma Smith points out, 'Branagh's film does not glorify or underestimate the costs of war', and 'does not mini-mise Henry's individual heroism' in its 'parable of personal decency and bravery in a brutal situation'.[8] Branagh's Henry, among his mud-stained comrades, delivers the 'Saint Crispin's Day' speech, like Olivier, from a wagon, but here the faces around him are familiar, identifiable as those who have accompanied him closely on his campaign. His own features do not have the film-star handsomeness and quasi-aristocratic grace of Olivier: he is a leader among his men (Figure 5.2). Other commentators have been less favourable than Smith. In a searching analysis of the film's cultural and (so to speak) real-world politics, Donald K. Hendrik has argued that it 'studiously maintains . . . a conservative rather than a criti-cal ambivalence, progressive merely in the weakest sense of its openness toward some undecidability, but undecidability is here really an alibi for a tactical indecision'.[9]

There are two effective figures of authority within each film: the king and the Chorus. In Olivier's the king's authority is elided with that of the Elizabethan actor who plays him, and when the Chorus appears he remains the figure we saw at the playhouse. Branagh's cho-rus, first seen turning on the working lights of a sound stage and then conducting us towards the historical setting, is a time-travelling war

Figure 5.2. 'Warriors for the working day': Henry V addresses his troops before Agincourt (Kenneth Branagh, 1988).

correspondent. Like the muddy carnage of the battlefield, this suggests comparisons with more recent reporting or fictional depictions of war, and brings the film closer to the kind of implicit acceptance of war as a grim necessity that some critics have taken issue with. The Chorus remains, though, an enthusiast rather than an objective reporter. Branagh's *Henry V* is a stirring, accomplished achievement, in some respects more disturbing than Olivier's film, but not always, perhaps, in the ways its scriptwriter, director, and leading actor intended. It carries, as Kenneth Rothwell observes in a sympathetic discussion of the film and its critics, 'a heavy freightage of ambiguity about the true nature of the young king', and the controversy surrounding it has served to highlight the fact that for better or worse Branagh 'can make an anti-war movie that also glorifies war'.[10]

In *Richard III* Lord Hastings, summarily condemned to death on a trumped-up charge of treason, may exclaim 'Woe, woe for England!' (3.4.80) but here political manoeuvres and the glamour of a homicidal usurper, rather than the state of the nation, are the dominant concern. Given their differences in temperament and technique, it is hardly surprising that Laurence Olivier's Richard in his 1955 film is more of an 'actor' than Ian McKellen's in 1995. Olivier's is a colder, more distant personality towards those around him and – even when he confides in it – the camera. The precision and agility of Olivier's speaking, his ability to colour each phrase subtly, are set against the restrained Buckingham of Ralph Richardson and the nervously apprehensive Clarence of John Gielgud. The sexual politics of Olivier's script include a strategy that minimizes the speaking roles of its women, the treatment of Lady Anne and the value added through a new, non-speaking character, Jane Shore (Pamela Brown), the mistress of King Edward, whose sly, knowing sensuality suggests a level at which politics and sex work together. She is introduced on camera when Edward and his retinue sweep past and he promises to celebrate his confirmation on the throne with 'all the pleasure of the court' (3 *Henry VI*, 5.7.44); she reappears when Hastings (her new lover) is freed from prison; and is present at the bedside of the dying king. Mistress Shore has staying power, and clearly has the measure of the peers.

The same cannot be said of Lady Anne (Claire Bloom), wooed by Richard in two scenes – Richard's plot against Clarence and his arrest being interpolated – so that the credibility of the transaction might be enhanced. In effect, her first appearance, following her husband's corpse (not, as in the original, that of her father-in-law Henry VI), is marked by a degree of sensuality as she folds back the pall from his open coffin and caresses the (unseen) body. The camera frames her closely as she leans over it, and then pulls back for the first words of her curse on the perpetrator of the crime ('O cursèd be the hand that made these wounds': *Richard III*, 1.2.14) then moves back closer until she rises and starts as she hears Richard's 'Stay, you that bear the corpse, and set it down' (33). A shot from her point of view shows him to us as he stands under a Gothic arch. He moves forward, beating away the guard who tries to intervene, and in the course of the next exchange it is clear that she can hardly resist his gaze. Even after she has set off again with the coffin and its bearers, she is drawn to look back towards him, but she is able to resist the impulse and crosses herself. The preparation has been made for the later scene in which Richard accosts her as she kneels at her husband's tomb. Now the surrender to Richard's sensual appeal is almost complete, and she is close to kissing him even when, after spitting on him for a second time, she insists that 'never came poison from so foul a toad' (147, replacing 'hung . . . on' with 'came . . . from'). By the end of the scene she is close to total abandon, and after she has left and Richard has mused on his sudden attractiveness, he moves towards the door through which she exited and pushes it open with his foot. A bed is seen in the background, with the skirts of her gown to one side of it, and the shot closes as his shadow falls across the bed and the partially concealed figure. Bloom, who had an affair with Olivier that lasted for the duration of the filming, testifies in her memoir *Leaving a Doll's House* to his 'immensely seductive' effect in character, 'his grey eyes mesmeric and his invective bitingly incisive'. As himself, she reflected in retrospect, he had 'a dryness, a lack of spontaneity' and was 'careful, somewhat plodding, full of theatrical mannerisms . . . brimming with a kind of false charm'. (Nevertheless, she 'ignored all the evidence'.)[11]

Olivier's use of shadows throughout the film, together with musical underlining by William Walton that would not be out of place in a horror film, asserts Richard's control over the minds and lives of others – here with a distinctly sexual flavour. After the assertion of his authority through the treatment of the augmented opening soliloquy, the script is shaped to maintain Richard's pre-eminence as a speaker by the removal of speeches by other characters, notably Clarence's pleading with the murderers (1.4), Buckingham's speech on his way to execution (5.1), and, most notably, the denunciation of Richard by Queen Elizabeth after the murder of her children (4.4). Queen Margaret is absent altogether.[12] As Jack J. Jorgens suggests, 'if the lesser characters have any depth, it is forced upon them by Richard'.[13] The film's depiction of the exercise of power is complemented by Olivier's power as actor and director, handing control over to Richard, although the ironic effect of the sinister shadows and other elements of mise-en-scène can be said to do the work of some of the lines that had to be removed from this exceptionally long play in order to make a workable film script. But comparison with the McKellen/Loncraine film shows what might be done to qualify the authority of the protagonist without diminishing his magnetism.

I suggested in Chapter 1 that the 1930s setting in the 1995 *Richard III* presents difficulties for the final working-out of its plot, but for most of the film this does not matter, so long as the focus is on the devious means by which Richard achieves his goals. His manipulation and elimination of his allies, and wooing of Lady Anne (1.2) have a momentum and seductive ingenuity that carry the picture for most of its way.[14] After a title card outlining the situation – 'Civil War Divides the Nation' – and identifying the factions and their family relationships, the startling prologue has a tank crashing through the wall of Prince Edward's field HQ and Richard, in a gasmask, killing him and the frail Henry VI. The action then swings towards the 'victory ball', establishing along the way 'Earl Rivers' (Robert Downey Jr) as a playboy, brother of the American Queen Elizabeth (Annette Bening). This casting was prompted (or, at least, justified) by the desire to draw analogies with Wallis Simpson's relationship with the Prince of Wales who was briefly King Edward VIII until his abdication in 1936.[15] In the palace a dance band is playing Marlowe's 'Come live with me and be my love' in a pastiche 1930s musical setting. Clarence (Nigel Hawthorne), an amateur photographer, is hustled away, the first hint of what is going on behind the scenes. After Richard's public performance of the play's opening lines (from 'Now is the winter of our discontent' to the first word of line 11, 'He . . .'), for the rest of the speech the camera finds him as he enters the gents' lavatory and leans over a urinal and continues with a sardonic repetition of lines he has just spoken to the court, taking the text up with 'capers nimbly in a lady's chamber' (1.1.11–12). As well as establishing his ability to command respect and affection, the sequence also shows Richard's virtuosity in executing simple (private) actions with his one functioning hand. He is seen as man of skill even before his organizational abilities become apparent. In the wooing scene, which takes place in a hospital mortuary, he sucks the ring from his own finger and holds it in his mouth before placing it on that of Lady Anne (Kristin Scott Thomas). His suavity and delight in his power to win friends and influence people extend to his relationship with the audience. To be taken into his confidence is a privilege.

The locations, the formal suits of the politicians and the Lord Mayor, and the SS-like uniforms of Richard's faction, which gradually prevail over ordinary khaki, all situate the action in terms of familiar imagery from the 1930s. The most direct connection with the methods of Nazism is not so much the massed rally with which Richard establishes his claim to the crown as the brutality of the murders. Clarence is stabbed to death in his bath, its water rapidly suffused with his blood; Rivers is skewered from beneath his bed while being fellated by an air hostess; Buckingham is garrotted with wire; Hastings is hanged, his body shooting down towards the camera from an iron grating; and we see one of the princes smothered with a red cloth. Like Olivier's film, the script omits Queen Margaret, but gives some of her lines to the Duchess of York (Maggie Smith), who reminds Queen Elizabeth with more truth than tact 'you are a dream of what you were. A breath./A queen in jest' (adapted from 4.4.88–91) before leaving for France by aeroplane. The women's grief as they are forbidden to visit the princes in the Tower (a radically abbreviated version of 4.2) allows them a fuller voice than in Olivier's version, but their presence in the film is not so much a matter of spoken lines as of images of family life either precariously maintained or disrupted. The marriage of Richmond and the younger Elizabeth the day before the battle and the scene in which we see them in bed together the next morning contrast with the evident barrenness of Richard's relationship with Lady Anne – whom he ignores as she stands invitingly on a staircase in one scene. She disintegrates into dependency on drugs until ('grievous sick') she is dead in bed, staring lifelessly at the ceiling as a spider scuttles across her face.

Although the film identifies him with fascism, Richard (unlike Hitler or even Mosley) has no political programme beyond the achievement of power. Bertolt Brecht, in *The Resistible Rise of Arturo Ui* (1941; first produced 1958) used Shakespeare's play as the framework for an indictment of the social and political forces that allowed Hitler's ascendancy. The analogies serve Loncraine and McKellen more simply as a means of bringing the story of Richard alive for a modern audience, without any searching analysis of the political process. In some respects this is a gangster film, in others an 'English heritage drama'. The military denouement is achieved with explosive vigour but lacks the assurance of a restored peace that the play insists on. Richard and Richmond confront each other on girders high above the floor of the ruined power station where the final battle takes place. The last Plantagenet falls to his death as he extends his hand towards Richmond, smiling in triumph as he topples into the fire that then engulfs the screen. Richmond's ambiguous smile suggests recognition if not complicity. As Richard falls, Al Jolson's voice rings out, with 'I'm sittin' on top of the world'. McKellen, in his notes to the screenplay, acknowledges the ambiguity of the exchanged looks, recalling that when he first heard the song overlaid on the shot it seemed to underline the fact that both men 'simultaneously feel, in the moment when their fates collide, that they are sitting on top of the world'.[16] Unlike the death of Olivier's Richard, fighting desperately to the last, impaled on the spears of soldiers and given the death blow by Richmond, then slung contemptuously across a horse's back – he has achieved the mount he had called for in desperation earlier – McKellen leaves the film with a heroic brio that has been compared to that of James Cagney as Cody Jarrett on top of an exploding petroleum tank in *White Heat* (1949).[17] Jarrett, though, was proving himself to his dead mother and claiming fulfilment of his manhood: Richard has no such agenda, and this modernized version of a medieval devil, filtered through Tudor historiography and twentieth-century history, is falling into the flames of a Hell he may not believe in.

Both *Julius Caesar* and *Coriolanus* include scenes of political manoeuvring, with the common people at the mercy of rousing rhetoric in the former and exploited by politicians for their own ends in the latter. Fiennes's *Coriolanus* identifies the leading citizens (the play's plebeians) with an activist cell, prominent in the assault on the grain silos at the beginning of the film and in all confrontations with Caius Martius and the aristocrats. They confer in a cheerless flat in a bleak housing development, and one of their leaders is a woman. The tribunes' business suits set them apart from them, and there is no suggestion that they are easily fooled – though in the end they are successfully manipulated. But this is a modern political world in which everyone is liable to be manipulated, not least Caius Martius himself. Without resorting to the kind of slant Brecht attempted in the stage version of the play left unfinished at his death, Fiennes manages to suggest that in a properly ordered society, such figures as this hero would be irrelevant – but the world is not run properly and, unlike Brecht's additional scene with the death of Coriolanus reported in the Senate and the tribunes moving 'next business', there is no suggestion that it might be.[18]

Mankiewicz's 1953 *Julius Caesar*, as has been noted, uses its black-and-white cinematography to reinforce similarities between its action and recent events in Europe. However, it stops short of what was planned as a moment of graphic political violence: it lacks the scene (scripted and shot but not included) in which Cinna the poet is murdered by the rioting plebeians, who initially take him for Cinna the conspirator and then decide to kill him anyway 'for his bad verses'. The producer John Houseman thought that after the mob had been stirred to rebellion by Mark Antony's speech, 'this minor lynching was anticlimactic'. The shooting script, though, shows that it would have revealed a further element of the orator's cynicism. As he pauses to master his emotions with 'My heart is in the coffin there with Caesar' (3.2.103), the script has him '[turn] his back to the mob, his hand to his eyes. Safely unobserved, his eyes reveal their alertness to the changing mood of the mob'. Later, as they wreck the market, he 'turns to the CAMERA. His sweaty, tense expression relaxes into a grim smile'. The crowd would have pursued Cinna into the forum, and in the final two shots of the sequence Antony would have watched the murder, 'his look . . . an impassive one'.[19] The low-budget amateur film made by David Bradley in Chicago in 1950 has an effective version of Cinna's fate: the poet has been trapped in an alley or the corner of a portico by a sinister-looking group of men, and the scene is framed by superimposed flames, so that it is subsumed into the general sense of mayhem and conflagration. There is then a cut directly to the flame of a lamp as the triumvirs discuss the proscriptions that decide who else should be assassinated.

The representation of political processes in Mankiewicz's film, emanating as it does from a major studio in the early 1950s, demands interpretation in the light of the Cold War. But such decoding is by no means straightforward. Maria Wyke, in a study of the historical Caesar's significance in American history, notes that 'the colossal statuary and monumental architecture, the military pomp and adulation, the cult of personality, and the arrests and purges ... constitute characteristics common to the European dictatorships of the 1930s and 1940s'. She considers Louis Calhern's Caesar most likely to be identified with Stalin, physically frail, the object of 'a nascent conspiracy', and anxious about 'the dangerous men who surround him'. This fits the film neatly into the anti-Soviet propaganda of the time, and reviews and magazine articles support this view of its reception. Wyke concludes, though, that 'the rich intertextuality and the complex construction ... open up the possibility of additional, even contradictory, readings of the film's Caesar'.[20] John H. Lenihan suggests that Brutus in Mankiewicz's film is not a noble spirit worked on by a subversive 'proto-Commie' Cassius, but an idealist 'wrongly labelled as a traitor by a conniving demagogue' – Antony.[21] Jack J. Jorgens captures the subtlety with which the ambivalence of Antony is suggested elsewhere in the film: 'The definitive image of Antony occurs in his prolonged entrance to join the conspirators by the body of Caesar. As he moves along a corridor lined with pillars, light and shadow are alternately thrown across his face, embodying the problem faced by the conspirators and audience alike: Who and what is Antony?'[22] In Stuart Burge's 1970 *Julius Caesar* Charlton Heston, returning to the role he played in David Bradley's 1950 version, is at once a more histrionic and less dangerous Antony. The production, handsome enough but lacking the monumentalism of the MGM film, has Gielgud as Caesar among a distinguished cast, but Jason Robards delivers a fatally incommunicative Brutus, locked in his inwardness and draining the energy from every scene he appears in. Despite the sterling performances of Richard Burton and Rex Harrison as Caesar and Antony in *Cleopatra* (1963) – in a script that seems to devote a good deal of effort to the task of not being by Shaw in the first half or Shakespeare in the second – and Heston's return to Antony in the lavish but unconvincing *Antony and Cleopatra* (1972) he directed himself, the 1953 *Julius Caesar* remains the most persuasive presentation in the cinema of the dictator and his enigmatic eulogist.[23] Its political ambiguities may be the reason for its remaining intriguing and effective after six decades.

Beyond Shakespeare

Given the simple tripartite template proposed by Deborah Cartmell and cited in the Introduction, (p. 1) of transposition, commentary, and analogue as three types of adaptation from text to screen, all Shakespeare performances that shift (or transpose) the plays to new periods and circumstances might count as adaptations.[1] This chapter examines that additional level of alteration that takes the play beyond the sense of a film as a production of the play by other means, and into profitable realms of infidelity not available even when *Love's Labour's Lost* becomes a pastiche thirties musical or *Hamlet* is situated in 'Manhattan, 2000'. In the freer kinds of adaptation discussed here the 'English-speaking' aspect is important, as a crucial marker of the liberty gained by the decision not to use a play's language – or at least, most of it – but to work either within the self-imposed bounds of its construction and incidents, or to range more freely while reminding the audience of what is not being used by some degree of allusiveness.

Like *Men of Respect*, the mafia *Macbeth* discussed below (pp. 145–148) a few films that we can count as appropriations rather than 'the play performed by other means' have followed their original closely. Among the most entertaining of these are the two comedies *Scotland PA* (2001), which situates *Macbeth* in the cut-throat competitive world of rival fast food restaurants, and *Gnomeo and Juliet* (2011), an animated feature in which the familiar play is the pattern for feuding and love among rival garden ornaments. Cultural capital is deftly reinvested by both films, with a nod towards the seriousness they respect but undermine. It is significant that both use plays whose outlines, if not detail, are widely known. Billy Morrisette, the director of *Scotland PA*, who first encountered the play in high school, declared that he was making it for 'kids ... who were reading *Cliff's Notes* [*sic*] and getting stoned'. Gnomeo even consults the statue of Shakespeare (voiced by Patrick Stewart) to find out where his story is heading, but the outcome defies Shakespearian precedent and secures a happy ending for the principals and their supporters. There are passing references to other plays, and the 'balcony scene' makes use of a garden pond in a manner suggestive of Luhrmann's *Romeo+Juliet*.[2]

Many films have drawn on the plays as a dominant structural or thematic source for their story but without adopting their plot so fully. In some, a Shakespearian element underlies the plot – for example, *Hamlet* in Disney's *The Lion King* (1994) or *King Lear* in *The Godfather, Part Three* (1990), *A Thousand Acres* (1997, from the novel of the same title by Jane Smiley), *King of Texas* (2002), and Kristian Levring's *The King is Alive* (2000). In Levring's film, a group of Western tourists stranded in an abandoned mining town in Namibia reconstruct what they – or one of their number, the former actor Henry (David Bradley) – can recall of *King Lear* as they wait for rescue. Levring's strict application of the austere rules of the Dogme 95 group (their 'rules of chastity') produces a vision of the play and its relationship with human interactions and personalities even starker than that of Brook's *King Lear*. Henry is a Hollywood screenwriter, and interrogation of the tenets of 'mainstream' movie-making complements scrutiny of the fragile cultural and social status accorded Shakespeare's text in Western society. This challenging and fascinating work is, as Thomas Cartelli and Katherine Rowe point out, 'unaccommodated' film-making.[3] The quasi-documentary aesthetic of *The King is Alive* ensures that the characters' ordeal is shared by the audience, who may also suspect that it was endured by the actors themselves, at least during the long hot days of filming.

Meanwhile, back in the mean streets of the mainstream, *The Godfather, Part Three* does not foreground the congruence of play and film but has it emerge gradually. Michael Corleone is not dividing his 'kingdom' up so much as seeking retirement by legitimizing it and gaining respectability for the family and himself through charitable generosity, but the presence of his brother's illegitimate son at times suggests the dynamic of the Gloucester plot. The influence of *King Lear* is felt most strongly when his daughter Mary is killed by an assassin aiming at Michael, and dies in his arms on the steps of the Teatro Massimo in Palermo. In memoranda documenting the scripting process, Shakespearian tragedy is invoked more than once by the collaborators, with references to *Timon of Athens* and *Macbeth* as well as to *King Lear*.[4] The impression these give is of Francis Ford Coppola's desire to fashion a tragedy out of his material, generating Shakespearian resonances and only 'quoting' a play directly in the scene of Mary's death and Michael's agonized scream. The whole of the *Godfather* saga has qualities (and ambitions) in common with older tragic drama and in particular with both *King Lear* and *Hamlet*: as Vito explains to his son Tony in *Part Three* 'every family has bad memories', and the modus operandi of their business has been 'reason, backed up by murder'.

Another, less glamorous, example of this mode of appropriation, profiting from an 'original' but with more allusion than citation, is Edgar G. Ulmer's *Strange Illusion* (1945), which has production values so low that it only just scrapes in the 'B-movie' category, but is as effective in many respects as some better-known films in its application of the elements of a Shakespearian original to a new story. Paul Cartwright, a young man barely out of his teens, dreams that the death of his father and the emergence of a successor as his mother's prospective husband are the result of shady dealings, including murder and a hidden identity. The plot does not include a ghost, but the dream is not explicable as being other than supernatural as it includes information – later confirmed – that could not have come in any other way. Paul has already shown his hostility towards the newcomer, an attitude that has worried his mother and caused a breach between him and his sister Dorothy. Paul's girlfriend, a less developed character with some of Ophelia's functions, remains committed to supporting him. The 'ghost' effect is reinforced by the eccentric decision of his dead father, a criminologist and judge, to leave behind sealed letters to be delivered to his son. Because the latest posthumous missive directs him to complete his father's book on unsolved crimes, Paul is soon on the track of his mother's new beau, but he is temporarily thwarted by the villain's conspiracy with a local psychiatrist to have him confined in his private mental hospital.

Intriguingly, this subsidiary villain offers a partly 'Freudian' interpretation of the situation, as he explains why a spell under his close watch would be beneficial: 'In some cases, filial devotion to a mother goes beyond the borderlines of normality – it can frequently produce hallucinations'. Given his early career in Weimar Germany as well as the vogue for psychoanalysis in 1930s America, especially Hollywood, Ulmer would have been aware of the missing element here: there is no suggestion that Paul has a subconscious desire for his mother or a suppressed wish to commit parricide. The prospective husband is duly unmasked as a fraud and a homicidal and sexual predator – he has tried to strangle Paul's girlfriend – who had already killed a young bride for her fortune and then faked a new identity. In a reprise of the 'illusion' sequence, with swirling fog, that began the movie, we see Paul, his sister, his mother, and the reassuring figure of the amiable local doctor who is now in line for her hand as they stroll confidently towards the future. *Strange Illusion* is an intriguing demonstration of how far an ingenious and gifted film-maker, despite being confined to poor resources, could go without carrying through every aspect of a Shakespearian model. The film is not so much a *Hamlet*, as *Hamlet*-ish.

In some cases a Shakespearian text forms a 'play within a film', so that the references in the plot that frame it are in counterpoint to direct quotation, not merely of lines but of whole scenes. *Kiss Me Kate* (Jack Cummings, 1953 – without the stage musical's comma before 'Kate') is a Technicolor (and 3-D) adaptation of the great 1948 musical that itself adapts *The Taming of the Shrew* as a parallel to the off-stage lives and loves of the divorced couple who are playing its leads. The book by Bella Spewack is, as Irene G. Dash points out, the first adaptation of the source to be made by a woman, and in giving Lilli Vanessi/ Katherine a soliloquy, 'I hate men', it allows her a voice denied to her in all other versions, including Shakespeare's, while her husband Fred Graham has some hard thinking of his own to do.[5] In this respect, with its sophisticated (but also, in movie terms, traditional) structure of a play within the musical, *Kiss Me Kate* is a commentary on the original as well as a major work in its own right.

A comparable juxtaposition in a tragic vein is George Cukor's *A Double Life* (1948). Ronald Colman plays Anthony (Tony) John, an actor whose career, though successful, has settled into the rut of facile Broadway comedies. He has long thought of appearing as Othello, but has an instinctive fear (justified, it turns out) that it will unleash impulses he had better not explore. In learning to become a good actor rather than a 'hambone' Tony has acquired the ability to tap into his own emotions in the approved Stanislavskian manner. But this has its dangers. When he finds himself impelled to strangle his ex-wife, who is playing Desdemona, the only way he can deal with the desire is to 'become' Othello in the bedroom of a waitress with whom he has had an affair and kill her. George Cukor's film interweaves the performances of scenes from the play, principally its conclusion, with the actor's off-stage life. Effectively, the story itself is one of the leakage of Shakespeare into reality, as the play becomes the medium by which darker forces possess the mind.

An actor's identification with a tragic role figures in *The Dresser* (1983), but here there is not the same intensity of psychological exploration. A Shakespearian actor of great power but with an old-fashioned, heroically overpowering technique is touring his familiar repertoire in wartime England. The endeavour is in itself heroic, and the classic 'the show must go on' element of this backstage drama is provided by the struggle to achieve the storm in *King Lear* with enough force when one of the already depleted company is missing. 'Sir' (Albert Finney) is accompanied by his dresser Norman (Tom Courtenay), a pathetic but comic figure who plays the fool to his Lear off-stage. After a commanding performance of the play, 'Sir' dies, and the dresser discovers that, contrary to his promises, the actor has not dedicated his unfinished memoirs to him. There is no division of the kingdom as such, but the actor's performance as the king in the storm onstage is complemented by his behaviour outside the theatre and in the dressing room. In one scene he rages alarmingly in the streets of the Northern town where he is playing, and it is clear that he has a rather specialized conception of the war itself. Norman has to tell him not to take the bombing of the Grand Theatre, Plymouth personally (Herr Hitler 'is making it very difficult for Shakespeare') and when he encounters a disconsolate old man sitting by the ruins of his bombed house, the actor gives him a pair of tickets for the evening's performance. Harwood, author of the screenplay as well as the play of the same name, had been dresser to Sir Donald Wolfit, the actor on whom 'Sir' is based, and wrote an account of his life in the 'unfashionable theatre'.[6] 'Sir', though, is not Wolfit, who did not die during the war and enjoyed a considerable career after it. But the domineering actor, insistent both on his privilege of taking the stage at others' expense and the importance of his art, makes the analogies with Lear effective. Shakespeare serves in *The Dresser* as a marker of cultural values as well as the provider of material for the screenwriter, director, and actor.

In many respects, this is as much a fable of 'seeing it through' as many films actually made in wartime, not least Olivier's *Henry V.*

The political significance of Shakespearian performance in a former British colony is a dominant element of *Shakespeare Wallah* (1965), directed by James Ivory and produced by Ismail Merchant, in which a small troupe of travelling players struggle to come to terms with the gap between the theatrical fare they found a welcome for before Indian independence and the realities of a new regime in which their mannered, old-fashioned presentations of English classics seem at best irrelevant, at worst a reminder of imperialism. Based on the career of Geoffrey Kendal and his wife and leading lady Laura Lidell, the film features their daughter Felicity as Lizzie in a role paralleling her real-life experiences, except for the important fact that the fiction has her father rueful but glad that Lizzie is departing to try her chances in England.[7] Kendal was in fact bitterly opposed to Felicity's departure, regarding it as a betrayal and taking some years to become reconciled to it. The burgeoning Bollywood film industry, personified in a jealous star, Manjula (Madhur Jaffrey), provides rivalry for the values of the colonial past as well as for the Kendals' daughter, who falls for Manjula's lover, a rich young film director, Sanju (Shashi Kapoor). *Shakespeare Wallah* does not adopt or adapt Shakespearian texts for its storyline, but the scenes from performances of *Antony and Cleopatra* ('Let Rome in Tiber melt/And the wide arch of the ranged empire fall') and *Othello* have a particular resonance in this context, and 'Shakespeare', the congeries of cultural, social, and political attitudes, is a potent signifier for the values that are now in question in the evolution of a new India.

Other films have made the performance of one of the plays a key event in the emotional development of a character, sometimes in an educational context, as in *Dead Poets Society* (1989) or the comedy *Were the World Mine* (2009), in which a young gay man finds acceptance of his identity in a production of *A Midsummer Night's Dream.* In the latter film, the discovery of a magic herb helps the student turn the whole town gay, reversing, so to speak, the polarity of prejudice, while at the same time making *Fame* (1982) and *High School Musical* (TV movie, 2006) and their offshoots seem like empty celebrations of hyped-up youthful aspiration. (Not that this is necessarily a bad thing in itself or a new phenomenon: a previous generation found its fix in the Judy

Garland/Mickey Rooney musicals.) The alleged ability of Shakespearian performance to change lives for the better is central to Kenneth Branagh's *In the Bleak Midwinter* (1995, released as *A Midwinter's Tale* in the United States). The film opens with the sound of Noël Coward singing the verse of 'Why must the show go on?' but interrupts him before the chorus with its all-important question. It subsequently delivers an optimistic answer. A no-budget benefit performance of *Hamlet*, organized in aid of a rural church by an idealistic young director (Michael Maloney) unites a disparate group of actors, brings them to an understanding of each other and themselves, and gives hope to a moribund community called, appropriately, Hope. When the actor–director (playing the prince) is tempted by the chance of a role in a Hollywood sci-fi epic, the project seems likely to crumble, but the show does go on. The ending is, as Branagh recognizes, likely to be found sentimental:

Actors are sentimental. It's one of our weaknesses. But I believe at times one of the gloriously silly ones. It may not translate into action on all occasions ... but in this instance I wanted the happy ending, which we beggarly actors so long for, and rarely find.[8]

Although the play does not provide the pattern for the film's script, it represents a partial solution for the spiritual and cultural as well as economic deprivation the young idealist within the film wants to address. As Samuel Crowl notes, the film is in some respects an act of homage to the dominantly warm-hearted (though often slyly acidic) comedies made by Ealing Studios in the middle decades of the century, which are evoked by its use of black-and-white photography, the gallery of sharply defined character types, and the warmth of human feeling evinced by the ending.[9]

Hamlet functions as a symbol of civilization in very different circumstances in Ernst Lubitsch's *To Be or Not To Be* (1942), in which Joseph Tura ('the great Polish actor' as he likes to think himself) is disturbed by the departure of a young man from the front orchestra stalls as soon as he begins the famous soliloquy, but the speaking of 'Hath not a Jew eyes?' by a Jewish actor is the more serious Shakespearian element of this comedy set in Warsaw during the first weeks of the Nazi occupation. Other examples of what might be called significant but incidental Shakespeare are the drawing room performance of the balcony scene from *Romeo and Juliet* by the young, ambitious, and embarrassingly drunk actress played by Katherine Hepburn in *Morning Glory* (1933), and the appalling not-far-enough-off-Broadway production of *Richard III* in *The Goodbye Girl* (1977) in which a young actor follows his director's insistence that Richard of Gloucester must be played as an outrageously camp gay man.

The most thorough application of Shakespeare's plays – both plots and dialogue – to the story of a theatrical career is *Shakespeare in Love* (1999). The playwright (Joseph Fiennes) suffers from writer's block as he struggles to rise above the conventional though successful level of *The Two Gentlemen of Verona*, resisting the pressure from the manager, Henslowe, to stick to the proven formula ('love – and a bit with a dog'). He heeds the advice of Christopher Marlowe (Rupert Everett) that his new play's working title, *Romeo and Ethel the Pirate's Daughter*, leaves something to be desired and accepts his advice about reshaping the plot, but it is not until he falls in love with the unattainable Lady Viola de Lesseps (Gwyneth Paltrow) that inspiration returns. After seeing her at a ball he climbs up to her balcony – and falls off – but his desire to be with her coincides with her longing to be an actor, and their paths cross at the playhouse where she presents herself in disguise as a young man anxious to join the company. The course of true love leads to time in her bedchamber and the composition of the play, by now known as *Romeo and Juliet*. In one scene they read newly written dialogue in her bed, with her taking her lines as Romeo and Shakespeare reading as Juliet, until they find themselves exchanging roles. Intercut with this, in a circling camera movement that matches with that used for the bedroom, is the rehearsal in the theatre, where she speaks Romeo's lines to the boy playing Juliet. Events conspire to part the lovers, specifically her newly rich father's insistence that she marry an impoverished nobleman, Lord Wessex, who will take her off to seek their (rather, his) fortune in America. After this has been settled, she manages to escape from her bridegroom to attend the opening afternoon of the new tragedy, where Shakespeare is standing in for the injured Burbage (Martin Clunes) as Romeo. Suddenly the voice of the boy player breaks in mid-performance. Viola takes over, and Juliet is played with a naturalistic authenticity that astonishes the audience and effectively jumps across a few centuries of theatre history. The company's triumph at the end of the play is interrupted by the arrival of the Master of the Revels, who denounces the company for having a real woman on stage, but punishment is averted when Queen Elizabeth (Judi Dench) intervenes. In defiance of another aspect of theatrical history, she has been attending a public playhouse. The happiness of the ending is qualified. Viola still has to marry Wessex, and Shakespeare – who now has the money to buy a share in the company – undertakes to write a new play. Thoughts of Viola lead him to what will become, somewhat prematurely, *Twelfth Night*, not performed for at least another five (historical) years. Meanwhile, Viola and Wessex are shipwrecked off the coast of a foreign land. He is drowned, but she is washed up on the shore, and strides off towards the trees that fringe landward side of the beach. The camera rises in a crane shot, and the screen fades to black: in the penultimate cut, in an exchange not included in the released film, she meets two men on the beach and asks what country this is. Told that this is 'America, lady', she pauses for a second, then says 'Well – good' and starts her solitary walk. In the shooting script's version of the scene, the towers of Manhattan would have been seen, in ghostly silhouette, beyond the trees. In his audio commentary, the director observes that the inclusion of a direct reference to *Twelfth Night* would have taken the film 'to a place we didn't want to be', and instead Shakespeare is seen beginning his script of the play but stopping short after inserting a colon after the first speech-heading.[10]

Marc Norman and Tom Stoppard's script is full of lines that will eventually reach the *Complete Works*, as well as the play Shakespeare is currently writing, and the representation of the playwright as a young man finding himself – and his distinctive voice as a writer – is engaging. It has been pointed out that he is never seen reading, which would after all be much less exciting than his amatory adventures, and he has a talent that comes from instinct and is nurtured by experience rather than study.[11] In that respect, Shakespeare is made less formidable for the modern audience – one of the lads, with a healthy appetite for a succession of muses, although (as he tells a quack doctor he consults) lately his pen has been running dry, literally and metaphorically. Parallels with Hollywood and the modern theatre include the financial tribulations of Henslowe and their solution, which amounts to creative accounting. Henslowe points out that the actors will get a share of the profits, but the moneylender quickly explains that there will be none. We witness the birth of the creative manipulation of compensation through percentage points on the net profits as distinct from gross so as to ensure that those allotted them are unlikely to receive any money.[12] The waiters at a tavern are all out-of-work actors, and even a Thames boatman has a script he wants Shakespeare to read. 'The show must . . .' Henslowe begins at one point, but trails off. 'Go on', Shakespeare insists, and we are in on the birth of a cliché. The recurrent joke, though, which works mainly by implication, is not only that the Elizabethan theatre resembles the modern performance media, but that Shakespeare has no sense of what posterity will make of him. He is ambitious, but in an unfocused, genial way, and he is fulfilling our biographical expectations with charming insouciance.[13]

Shakespeare in Love, like *The Dresser*, *To Be or Not to Be*, and the other 'backstage' films discussed above, draws on and (affectionately) mocks the cultural capital accumulated in the dramatist's name. The particular appeal of Madden's film lies in its following a pattern common to many films about young people developing, some of them 'teen movies', some more searching in their designs on the viewer and in their use of the Shakespearian material. The first of the individual films discussed in the pages that follow adopts elements of two plays to this end. The others include treatments of their originals that vary from direct quotation and the adoption of a play's plot as a framework, to a less direct 'plagiarism' (in Renoir's sense), with or without an overt invocation of the playwright's name and works. In at least one case, the film may be considered a commentary on the play, even if that is not its principal intention.

Prince Harry by Other Means: *My Own Private Idaho*

In Gus Van Sant's *My Own Private Idaho* (1991) a Shakespearian framework – the rebellion of a king's heir apparent and his search for his true family at a lower level than the court – is integral to the narrative, into which scenes in an approximation of the language of the original *Henry IV* plays are folded. The film intertwines the stories of Scott Favor (Keanu Reeves), a modern-day Prince Harry, and Mike Waters (River Phoenix), a narcoleptic gay hustler in search of his true family. Scott has a substitute for the father against whom he is rebelling in Bob Pigeon (William Richert), a Falstaff figure loved and celebrated in the street-life of Portland, Oregon. 'Fat Bob' arrives in town with a sidekick, exchanging reminiscences that are versions of those of Shallow and Falstaff in 2 *Henry IV* – 'Jesus, the things we've seen'– and soon he is back in his element, surrounded by his admirers in a derelict hotel, where Scott and Mike pick his pocket to find his drugs. When he wakes and asks what time it is, the reply is a paraphrase of Prince Harry's speech in the second scene of 1 *Henry IV*: 'You wouldn't look at a clock unless hands were lines of coke, dials were like the signs of gay bars and time itself were a fine hustler in black leather'. Scott leaves the hotel, kicking open a padlocked back door, and pauses at the exit to the street to reflect on his intention to make a prodigal's return to the mayor, his father:

When I turn twenty-one I don't want any more of this life. My mother and father will be surprised at the incredible change. It will impress them more when such a fuck-up like me turns good, than if I had been a good son all along. All my bad behaviour I will throw away to pay a debt. I will change when everybody expects it the least.

Bob is behind Scott during this, in an echo of the staging in Welles' *Chimes at Midnight*. Van Sant stated in an interview published with the script that he 'didn't fully know who [Scott] was' until he saw Welles' film, but that once he began work he tried to forget it because he 'didn't want to be plagiaristic or stylistically influenced by it, even though it had given [him] the idea'.[14] Admitting the lack of correspondence between Scott's being the mayor's son and the position of a king's heir apparent, Van Sant reflected that 'the reason Scott's like he is, is because of the Shakespeare, and the reason the Shakespeare is in the film is to transcend time, to show that those things have always happened, everywhere'.[15]

The changes in the language are carefully modulated, not simply in the retention of some words and paraphrasing of others. 'Shakespeare', Anthony Lane has observed, 'is all but banished from the dialogue, but he lingers like a drug in the rough, melancholic joys of the film's camaraderie; he gets into its bloodstream in ways that we can't always trace, and at times when you think he is long gone'.[16] Lane may be depriving Shakespeare of some of the credit due to him: the long scene between Fat Bob and Scott after the robbery modelled on the Gadshill episode follows closely the play's 2.5, albeit with many cuts, and although the playing out of Harry's interview with his father was omitted in the final cut, it was filmed, including Scott's 'I do' in answer to Bob's plea on his own behalf not to be cast aside (Figure 6.1).[17] Bob's place as a surrogate father is pointed up repeatedly, making a straightforward commentary on this aspect of the play and at the same time emphasizing the parallel with Mike's search for his family, a quest that lends the film the quality of a road movie, albeit for most of the time a very sad one. In the penultimate scene of the Falstaff/Harry plot, Bob and his cronies invade a fashionable bar where the reformed Scott, enriched with his inheritance, turns his back on his old familiar, who kneels to him before he is removed by the management. 'I don't know you, old man. There was a time when I needed to learn from you, my father and psychedelic teacher'.

The beauty of the photography, especially notable in landscapes, also transforms such scenes as that in which the young people sleeping rough on Portland rooftops see Fat Bob approaching and call across to each other that he has come back to town. The use of variations on 'America the Beautiful' on the soundtrack is only partly ironic: there is daily beauty even in the lives of the hustlers and addicts. The Shakespearian superimposition of lyrical and expressive language on the sordid milieu of Eastcheap has its equivalent beyond the dialogue.

Figure 6.1. *My Own Private Idaho* (Gus Van Sant, 1991): Bob Pigeon (William Richert) and Scott Favor (Keanu Reeves) the morning after the abortive robbery.

When a rival, carnivalesque funeral celebration for Bob takes place at a distance from the stiffly formal obsequies of Jack's father, the low-life values reassert their appeal.

Van Sant's rich and beautiful film uses Shakespeare as a moral and poetic touchstone, and the scenes that paraphrase episodes and speeches from the *Henry IV* plays withstand comparison with those in *Chimes at Midnight*. Arguably, they better the Wellesian original. Reeves, subtler and more effective than in his 'real' Shakespearian role as Don John in Branagh's *Much Ado*, delivers a Prince Harry to rival Keith Baxter's, while Richert's Falstaff is more intimate and affecting than that of Welles, though it cannot rival it in physical and vocal power. In this, though not in all respects, an adaptation that seems to start from a distance is closer to its original than Welles' adaptation, claiming to deliver the essence of Falstaff (or 'Merrie England'). There is something oddly inauthentic in the tavern milieu of *Chimes at Midnight*, a fault that has nothing to do with any (in)fidelity to the original but which stems from the lack of a real social context for the goings-on in the Eastcheap world. *My Own Private Idaho* has a seriousness and understanding of the fragility and value of mere play in the context of a (street) life as it is lived that Welles cannot achieve.

Enchanted Islands: Two Variations on *The Tempest*

Paul Mazursky's *Tempest* (1982) follows *The Tempest* closely in situations and characterization, although its story is one of self-imposed exile as a result of a late-twentieth century emotional diagnosis: the male mid-life crisis. It parcels out the exposition through a series of flashbacks on a 'need to know' basis rather than having everything made clear in an equivalent of Prospero's long narration in 1.2. We learn in stages how the successful New York architect Philip Demetrius (John Cassavetes) comes to be on a Greek island along with his daughter Miranda (Molly Ringwald), a live-in companion Aretha (Susan Sarandon) with whom his relationship is that of a celibate, and a seemingly demented goatherd Kalibanos (Raul Julia) who was once the 'boss' of the island but now serves Philip. The tempest itself does not occur until the last half-hour of this long (143-minute) film, when Philip is able to conjure up a spectacular electrical storm, wrecking the speedboat in which his estranged wife Antonia (Gena Rowlands), her lover the multi-millionaire Alonso (one of Philip's former clients), and his entourage are on a sight-seeing expedition. The flashbacks have by now explained that Philip has entered a mid-life crisis in which his resentment of Antonia's return to the theatre, his contempt for her new associates and – decisively – her affair with Alonso have prompted him to escape to Greece with their daughter and their dog. They strike up acquaintance with Aretha in Athens, where, after an encounter with Antonia and her party in a night club where Aretha is singing, Philip persuades her to accompany him to the island where he hopes they will be out of reach of the shallow society represented by Alonso and his associates. Aretha thus becomes in some respects a mentor to Miranda, in others an Ariel to counter the effect of Kalibanos who, like Caliban, lusts after Miranda. Before the wreck of the launch, Miranda has already encountered Alonso's son Freddy – she is swimming underwater, he is scuba-diving – and Antonia's affair with the ailing Alonso is already on the wane.

After the storm, Mazursky manages to weave in an impressive amount of the play's business, including a drunken comic interlude with the 'court jester' and doctor from Alonso's entourage; a moment when Aretha advises Philip that 'it's time to forgive'; a passing nod to Gonzalo's 'plantation of this isle' speech ('My God Harry, we could start an ideal society', says a spaced-out consort of one of the yacht's party); and a celebratory dance in which Philip and his wife are reconciled and at least some of the others have achieved self-knowledge. At the end of the film, Philip, Antonia, Miranda, and their dog arrive in New York by helicopter, landing on a helipad in front of the World Trade Towers, with swooping aerial shots of the city accompanied by Dinah Washington's performance of Rodgers and Hart's 'Manhattan' on the soundtrack – 'We'll make Manhattan/Into an isle of joy'.

A recurrent theme is the theatre, both the congested and implicitly meretricious urban glamour of Broadway – in the first flashback Antonia, Philip, and Miranda are stuck in traffic in Manhattan's theatre district – and the roots Philip hopes to return to: he is building an amphitheatre on the island. Is it significant that Kalibanos, a goatherd, may not merely represent the Dionysiac forces Philip tries to contain through his celibacy and in protecting the rapidly maturing Miranda, but is also, by virtue of his calling, the creator of a 'goat song', thus indirectly invoking one of the alleged derivations of the word 'tragedy'? In one scene Kalibanos charms the goats with his clarinet as they assemble in the unfinished amphitheatre, and he, who showed Philip such mysteries as how to find olives, is the true master of the island. Mastery of the roots of art in nature has been identified as instinctive in a person who seems 'half mad'. The final credits begin with a curtain call which seems to unite the ancient and modern theatre. Each character is identified as he or she enters through the blue door of the island home to join a line-up on the terrace. Like the play's epilogue, this returns the spectators to their own world, though a wordless curtain call within the frame of the screen image and in its principal setting cannot have the force of the lines in the live theatre, where the character Prospero returns to being an actor at the moment when the narrative takes the character away from the island.

Tempest does not quote the language of the play's dialogue directly, but some lines sound like a paraphrase and many situations correspond closely. At some points the film offers a wry commentary that might apply to the original as well as to itself: one of the shipwrecked party remarks that 'there seems to be some question of authority on this island'. 'Who's Kalibanos?' asks Freddy/Ferdinand, to which Miranda replies, 'He's your long-lost ancestor'. Kalibanos may not be a 'savage and deformed slave', and far from being reluctantly colonized he longs for the arrival of tourists in his slightly crazy way. One of the artefacts he hopes to peddle is a group of assertively phallic terracotta statues, he is capable of technological innovation – rigging up his TV in an attempt to seduce Miranda with episodes of the Western series *Gunsmoke* (dubbed in Greek) – and he is a natural if untaught clarinettist. There is no pathos in his being left in possession of the island, and he is unfailingly optimistic and cheerful, fond of his goats and resentful only of his lack of progress with Miranda. It is hard to credit Philip's access to magic in summoning the storm – his secret studies seem to consist mainly of fathoming baseball batting averages. He refers to magic on a number of occasions, telling Aretha that if he slept with her it would lead to 'storms, nightmares, waves, electricals' and embracing the violent storm that breaks over Manhattan when, after drunkenly disrupting a party, he takes the decisive step towards separation from Antonia. In a film that appropriates *The Tempest* for a sophisticated fable of 'relationships' and 'finding oneself' the literal exercise of supposedly supernatural powers seems out of place.

However, the true summoner of the storm may be not Philip but the island itself – or even Kalibanos.

The significant but more limited use of a Shakespearian original in the science-fiction spectacular *Forbidden Planet*, directed by Fred M. Wilcox (1956), contrasts usefully with Mazursky's *Tempest*. There is an undeniable disparity in genres and production regimes – this is a high-budget product from MGM – and in the difference in ethos of the film-makers and their chosen milieu. However, both films draw on elements of the play to support propositions about human nature and conduct, though those of *Forbidden Planet* are less sophisticated and are subservient to the need for a simple adventure story with a distinctive moral message. Both stories warn about forces from within that need to be controlled.

Forbidden Planet's special effects range from a certain camp charm – the landscape of the planet Altair 4, the flying saucer, Robby the Robot, the domestic labour-saving devices of Dr Morbius's household – to the still impressive realization of the underground installations and nuclear reactor built by the planet's former inhabitants, the Krell. What hideous power destroyed that race of super-intelligent beings, killed all but two (Morbius and his daughter) of the survivors of a crashed spaceship, and now menaces the team who have come in search of the ship and its survivors? In the far reaches of the universe, even in the last decades of the twenty-first century, humans, having united on their own planet and proceeded to 'the conquest and colonisation of deep space', still have much to learn. But the answers on Altair 4 take them back to a psychological explanation so outmoded that the concept of the id has to be explained to space travellers trained in strictly materialist thinking, whose assumption is that everything can be boiled down (or up) to atomic science. The available language is resolutely old-fashioned, reaching back beyond Jung and Freud – 'some devilish thing that never showed itself' and 'some dark terrible incomprehensible planetary force'. In dialogue omitted in the final cut it is suggested that even the ability of Altaira/Miranda to charm wild beasts may be better explained by talk of ladies and unicorns than appeals to science. In another deleted exchange, the crew's resident intellectual can still insist 'personally I prefer the medieval explanation'.[18] One of the crew, looking at the planet on the spaceship's viewing screen, reflects that 'the Lord sure makes some beautiful worlds', a passable and homely equivalent for 'O brave new world' and an intimation of an alternative, religious, view of the universe. As for the Krell, 'after a million years of shining sanity, they would hardly have understood what power was destroying them'. Yes, these were the 'monsters from the id', capable of tearing other creatures apart but emanating from Morbius's own subconscious and (it is made clear) connected with the unconscious desire that motivates his anxious protection of his daughter's virtue (Figure 6.2).

It does not pay to enquire too closely into the logic of much of the film – why spoil an exciting story? Altaira's naivety, pulchritude, and instinctive preference for short skirts and Grecian-style tunics that border on lingerie by Frederick's of Hollywood, together with the fact that she has never encountered any human males, make it inevitable that she will respond to the chaste but unequivocal attentions of Adams the spaceship's commander (Leslie Nielsen) who teaches her to kiss. The newly arrived space crew includes a cook whose principal function is to engage Robby in the production of Bourbon (in vast amounts) and to give voice to the sentiments of crewmen who, after 380 days' space travel, will be enthusiastic at the prospect of female company. The play's dialogue is shadowed on a number of occasions: Robby's command of a phenomenal range of languages and dialects prompts the equivalent of Ferdinand's surprise on discovering that Miranda speaks his language; and we are told that the Krell's civilization had 'cloud-piercing towers'. As Morbius, Walter Pidgeon has the gravitas and diction of an

Figure 6.2. Another brave new world: Altaira learns how to kiss (Fred M. Wilcox, *Forbidden Planet*, 1956).

old-fashioned Prospero, which suggest that if the original character's words came to mind he would do them justice.

Behind the borrowings in plot and situation from *The Tempest* is the desire of the film's makers to combine the play's aura with the well-established and respectable tropes of science fiction. Even with all the advantages that technology can offer, and specifically those of atomic science, humans (or creatures in general) can be 'victims of human greed and folly'. The Krell's achievements, on a grander scale but comparable by inference with the achievements of atomic science in the late 1940s and 1950s, have created the means of empowering their own destruction at the hands of their baser instincts. In a comparison with another classic science-fiction film from 1957, Barry Keith Grant points out that 'whereas *Invasion of the Body Snatchers* warns us to watch our relatives and neighbours, *Forbidden Planet* exhorts us to examine our inner lives. The Krell, with their new technology for transforming thought into matter, are like the human race, facing the dilemma of the atomic age'.[19] In this respect, although *Forbidden Planet* cannot be aligned closely with American paranoia about infiltrators from alien (communist) cultures, it speaks directly to another dominant anxiety of its time. In this it is a profoundly humanistic and in some respects conservative film. The appeal to psychoanalytic theory predominates, but religion is not absent from its imaginary.

When the explanation for the mayhem has been arrived at, we are told that 'we've all got monsters in our subconscious. So we have laws and religion'. As for Morbius, he has to be told, in a memorable line, that 'That thing out there – it's you!' He must die, and his new-found planet with him, for the safety of the greater number – that is, presumably, the rest of the universe – and the space ship heads back to Earth with Altaira and, happily, Robby on board. There is enough of *The Tempest* to serve the film's ends – no Ariel is needed on Altair 4 – and unlike Caliban, Robby will be available for spin-offs, if not for a sequel. Moreover, as a space-age Jeeves, he is to be a prototype for C-3PO in *Star Wars* (1977).

Tragic Gangsters: *Men of Respect* and *Joe Macbeth*

In an influential *Partisan Review* essay on the American gangster as tragic hero, Robert Warshow observed in 1948 that '[a]t a time when the normal condition of the citizen is a state of anxiety, euphoria spreads over our culture like the broad smile of an idiot', and that in these circumstances opposition to optimism had to be disguised: 'The gangster film is remarkable in that it fills the need for disguise (though not sufficiently to avoid arousing uneasiness) without requiring any serious distortion. From its beginning, it has been a consistent and astonishingly complete presentation of the modern sense of tragedy'.[20] Sixty years on, the force of the imperative in the American media to pretend and promote euphoria may have diminished, but the potential for the gangster to stand out as at least in some sense a tragic hero has not: the family background of the *Godfather* trilogy (especially the *King Lear* aspect of Part Three) and other notable films and the TV series *The Sopranos* have continued the critique of optimism and conventional domestic pieties.

Men of Respect, directed by William Reilly, transposes *Macbeth* to the New York mafia and is unusual among adaptations in following its source play methodically, often scene-by-scene and speech-by-speech. Released in January 1991, at a point in the season described by Janet Maslin in her *New York Times* review as 'traditionally the burying ground for the year's most unclassifiable releases', it stood out as 'hard to beat when it comes to eccentricity, weird inventiveness and sheer nerve'.[21] These qualities give the film considerable appeal, and its close attention to the play's text makes it a stimulating commentary as well as a fast-moving thriller, albeit one with limited means at its disposal. Reilly shows much ingenuity and skill in staging his low-budget gangster movie, although it is hard to resist comparisons with the far more lavishly funded *Godfather* films. Much of the action takes place in the Greenwich Village restaurant owned by Mike Battaglia (John Turturro), who has distinguished himself in a heroic shoot-out that eliminates a traitor and the heads of a rival gang he is in league with. This earns him admission to the select group of 'men of respect', a bond sealed by blood-brotherhood with the padrino Charlie D'Amico (Rod Steiger), but Battaglia and his comrade Bankie Como have encountered a fortune-teller (Lilia Skala). Her predictions prompt him to aim higher, and his wife Ruthie (Katherine Borowitz) urges him on. The murders are graphic and bloody and Reilly makes the sexual dimension of the Battaglias' relationship clearer than even Polanski's *Macbeth*: Ruthie is a formidable, gaunt presence stalking through the restaurant and its backyard on high heels during the celebration of Mike's promotion and the victory over the rivals. In this Borowitz complements Turturro's manic, staring performance, and together they seem dangerous from the very beginning. Bankie is a more homely character, an enthusiastic amateur cook and less obviously criminal than Mike, and the family dimension of the mafia milieu makes this aspect of his character credible. At the same time, appeals to *omertà* and the safeguarding of 'our thing' – as Cosa Nostra is appropriately translated in the dialogue – are not the same as the play's invocations of the legitimacy and sanctity of kingship.

The language may be more of a problem, because the actors sometimes seem anxious to avoid falling back on the original lines. The equivalence is often very close: 'Corvo's loss, that's Battaglia's gain', says Charlie when he learns about the death of the traitor; Bankie voices his reservation that he will do what's necessary 'just so I don't have to do anything so I can't look at myself in the mirror' (compare 2.1.26–9, where Banquo is anxious to 'keep [his] bosom franchised and allegiance clear'); and Battalgia angrily declares 'I don't want no more reports' when he is told the enemy is closing in. One of the most striking paraphrases is Ruthie's 'I know what it is to have a life inside me and squashing it out because it's not the right time for it' (compare 'I have given suck . . .' at 1.7.54–8) which adds a new element to the character. In her decline into madness, Ruthie complains that the restaurant's supplies of linen are all dirty, and she compulsively scrubs the bath where she and her husband had washed the blood from their hands and clothing. After a version of the sleepwalking scene, Mike finds her slumped with her neck against the side of the bath, her throat cut and streaks of her blood staining the now spotless enamel. One aspect of the play's action is harder to parallel than the rest in this urban world: in the absence of an arboreal equivalent for Birnam Wood, Mike is told that he is safe until the stars fall from the sky, and this is achieved by a firework display that coincides with the final siege of the restaurant. In the combat with his nemesis, Battaglia learns that Duffy had indeed been born by a posthumous caesarean section and the death blow is delivered with a long knife of the kind used to kill Duncan and his minders.

The play's placing of events – as Banquo places himself – 'in the great hand of God' is more difficult to achieve in the gangster world than in medieval or renaissance Scotland, even in Polanski's largely religion-free version. In Reilly's film the final exchange between Battaglia and Duffy is unfortunate in its bathos, but also marks the limitations of this conception of his adopted genre: 'Shit happens', says Duffy, to which Mike replies 'Ain't that the truth'. *Men of Respect* ends with the confirmation of Mal (Stanley Tucci) as Charlie's successor, and a twist not unlike that of Polanski's final shot of Donalbain going to consult the weird sisters when we see Fleance as an onlooker, clearly awaiting his chance for the power prophesied for him. There may have been an act of vengeance, but the outcome is merely the reinforcement of the security of 'our thing' and those now sworn to defend it. Battaglia's final exchange of words with Duffy corresponds directly to nothing in the play's dialogue (at 5.10.16–34), and its rueful lack of dignity or energy pales beside the famous last words of heroic hoodlums from the past, such as Edward G. Robinson's dismayed 'Can this be the end of Rico?' in *The Public Enemy* (1931) or Jarrett Cody's defiant 'Top of the world, Ma' in *White Heat* (1949).

Moralizing dialogue after the demise of the villain/hero, or extra-diegetic commentary asserting that crime does not pay, are not uncommon in Hollywood gangster films after the mid-1930s, but the substance of the narrative frequently renders this self-evident as the formality it is. The transgressors are usually charismatic figures whose success we encourage as a vicarious victory over society's laws, even as we acknowledge their iniquities. Jarrett Cody, as Jack Shadoian points out in his study of the American gangster film, may have been 'the most vicious gangster hero to date', but he is also 'the most tortured and suffering', fixated on his dead mother and taking on the world he is now 'top of' by his spectacular suicide. 'Cody', writes Shadoian, 'is associated with nature, mother love, personal integrity and loyalty'.[22] Nothing of the kind can be claimed for Battaglia, but Shakespeare's hero has a sense of himself in relation to God, the Devil, and eternity. The remarkable B-movie *Joe Macbeth* (1954), directed by Ken Hughes and produced in England with American leads (Ruth Roman and Paul Douglas), has a superb showdown, in which Joe, deserted by his henchmen, takes on the outside world and its machine guns in a darkened dining room, its French windows shattered by the gunfire of his enemies and himself while a distant bell on a lakeside jetty tolls, reminding him of the drowning of Duncan. When his wife opens the doors at the end of the room he accidentally shoots her and she falls forward onto the floor. After a few more moments of desperate defiance he dies at the hands of Lennie, the Macduff figure. The sinister butler Seyton (pronounced 'Satan') asks whether he will be taking over the house that has been the emblem of gang leadership, but is told that he had better pack his bags and leave. After Lennie himself exits, sirens and a burst of machine-gun fire off screen suggest that the forces of law and order have completed the process of rough justice. Over the final shot of the butler standing by Joe's body, an on-screen reminder, attributed appropriately, tells us that 'blood will have blood'.

Teenagers in Love: *10 Things I Hate About You*

The international popularity of soap operas and film comedies set in American high schools offers a ready-made set of intelligible plot and character conventions that lend themselves to at least some aspects of the comedies of love. Shakespeare is borrowed as a starting point in a number of films catering to the teenage market with affectionate satire of this milieu. The heroine of *She's the Man* (Andy Fickman, 2006) disguises herself, Viola-like, as her brother Sebastian – conveniently absent abroad – to get onto the soccer team of an all-male school when her own school's team is disbanded. In *Get Over It!* (Tommy O'Haver, 2001) a musical version of *A Midsummer Night's Dream*, at first incomprehensible to the pupils, becomes intelligible when they find themselves involved in a play where their own situations are found to correspond to those of the characters. In *Were the World Mine* (Tom Gustafson, 2008) a production of the same play enables a gay teenager to find respect and – helpfully – the 'love juice' that will turn the small town's homophobes gay for a while and teach them a lesson. In *Hamlet 2* (Andrew Fleming, 2008) burnt-out, ego-driven British actor (Steve Coogan), stranded as a drama teacher in a Tucson high school, faced with the cutting of his already downgraded drama class, presents a wildly eccentric riff on a 'classic' play: Jesus Christ and the Prince of Denmark use a time machine to pre-emptively save Gertrude and Ophelia from the fate that awaits them. Advertising copy for *She's the Man*, with key verbs picked out in bold, suggests the kind of adolescent emotional stew that the genre thrives on: 'Duke **wants** Olivia who likes Sebastian who is really Viola whose brother is

dating Monique so she **hates** Olivia who's with Duke to **make** Sebastian **jealous** who is really Viola who's **crushing** on Duke who thinks she's a guy'.²³ In addition to these cross-currents of desire and enmity, the characteristics of the 'teen movie' include discrimination between rival lifestyles, the process of finding one's 'true' identity, clashes with parental and academic authority, and the tribulations of what in most cases is only temporary heartbreak. Ritual occasions – notably the prom, the sports event, and the high school play – provide the occasion for the conflicts to arise and be resolved, while the promise of a future beyond school offers reassurance of a kind that may be qualified by anxiety but usually promises a new lease of prolonged adolescence at college before the allegedly 'real' world closes in.

Gil Junger's *10 Things I Hate About You* (2002) is the most skilful blend of these ingredients in a 'Shakespearean' adaptation, and their effective deployment suggests that the genre's plot and character conventions correspond in many respects to those of the *The Taming of the Shrew*. There are references to Shakespeare's sonnets in a classroom scene, and the presence of a student who is a Shakespeare enthusiast, but only one line from the play is quoted in the dialogue: on his first day at the school Cameron (Lucentio) sees Bianca Stratford and says 'I burn, I pine, I perish' (1.1.149). (Advertising for the film carried an amended version of Elizabeth Barrett Browning's 'How do I love thee? Let me count the ways', with 'hate' replacing 'love'.)

Padua High School is an idyllic combination of Gothic academic architecture (tradition) and modern facilities (education as it should be), and in this well-heeled suburb many of the students have their own cars. The opening scene introduces what an Elizabethan author might have called the humours of high school, the eccentric groups that teenagers form to express their solidarity with one fashion or another, and their desire to be both exclusive and included: 'cowboys' who have never seen a cow and white pseudo-Rastafarians who wish they were West Indian, and so on. The newcomer Cameron (Joseph Gordon-Levitt) is shown around the school by a genial, geeky (and lovable) mentor, Michael (David Krumholz). This is the equivalent of the opening scene of the play proper in *The Taming of the Shrew*, the arrival of Petruchio and Grumio in a new city and the explanation of its characters. The motor of the plot is a father's refusal to allow his younger daughter Bianca (Larisa Oleynik) to date (rather than wed) until her recalcitrant sister Kat (Julia Stiles) does so, and Joey, one of Bianca's rival suitors (not both, as in the play) pays a tough and rebellious fellow student, Patrick (Heath Ledger), to tackle Kat. The psychological motivations of the father and his elder daughter are specified, his being stated early in the story. He is a gynaecologist whose wife has left him, and whose experience of the results of unwanted pregnancy among unmarried mothers has made him excessively protective of his daughters. In one scene he insists that Bianca wear a harness-like contraption that simulates the bulk and weight of pregnancy in order to warn her what a date might lead to, and he is unable to imagine that going out with boys could lead to anything short of sleeping together.

Kat, for her part, is a man-hating feminist, frequenting a women-only night at a bar and generally devoted to giving men a hard time. She denounces the choice of texts in her English class, rejecting Hemingway as 'an abusive alcoholic misogynist, who spent half his life hanging around Picasso trying to nail his leftovers', and she asks why the syllabus shows no sign of Sylvia Plath, Charlotte Brontë, or Simone de Beauvoir. Later she is seen at home reading *The Bell Jar*, and in a bookshop scene where Patrick tries to woo her by asking where he can find Betty Friedan's *The Feminine Mystique*, she deals with him by slamming a copy against his chest. Against her father's will she has applied to and been accepted by Sarah Lawrence, a women's college on the other side of the country. Patrick rescues her from a drunken party where she has made an exhibition of herself dancing sexily on a table, and they come near to kissing – until she leans over and vomits on the grass. Love is in the air, but it has a little way to go. Patrick's wooing approaches success when they realize that both of them behave badly because they share the desire to think for themselves: he asks 'What's your excuse . . . for acting the way we do?' – note the complicity of that 'we' – and she replies, 'Why should I live up to other people's expectations instead of my own?' After a scene with Bianca in which Kat realizes the selfishness of her behaviour in refusing to go to the prom (and thus preventing her sister from getting their father's permission to do so) she and Patrick seem to be heading for a happy ending, but the rich and vain Joey, stood up by Bianca in favour of his rival, complains publicly that he hasn't had his money's worth from the deal he made. Kat feels cheapened and betrayed.

However, she cannot shake off the feelings she has discovered in herself, and her literary enthusiasms are the vehicle for her tearful acceptance of her love for Patrick, in a 'sonnet' she has written in response to a class exercise that called for a new version of Shakespeare's Sonnet 121 ("Tis better to be vile than vile esteemed/When not to be receives reproach of being'). Kat's poem is not a sonnet, but it conveys the unvarnished truth about her feelings: 'I hate the way you talk to me/And the way you cut your hair', it begins, and goes on for a number of lines in the same vein but ends with an admission that she loves the person addressed. She leaves the class in tears, as Patrick looks on, pensively. The resolution of the dilemma follows quickly: when she gets to her car she sees a Fender Stratocaster on the driving seat, a guitar he had recently seen her trying out in a music store and which he has bought with the money from his bargain with Joey. Amends have been made, and as they kiss the image transitions to a crane shot overlooking the school's forecourt and then to the view from a helicopter that circles around the top of the central tower, where her favourite rock group are singing 'I want you to want me'. Realizations about oneself are key elements in the working-out of the plot, accompanied by revelations about the origins of attitudes of a kind unavailable in *The Taming of the Shrew*. Kat tells Bianca that her man-hating was motivated by the fact that she once agreed to have sex with Joey, only to be dumped by him, and this moment of understanding between the sisters is followed by Kat's perception that she has been selfish. Their father tells Kat that she can go to Sarah Lawrence after all: 'You know, fathers don't like to admit it when their daughters are capable of running their own lives – it makes us become spectators. Bianca still lets me play a few innings, you've had me on the bench for years'. The sporting metaphor is the only way he can articulate his feelings, and the moment has a touching sense of his unease in addressing the truth. It mitigates at least partially the crudity with which he expressed his anxieties about their becoming pregnant, and provides a motivation that will serve in place of the play's specific brand of patriarchal concern.

The film's relationship with Shakespeare may be summed up by the (black, articulate) literature teacher who explains: 'I know Shakespeare's a dead white guy, but he knows his shit, so we can overlook that' and delivers the first lines of a sonnet as though it were rap.

Although the student who is a Shakespeare enthusiast is as affected as any of her peers, at least she gets together with Michael, the likeable helper. *10 Things I Hate About You* is able to enjoy rather than excuse its deviations from its original. *The Taming of the Shrew* provides a template for much of the structure and most characters, but the set speeches and many of the situations can be reshuffled or ignored with greater licence than even Zeffirelli allows himself: the wooing and reconciliation episodes in the play are distributed through a number of sequences, and the growth of a loving relationship between Kat and Patrick does not have to be 'cheated' into the script as is the case in Zeffirelli's film. The new medium, at least in its popular formation, demands gradual development over the running time, with a temporary reversal in what many scriptwriting gurus encourage one to think of as the third act of a movie – here it comes when Patrick's venal motivation is revealed at the prom. The names of the principal characters point towards the play, and the general effect is one of playful homage, with *The Taming of the Shrew* supporting the comedy without getting in the way of its need to fulfil contemporary imperatives of motivation and the light-hearted addressing of 'issues'. It could be objected that Kat's feminism is characterized simplistically in terms of aggression, and that it is explained as nothing more than a phase she is going through on her way to self-realization. But making her own choices is her basic aim in life, and the ending suggests that this will include loving Patrick. Seriousness may be said to creep in, without obtruding itself, and the self-conscious play with stereotypes, like that exercised in *commedia dell'arte*, may even support this sense of reality beyond the action or the privileged world of the characters. It is an escapist movie, but these have their uses: like the play promised to Christopher Sly in the induction to Shakespeare's play, it is 'more pleasing stuff' than 'a Christmas gambol, or a tumbling trick', and is in the end 'a kind of history'.[24]

Teenage Tragedy

In many respects the ideal Shakespearian vehicle for a tragedy of teenage love is *Romeo and Juliet*, and the influence of the musical *West Side Story* (1957) and the film version of it directed by Robert Wise (1960) can be traced in many stage productions of the play as well as in Baz

Luhrmann's film.[25] Arguably this makes the musical one of the most influential presentations of the play in its whole performance history. On the screen, the outstanding examples of the tragic (or partially tragic) stories of teenage love and rebellion remain *Rebel Without a Cause* (1955), in which James Dean plays the son of a wealthy family who clashes with the police as well as his parents and *The Wild One* (1954), with the somewhat more mature Marlon Brando as leader of a motorcycle gang. *Rebel Without a Cause* ends with two of the teenagers dead, but Dean's character, Jim Stark, is reconciled with his parents, and at the end a match between him and his girlfriend Judy (Natalie Wood) is seemingly in the offing. Jim's repeated question to his father suggests that finding one's (masculine) identity is the central theme: 'What do you do when you have to be a man?' *The Wild One* is notable for Brando's brooding and intense performance, and his response to the question 'What are you rebelling against?' – 'What have you got?' In *West Side Story* the problem of juvenile delinquency is identified with ethnic rivalry: the conclusion has been thought fragile, as the rival gangs line up to carry off the dead lovers, but Leonard Bernstein's score lends the moment a strong suggestion of transcendent hope, an equivalent of the 'glooming kind of peace' that is achieved at the end of the play.

Comedy has been favoured more than tragedy in films that adapt the plays to the world of American teenagers: angst has been largely confined to the problems, outlined above in respect of *10 Things...*, of love and status, with delinquency either harmless or even (as in the case of that film's Patrick) a sham. *O*, directed by Tim Blake Nelson, is a notable exception. Production had been completed by early 1999, but the film was held back on account of the shootings at Columbine High School on 20 April of that year, and it was not released until 2002. *Othello* becomes a story of jealousy and envy in a private high school, where Odin James, known as 'O' (Mekhi Phifer), is the star of the basketball team and the only black student. When he is awarded the accolade of player of the year, the team's coach publicly declares that he loves him like his own son. Hugo (Josh Harnnett), the coach's son, is irked by Odin's choice of Mike Cassio (Andrew Keegan) as his 'go-to guy' in the team as well as what can only be a loss of his father's esteem. He enlists a spoilt rich kid, Roger, to be his accomplice in alienating Odin from his girlfriend Desi (Julia Stiles), who happens to be the daughter of the Dean – the head of the school. The first stage in this is a trumped-up charge that Odin has 'forced himself' on her, which is effectively denied but brings out the latent racism of the Dean. The ensuing plot follows the play closely, with basketball taking the place of military prowess as the hero's ticket of admission to a predominantly white society, and the authority of the coach (Martin Sheen) assuming the functions of the Venetian state while the Dean becomes an equivalent for Brabantio. Summoned to the coach's office after Roger has made his accusations against the couple, Desi refuses to tell her father exactly what has gone on between her and Odin, which at this stage amounts to no more than lying on a bed half-dressed. The Dean, who has not been told of the relationship, warns Odin: 'She deceived me – what makes you think she won't do the same to you?' In due course, the affair is consummated when the pair go to a motel together, but by now Odin's mind has been poisoned by Hugo and as they make love he looks up and in the mirror at the end of the bed imagines that he sees Mike in his place. The immediate consequence of this is to madden Odin, who makes his thrusts so hard and the rhythm so urgent that Desi repeatedly asks him to stop: she is becoming afraid of his aggression.

The sex scene is explicit, and together with the frequent 'bad language' and violence it earned *O* an 'R' rating in the United States. It is disturbing not so much because of its graphic erotic content as the suggestion that it confirms the common racist motif of the over-sexed black man deflowering a white girl. The cliché is referred to jokingly by Odin and Desi in an earlier scene, where he points out that he can use the word 'nigger' while she can't and talks about his visits to her dormitory as 'playing the black buck loose in the big house'. Desi has made what in retrospect must be a mistake in telling Odin 'You can do what you want with me . . . I want you to have me however you want'. Later this re-emerges when Hugo in the major 'temptation' scene talks about white girls being 'snaky' and refers to Odin's having grown up 'in the hood' and not knowing their ways. (The equivalent passage in the play is 3.3.201–4: 'In Venice they do let God see the pranks/They dare not show their husbands . . .'). Hugo tells Mike, who has been disgraced and banished from the team for two games after a brawl in which Roger has been injured, that he should 'hang with Desi' to get her to intercede on his behalf with Odin and, through him, the coach.

Consequently, Odin sees Mike and Desi together in the bleachers during games and around the school, and his jealous suspicions grow. What has been a subtext, uneasily implied earlier, gradually comes to the surface. Contact with a drug dealer, introduced to him by Hugo, and rap music on the soundtrack underline the largely unspoken issue of Odin's origins. After he has yielded to the temptation to take a performance-enhancing drug and disgraced himself by uncontrolled anger during a 'slam-dunk' contest, even Mike tells Hugo (as Odin eavesdrops) that 'the nigger's out of control'. The racial stereotypes now seem to be confirmed on both sides, with some of the whites emerging as racist and the black hero appearing to confirm their views. However, the film breaks with the gender assumptions of the play subtly and decisively. It is made clear throughout that Desi is her own woman. She does not take any nonsense from the men around her, and Stiles responds convincingly to Odin's extreme behaviour in the motel but forgives him and refuses to accept Emily's suggestion that he forced himself on her, an accusation that would destroy his career at once. Unfortunately she is deprived of all but the briefest equivalents of Desdemona's speeches in the final scene: Odin strangles her convincingly with his bare hands, and she does not speak to exonerate him before she expires.

The most remarkable adjustment of the play's strategies is the use of a prologue and epilogue in which we hear Hugo's voice, accompanied by images of white doves in the cupola above a staircase, and by the team's mascot, a hawk, that Hugo subsequently steals and hides: 'All my life I always wanted to fly. I always wanted to live like a hawk. I know you're not supposed to be jealous of anything, but . . . to take flight, to soar above everything and everyone, now that's living'. On the soundtrack we hear the 'Ave Maria' from Verdi's *Otello*. In the absence of formal soliloquies this provides some insight into Hugo's motivation, though it does not encompass his racism except in his use – which seems admiring – of the word 'dark' to describe the person or force he would like to be. It is formulated in terms of psychological need absent in Iago's various accounts of his motives, all of which are simpler rationalizations in terms of wrongs done to him, or plain statements of envy or jealousy. Hugo, though, is a twentieth-century young man, aware that psychology has explanations to offer. The final sequence shows the aftermath of the denouement in which Odin shoots himself after strangling Desi in her bed and Hugo shoots his girlfriend Emily after she denounces him and reveals the truth about the handkerchief that (as in the play) she had purloined and which served as 'proof' of Desi's unfaithfulness. The bodies are removed by ambulance, media reporters assemble outside the dormitory, and Hugo is taken away in a police car. He gazes out of its back window towards the crowd. This is intercut with the images of the doves and the hawk, and a voice-over, part of which repeats the 'prologue' (up to 'Now that's living'). Now we hear a further development of the ideas:

But a hawk is no good around normal birds. It can't fit in. Even though all the other birds probably wanna be hawks; they hate him for what they can't be. Proud. Powerful. Determined. Dark. Odin is a hawk. He soars above us. He can fly. One of these days, everyone's gonna pay attention to me. Because I'm gonna fly too.

The defiant insistence by Iago that 'from this time forth [he] never will speak word', adopted in their films by Welles and Parker, is here partially contradicted, at least so far as the audience is concerned. The accompanying music includes both rap and the 'Ave Maria', as though these represent opposite poles in the culture of the protagonists.

In Odin's final speech, the equivalent of 'Soft you, a word or two before you go' (5.2.347–65) the underlying themes of class and racial prejudice are voiced more explicitly and in cruder language (and with a more pronounced Southern accent) than hitherto:

My life is over, that's it. But while all ya'll are out here livin' yours, sitting around talking about the nigger who lost it back in high school, you make sure you tell them the truth. You tell them I loved that girl! I did! But I got played! [*Points to Hugo*] He twisted my head up. He fucked it up. I ain't no different than none of ya'll. My mom's ain't no crack head. I wasn't no gang banger. It wasn't some hood rat drug dealer that tripped me up. It was this white, prep school motherfucker standing right there! You tell them where I'm from . . . didn't make me do this.

The catalogue of racist clichés is a list of negatives to be rejected, whereas Othello's reminder that he has 'done the state some service' is in terms that are entirely positive. Odin does not invoke the means by which he has risen above his alleged background in this elite and almost entirely white school: in this speech he does not even say he has been a basketball star. The elevation of 'O' made him an important emblem of the school's success: achievement in sport is a major factor in fund-raising for American private schools, colleges, and universities, and consequently the team coach as a figure of power and outstanding sporting ability can be a major priority in the enrolment of students from relatively deprived backgrounds. Ethnic and class diversity and 'affirmative action' are important issues, still hotly debated. Although some of these questions may be implicit in *O*, they are not explored as fully as might have been wished.

In any case, one might ask whether the *Othello* story is as effective a vehicle for social comment as the director seems to have expected. Productions of the play on stage and screen are now expected to reflect or at least take account of current attitudes to race, but when the play is borrowed in this way it is arguable that the pattern it provides is not up to the task. In *A Double Life*, the focus is entirely on the psychology of the actor who finds that playing Othello unleashes subconscious desires better left untapped, and the absence of reference to the play's racial implications is a relatively minor if regrettable consideration, a sign of what was taken for granted or ignored by the film's makers in 1948. In *O*, explicit in some respects about this dimension of the play it appropriates, a responsibility seems to be shirked or at least treated superficially. It seems reasonable to ask what a radical black director such as Spike Lee would have made in 1999 of the play's story, or indeed whether he would have considered using it in the first place. There may simply be too much Shakespeare in *O*, characterized by Kenneth S. Rothwell as a continuation of 'the fad for inserting teen/ pic *topoi* between Shakespeare's text and the filmic site', so that identifying the parallels and gaps becomes a distraction.[26] Perhaps comedy can bear this kind of effect, where tragedy suffers from it. 'Can one have too much of a good thing?' asks Rosalind. When the original is too dominant and the adaptation brings clichés rather than originality to the fore, and the new film has not gone far enough beyond Shakespeare, the answer is probably, 'Sometimes, yes'.

In writing the chapters of this book, I made a point of re-viewing films I had already watched many times – in some cases, had studied in some detail for other purposes – but avoided rereading the published commentaries on them in books and articles long known and valued. As the introduction explained, to engage appropriately with them would require more words than could be spared from discussion of the films themselves. After the first draft, I returned to this body of criticism and scholarship, though with some trepidation. Would I have unconsciously reproduced my colleagues' work? Would I suddenly find that I had erred in observing the action or interpreting the characters' behaviour or the film-makers' techniques? And what about the films I had failed to devote enough space to, or had simply decided not to discuss? My defence on these counts would be that the aim was not to achieve a proportionate treatment of films, calibrating them according to their worthiness as objects of study, or to attempt to get in every significant or relevant film. The choice of topics inevitably sidelines other possibilities: it would have been enjoyable to write a chapter solely on acting, for example. On the other hand, acting would creep into all the chapters, one way or another.

This book does not propose a canon of 'great Shakespeare films', but certain plays and films made from them have acquired iconic status, impressive accumulations of cultural capital. What is happening when a teenage boy, bored by Olivier's *Hamlet* (shown to his class by a teacher played by the actor's widow, Joan Plowright), imagines the prince replaced by the eponymous *Last Action Hero* in Arnold Schwarzenegger's 1993 (action) comedy? This is a Hamlet who makes up his mind pretty quickly: 'You kilt my fodder – big mistake', and he blasts Claudius away. With 'To be . . .' he pauses for a moment, then decides 'Not to be' and ignites an explosion that demolishes Elsinore. This clash of the icons, from 'high' and 'low' culture, is supported by a meticulous pastiche of the visual style of Olivier's *Hamlet*. The action movie is paying ironic homage to its Elizabethan equivalent by way of parodying the film teachers once loved to show in class. But what are the iconic Shakespeare films now? Has Zeffirelli's *Romeo and Juliet* been superseded in the classroom by Baz Luhrmann's *William Shakespeare's Romeo + Juliet*? Is it appropriate (let alone accurate) to divide the history of Shakespeare on film into periods before and after Olivier or Branagh? From the point of view of the waxing and waning confidence of 'the money' in Shakespeare as a co-author of screenplays, this may be true, but as a guide to understanding the cultural and aesthetic issues at stake, it is surely misleading.

This is not a defence against anticipated criticisms, but an invitation. The reader is invited to revisit these topics, to place them alongside the more detailed and thorough accounts of individual productions, to insist that such-and-such a film should get fuller (or occasionally, at least some) attention, and to take up the argument about – for example – the qualities of Welles *Macbeth*, the ethics of the *Henry V* films, the sexual and racial politics of the various versions of *Othello*, and the rival claims on our time of the various *Hamlets*. The best course of action, then, short of making one's own film or video from a Shakespeare play (well worth trying and very rewarding) or to outline a script of one's own, is to watch the films again — and again. To adopt a request from the age of the VHS tape and, before that, of those metal cans with their spools of film: now please rewind . . .

Details of each film have been confined to: title, director(s), nationality, and year of release. The national identity is conventionally identified as that of the principal sources of finance, rather than the location of filming and post-production work, and the year of release given in some sources may vary according to the 'territory' (USA, Europe, etc.) where the film was released rather than its actual origination.

Almost all the films discussed in this book and listed here are currently available on DVD, although some (notably Peter Hall's *A Midsummer Night's Dream*) have yet to be released in Britain or Europe, and at least one – *Joe Macbeth* – seems not to have appeared on domestic VHS or DVD. Others have ceased to be available, although the situation is constantly changing. In some cases, whole films, as well as extracts, have been uploaded to You-Tube, although the provenance of these is often uncertain and it is unwise to use them as references in writing about the productions. In addition to the titles listed here, mention should be made of two notable collections of films from the pre-sound era: the British Film Institute's *Silent Shakespeare*, initially available on VHS and reissued on DVD with a commentary by Judith Buchanan, which presents seven films; and volume 7 of the *Thanhouser Collection*, available at the time of writing from the Thanhouser Company Film Preservation, Inc. <http://www.thanhouser.org>, which includes versions of *The Winter's Tale* (1910), *Cymbeline* (1913), and *King Lear* (1917). Other silent Shakespeares available on DVD include the American tragedian Frederick Warde's *Richard III* (1912) and *King Lear* (1916) and the *Othello* directed by Dmitri Buchowetski, with Emil Jannings and Werner Krauss (1922). A restored edition of the remarkable 1920/1 adaptation of *Hamlet*, with Asta Nielsen as the prince/princess has been published by the Deutsches Film-institut (2011) in a two-disc set with extensive supplementary material in German and English. A number of titles are available with audio commentaries by directors and other artistic personnel: among the most informative are those accompanying the films by Julie Taymor (*Titus*, *The Tempest*), Baz Luhrmann (*Romeo + Juliet*), Kenneth Branagh (*Hamlet*), and John Madden's *Shakespeare in Love*. DVDs in the Criterion Collection, published in the USA and consequently available only in Region 1 (NTSC) format, often provide additional material – commentaries, documentaries, 'stills galleries', etc. – not available in British and European (Region 2) versions.

The Angelic Conversation, Derek Jarman (UK 1985)
Antony and Cleopatra, Charlton Heston (Spain/Switzerland/UK 1972)
The Asphalt Jungle, John Huston (USA 1950)
As You Like It

   Paul Czinner (UK 1936)
   Christine Edzard (UK 1992)
   Kenneth Branagh (UK 2006)

Bringing up Baby, Howard Hawks (USA 1938)
Caravaggio, Derek Jarman (UK 1986)
Chimes at Midnight, Orson Welles (aka *Falstaff*, Spain/Switzerland 1964)
Cleopatra, Joseph L. Mankiewicz (USA 1963)
Coriolanus, Ralph Fiennes (UK 2011)
Dead Poets Society, Peter Weir (USA 1989)
A Double Life, George Cukor (USA 1948)
The Dresser, Peter Yates (UK 1983)
Edward II, Derek Jarman (UK 1991)
Fame, Alan Parker (USA 1982)
Forbidden Planet, Fred M. Wilcox (USA 1956)
Get Over It!, Tommy O'Haver (USA 2001)
Gnomeo and Juliet, Kelly Asbury (UK/USA 2011)
The Godfather, Part Three, Francis Ford Coppola (USA 1990)
The Goodbye Girl, Herbert Ross (USA 1977)
Hamlet

   Cecil Hepworth (UK 1913)
   Eleuterio Rodolfi (Italy 1917)
   Svend Gade (Germany 1920)
   Laurence Olivier (UK 1948)
   Grigori Kozintsev (USSR 1964)
   Tony Richardson (UK 1969)
   Franco Zeffirelli (USA/UK/France 1990)
   Kenneth Branagh (UK/USA 1996)
   Michael Almereyda (USA 2000)

Hamlet 2, Andrew Fleming (USA 2008)
Henry V

   Laurence Olivier (UK 1944)
   Kenneth Branagh (UK 1989)

High School Musical, Kenny Ortega (USA 2006)
His Girl Friday, Howard Hawks (USA 1940)
The Hobbit, Peter Jackson (New Zealand/USA 2012)
In the Bleak Midwinter, Kenneth Branagh (UK 1995)
In Which We Serve, Noël Coward (UK 1941)
Joe Macbeth, Ken Hughes (UK 1954)
Julius Caesar

David Bradley (USA 1950)
Joseph L. Mankiewicz (USA 1953)
Stuart Burge (UK 1970)

The King is Alive, Kristian Levring (Denmark 2000)
King Lear

Grigori Kozintsev (USSR 1969)
Peter Brook (UK 1971)

King of Texas, Uli Edel (TV movie, USA 2002)
Kiss Me Kate, Jack Cummings (USA 1953)
The Lady Eve, Preston Sturges (USA 1941)
The Lion King, Roger Allen and Rob Minkoff (USA 1994)
Looking for Richard, Al Pacino (USA 1996)
Love's Labour's Lost, Kenneth Branagh (UK/France/USA 2000)
Macbeth

Orson Welles (USA 1948)
George Schaefer (USA 1960)
Roman Polanski (UK/USA 1971)

The Maltese Falcon, John Huston (USA 1941)
The Mark of Zorro, Fred Niblo (USA 1920)
Men of Respect, William Reilly (USA 1991)
The Merchant of Venice, Michael Radford (Luxembourg 2004)
A Midsummer Night's Dream

Max Reinhardt/William Dieterle (USA 1935)
Peter Hall (UK 1969)
Adrian Noble (UK 1996)
Michael Hoffmann (USA/Italy/UK 1999)
Christine Edzard (as *The Children's Midsummer Night's Dream*, UK 2001)

Morning Glory, Lowell Sherman (USA 1933)
Much Ado About Nothing

  Kenneth Branagh (UK/USA 1993)
  Joss Whedon (USA 2013)

My Own Private Idaho, Gus Van Sant (USA 1991)
O, Tom Blake Nelson (USA 2002)
Otello (Verdi), Franco Zeffirelli (Italy 1987)
Othello

  Dmitri Buchowetski (Germany 1922)
  Orson Welles (USA/Morrocco/Italy/France 1952)
  Stuart Burge (UK 1965)
  Liz White (USA 1980)
  Oliver Parker (UK 1995)

Une Partie de campagne, Jean Renoir (France 1936)
Prospero's Books, Peter Greenaway (Netherlands/France/Italy/Japan 1991)
The Public Enemy, Raoul Walsh (USA 1931)
Quo Vadis, Mervyn Leroy (USA 1951)
Rebecca, Alfred Hitchcock (USA 1939)
Rebel Without a Cause, Nicholas Ray (USA 1955)
Repulsion, Roman Polanski (UK 1965)
Richard III

  F.R. Benson (UK 1910–11)
  Laurence Olivier (UK 1955)
  Richard Loncraine (UK 1995)

Robin Hood, Alan Dwan (USA 1922)
Romeo and Juliet

  George Cukor (USA 1936)
  Renato Castellani (Italy/UK 1954)
  Franco Zeffirelli (Italy/UK 1968)
  Baz Luhrmann (as *William Shakespeare's 'Romeo+Juliet'*, USA 1996)

Rosemary's Baby, Roman Polanski (USA 1968)
Satyricon (aka *Fellini-Satryricon*), Federico Fellini (Italy/France 1969)
Scotland PA, Billy Morisette (USA 2001)
Sebastiane, Derek Jarman (UK/Italy 1976)
Shakespeare in Love, John Madden (USA 1999)

Shakespeare Wallah, James Ivory (India 1965)
She's the Man, Andy Fickman (USA 2006)
Skyfall, Sam Mendes (USA/UK 2012)
Strange Illusion, Edgar Ulmer (USA 1945)
Star Wars, George Lucas (USA 1977)
The Taming of the Shrew

    Sam Taylor (USA 1929)
    Franco Zeffirelli (Italy/USA 1967)

Tempest, Paul Mazursky (USA 1982)
The Tempest

    Derek Jarman (UK 1980)
    Julie Taymor (USA 2011)

10 Things I Hate About You, Gil Junger (USA 2002)
The Thief of Baghdad, Raoul Walsh (USA 1924)
The Thin Man, Hunt Stromberg (USA 1938)
A Thousand Acres, Jocelyn Moorhouse (USA 1997)
Titus, Julie Taymor (USA/Italy 1999)
To Be or Not to Be, Ernst Lubitsch (USA 1942)
Twelfth Night, Trevor Nunn (UK/Ireland/USA 1996)
I Vitelloni, Federico Fellini (Italy 1953)
Were the World Mine, Tom Gustafson (USA 2008)
West Side Story, Robert Wise (USA 1960)
White Heat, Raoul Walsh (USA 1949)
The Wild One, Laslo Benedek (USA 1954)

INTRODUCTION

1. Jean Renoir, *Renoir on Renoir. Interviews, Essays, and Remarks*, translated by Carol Wolk (Cambridge: Cambridge University Press, 1989), p. 233.
2. Julie Sanders, *Adaptation and Appropriation* (London and New York: Routledge, 2006), p. 20.
3. Deborah Cartmell and Imelda Whelehan, eds., *Adaptations: From Text to Screen, Screen to Text* (London: Routledge, 1999), p. 24.
4. Thomas Leitch, *Film Adaptation and Its Discontents* (Baltimore: Johns Hopkins University Press, 2007), pp. 123–125.
5. Colin McCabe, Kathleen Murray, and Rick Warner, eds, *True to the Spirit. Film Adaptation and the Question of Fidelity* (New York: Oxford University Press, 2011), p. 7.
6. Linda Hutcheon with Siobhan O'Flynn, *A Theory of Adaptation*, second edition (London and New York: Routledge, 2013), p. xv.
7. Mark Thornton Burnett, *Shakespeare and World Cinema* (Cambridge: Cambridge University Press, 2012).
8. See Judith Buchanan, *Shakespeare on Silent Film. An Excellent Dumb Discourse* (Cambridge: Cambridge University Press, 2009), pp. 147–189.
9. On Nielsen, see Tony Howard, *Women as Hamlet. Performance and Interpretation in Theatre, Film and Television* (Cambridge: Cambridge University Press, 2007), pp. 137–159.
10. Buchanan, *Shakespeare on Silent Film*, pp. 241–248.
11. On the film's significance in the relationship between sound and silent filming, and the relationship between this and its interpretation of the play, see Deborah Cartmell, 'Sound Adaptation. Sam Taylor's *The Taming of the Shrew*', in Deborah Cartmell, ed., *A Companion to Literature, Film, and Adaptation* (Chichester: Wiley-Blackwell, 2012), pp. 70–83.
12. Clinton Heylin, *Despite the System. Orson Welles versus the Hollywood Studios* (Chicago: Chicago Review Press, 2005).
13. On the effects of digital technology see two articles in *Cineaste*, XXXVII/4 (Fall 2012): 'From 35mm to DCP: a Critical Symposium on the Changing Face of Motion Picture Exhibition' (32–42), and 'Surviving a Nonlinear Way of Work: Veteran Film Editors Talk About Transitions' by Maria Garcia (43–47).
14. See Jennifer Barnes, '"Posterity is Dispossessed": Laurence Olivier's Macbeth Manuscripts in 1958 and 2012', *Shakespeare Bulletin* 30/3 (2012),

265–297, and Luke McKernan, 'Bloody Dreams: Laurence Olivier's MACBETH and the business of filming Shakespeare', in Olwen Terris, Eve-Marie Oesterlen, and Luke McKernan, *Shakespeare on Film, Television and Radio. The Researcher's Guide* (London: BUFVC, 2009), pp. 1–19.

15. On the relationships between 'creative' personnel and the studios, see Thomas Schatz, *The Genius of the System. Hollywood Film-making in the Studio* Era (New York: Pantheon Books, 1989). A valuable overview is provided by Douglas Gomery, *The Hollywood Studio System. A History* (London: BFI Publishing, 2005).

16. A version of Hall's stage production was recorded on videotape in 1959 during its first run; the American television series for which it was made did not complete its initial season and it was never shown. A (possibly unique) copy of the videotape is held in the RSC's archives at the Shakespeare Centre, Stratford-upon-Avon.

17. On the new millennium's revolutions in cinema (home) viewing and their effects, see Barbar Klinger, *Beyond the Multiplex. Cinema, New Technologies, and the Home* (Berkeley and Los Angeles: University of California Press, 2006) and J. Hoberman, *Film after Film, or, What Became of 21st Century Cinema?* (London and New York: Verso, 2012).

18. On David Bradley's *Julius Caesar*, see Kenneth S. Rothwell, *A History of Shakespeare on Screen. A Century of Film and Television*, second edition (Cambridge: Cambridge University Press, 2004), p. 153; on Liz White's *Othello*, Peter S. Donaldson, *Shakespearean Films/Shakespearean Directors* (Boston: Unwin Hyman, 1990), pp. 127–143.

19. An appropriately racy account of one important company is Peter Biskind's *Down and Dirty Pictures. Miramax, Sundance and the Rise of the Independent Film* (London: Bloomsbury, 2004).

20. Douglas Lanier, *Shakespeare and Modern Popular Culture* (Oxford: Oxford University Press, 2002), p. 89.

21. On the early stages of the introduction of synchronized dialogue, see Scott Eyman, *The Speed of Sound. Hollywood and the Talkie Revolution, 1926–30* (Baltimore and London: Johns Hopkins University Press, 1997).

22. Sarah Kozloff, *Overhearing Film Dialogue* (Berkeley, Los Angeles and London: University of California Press, 2000), pp. 174–175.

23. Victor Oscar Freeburg, *The Art of the Photoplay* (New York: Macmillan, 1918), p. 238.

24. Michael Tierno, *Aristotle's 'Poetics' for Screenwriters. Storytelling Secrets from the Greatest Mind in Western Civilization* (New York: Hyperion Books, 2002). Joseph McBride, *Writing in Pictures. Screenwriting Made (Mostly) Painless* (New York: Vintage Books, 2012), p. 43.

25. The decision to include Falstaff was made after rehearsals had begun. See Kenneth Branagh, *Beginning* (London: Chatto and Windus, 1989), pp. 231–232.

CHAPTER I

1. Daniel Albright, *Musicking Shakespeare: A Conflict of Theaters* (Rochester, NY: University of Rochester Press, 2007), p. 262.
2. Derek Jarman, *Dancing Ledge* (London: Quartet, 1984), p. 186.
3. Pascale Aebischer, *Screening Early Modern Drama: Beyond Shakespeare* (Cambridge: Cambridge University Press, 2013), p. 25.
4. Yolanda Sonnabend, '"The fabric of this vision": designing *The Tempest* with Derek Jarman', in Roger Wollen, ed., *Derek Jarman: A Portrait* (London: Thames and Hudson, 1996), pp. 77–79 (79).
5. William Pencak, *The Films of Derek Jarman* (Jefferson, NC and London: McFarland and Co., 2002), p. 101.
6. Julie Taymor, *The Tempest: Adapted from the Play by William Shakespeare* (New York: Abrams, 2010), p. 18.
7. Bernice W. Kliman's review in *Shakespeare on Film Newsletter* 14/1 (December 1989), 1, 9–10, analyses this aspect of the film in helpful detail.
8. Graham Holderness, *Shakespeare in Performance: The Taming of the Shrew* (Manchester: Manchester University Press, 1989), pp. 60, 61.
9. John Houseman, *Front and Center* (New York: Simon and Shuster, 1979), pp. 392–393. In Hollywood in 1942 Brecht tried to interest the director (and fellow expatriate) Wiliam Dieterle in the notion of a film *Caesar's Last Days*, but concluded that 'the industry [was not] making costume films' and was 'wary of the nightshirts' of such theatre productions as those of the Saxe-Meiningen company: 'in actual fact you could dye the tunics dark colours and have them elegantly cut' (Bertolt Brecht, *Journals, 1934–1955*, translated by Hugh Rorrison, edited by John Willett [London: Methuen, 1993], p. 219: diary entry for 8 April 1942.
10. Julie Taymor, *Titus: The Illustrated Screenplay, Adapted from the Play by William Shakespeare* (New York: Newmarket Press, 2000), pp. 178, 180.
11. Gary Crowdus and Richard Porton, 'Shakespeare's Perennial Political Thriller. An Interview with Ralph Fiennes', *Cineaste* XXXVII/2 (Spring 2012), pp. 18–23 (20–21).
12. Peter Brook, conversation (p. 25) and letter (pp. 240–241), quoted in Grigori Kozintsev, *King Lear, the Space of Tragedy: The Diary of a Film Director*, translated by Mary Mackintosh with a foreword by Peter Brook (Berkeley and Los Angeles: University of California Press, 1977).
13. *William Shakespeare's 'Hamlet' Adapted by Michael Almereyda* (London: Faber and Faber, 2000), p. xi.
14. *William Shakespeare's Hamlet*, p. xii.

CHAPTER 2

1. James Naremore, *The Magic World of Orson Welles*, revised edition (Dallas: Southern Methodist University Press, 1989), pp. 142, 144.

2. John Willett, *Expressionism* (London: Weidenfeld and Nicolson, 1970), p. 8 (on expressionism in general), p. 21 (on Strindberg), and p. 45 (on the 'Teutonic').

3. Janey Pace and Lowell Peterson, 'Some Visual Motifs of *film noir*' (1974) in Alain Silver and James Ursini, eds, *Film Noir Reader*, seventh edition (1996; New York: Limelight Editions, 2003), pp. 64–75; p. 67.

4. Foster Hirsh, *Film Noir: The Dark Side of the Screen* (New York: Da Capo Press, 2008), p. 57.

5. Hirsh, *Film Noir*, p. 68.

6. On the background of Welles' *Macbeth*, see Simon Callow, *Orson Welles: Hello Americans* (London: Jonathan Cape, 2006), chapters 20 and 22; on Olivier's *Hamlet*, Terry Coleman, *Olivier: The Authorized Biography* (London: Bloomsbury, 2005), Chapter 15. Budget details from Callow (p. 383) and Coleman (p. 199).

7. Michael Anderegg, *Orson Welles, Shakespeare and Popular Culture* (New York: Columbia University Press, 1999), p. 97.

8. On the distribution and reception of Olivier's film, see Sarah Street, *Transatlantic Crossings: British Feature Films in the USA* (New York and London: Continuum, 2002), pp. 106–109.

9. Penelope Houston, 'Orson Welles', in Richard Roud, ed., *Cinema: A Critical Dictionary*, 2 vols. (New York: Viking Press, 1980), II, pp. 1055–1068; p. 1054.

10. James McBride, *Orson Welles* (London: Secker and Warburg, 1972), p. 113.

11. Robert Garis, *The Films of Orson Welles* (Cambridge: Cambridge University Press, 2004), p. 138. Garis's analysis of the script is detailed and unsparing, but is qualified by his warm regard for the overall artistic achievement of this flawed film.

12. Roger Furse, 'Designing the Film "Hamlet"', in Alan Dent, ed., *Hamlet The Film and the Play* (London: World Film Publications, 1948), [unnumbered pp. 27–32; p. 28].

13. Raymond Durgnat, *A Mirror for England. British Movies from Austerity to Affluence* (London: Faber, 1970), pp. 112–113.

14. Bernice Kliman, *Hamlet: Film, Television and Audio Performance* (Rutherford, Madison and Teaneck: Fairleigh Dickinson University Press, 1988), p. 29.

15. Alexander Leggatt, *Shakespeare in Performance: King Lear* (Manchester: Manchester University Press, 1991), pp. 105–106.

16. Peter Brook, *The Shifting Point. Forty Years of Theatrical Exploration, 1946–1987* (London: Methuen, 1987), p. 204.

17. 'Interview with Keith Baxter', in Bridget Gellert Lyons, ed., *Chimes at Midnight* (New Brunswick, NJ: Rutgers University Press, 1988), pp. 267–283 (272–273).

18. Jarman, *Dancing Ledge*, p. 104.

19. Jarman, *Dancing Ledge*, p. 194.

20. Virginia Mason Vaughan, *Shakespeare in Performance: The Tempest* (Manchester: Manchester University Press, 2011), p. 188.

CHAPTER 3

1. Mulvey's article, 'Visual Pleasure and Narrative Cinema', first published in *Screen* in 1975, is included along with subsequent adjustments to, and applications of, its conceptual framework in E. Ann Kaplan's anthology *Feminism and Film* (Oxford: Oxford University Press, 2000).

2. Stanley Cavell, *Pursuits of Happiness: The Hollywood Comedy of Remarriage* (Cambridge, MA: Harvard University Press, 1981); Maria DiBattista, *Fast-Talking Dames* (New Haven and London: Yale University Press, 2001), p. 15.

3. Jeanine Basinger, *Silent Stars* (Hanover and London: Wesleyan University Press, 1999), p. 43.

4. Basinger, *Silent Stars*, p. 53.

5. Gaylyn Studlar, *This Mad Masquerade: Stardom and Masculinity in the Jazz Age* (New York: Columbia University press, 1996), p. 86.

6. Review by Sime Silverman, *Variety*, 4 December 1929, quoted in Jeffrey Vance and Tony Maietta, *Douglas Fairbanks* (Los Angeles: University of California Press/Academy of Motion Picture Arts and Science, 2008), p. 278. (Information on the budget and receipts is from the same source.)

7. Franco Zeffirelli, *The Autobiography of Franco Zeffirelli* (London: Weidenfeld and Nicolson, 1986), p. 216.

8. Barbara Hodgdon, 'Katherine Bound, or Play(k)ating the Strictures of Everyday Life', in *The Shakespeare Trade: Performances and Appropriations* (Philadelphia: University of Pennsylvania Press, 1998) pp. 1–38 (18).

9. A scene (the play's 3.4) between Margaret, Ursula, Hero, and Beatrice on the morning of the wedding, filmed but not included in the final cut, would have reinforced the impression of the women's solidarity as well as establishing Margaret (Imelda Staunton) more strongly.

10. Anthony Lane, 'House Parties', *New Yorker*, 24 June 2013, p. 84.

11. On Bottom's wife, see Russell Jackson, *Shakespeare Films in the Making: Vision, Production and Reception* (Cambridge: Cambridge University Press, 2007), pp. 31–32 and 54–55.

12. *New Yorker*, 17 May 1999, p. 97.

13. Michael Hoffmann, *William Shakespeare's 'A Midsummer Night's Dream'* (New York: Harper Entertainment, 1999), p. ix.

14. Celia R. Daileader, 'Nude Shakespeare in film and nineties popular feminism', in Catherine M.S. Alexander and Stanley Wells, eds, *Shakespeare and Sexuality* (Cambridge: Cambridge University Press, 2001), pp. 183–200 (193).

15. On Reinhardt's opening sequence see Jackson, *Shakespeare Films in the Making*, pp. 30–31.

16. Nunn has given a rueful account of the decision to add a spoken prologue, and his encounter with the 'amalgam of compromises' called for by film: *William Shakespeare's Twelfth Night: A Screenplay* (London: Methuen, 1996), pp. 12–13.

17. Patricia Lennox, 'A girl's got to eat: Christine Edzard's film of *As You Like It*', in Marianne Novy, ed., *Transforming Shakespeare: Contemporary Women's Re-visions in Literature and Performance* (New York: St Martin's Press, 1999), pp. 51–66 (61).

18. Arthur Eloesser, *Elisabeth Bergner* (Berlin, 1927), quoted by Russell Jackson, 'Remembering Bergner's Rosalind: *As You Like It* on film in 1936', in Peter Holland, ed., *Shakespeare, Memory and Performance* (Cambridge: Cambridge University Press, 2006), pp. 237–255 (243). Richard Burt notes the resemblance of Bergner's Ganymede to Greta Garbo as Queen Christina, and finds signs of a lesbian relationship between Celia and Rosalind in Czinner's film: *Unspeakable ShaXXXspeares: Queer Theory and American Kiddie Culture*, second edition (New York: St Martin's Press, 2000), p. 257, n. 16.

19. Nunn, *William Shakespeare's 'Twelfth Night'*, p. 9.

CHAPTER 4

1. On the problems with the bedroom scene in 1936, see Russell Jackson, *Shakespeare Films in the Making* (Cambridge: Cambridge University Press, 2007), p. 251, n. 36. Joseph Breen advised MGM that there might be problems with the British censors: 'We earnestly recommend to you that you play this scene so as to omit all action of them lying on the bed, fondling one another in a horizontal position, and pulling one another down, etc'.

2. On Garrick's version, and its emphasis on pathos, see Jill L. Levenson, *Shakespeare in Performance: Romeo and Juliet* (Manchester: Manchester University Press, 1987), pp. 19–30. Levenson also gives a detailed and perceptive account of Zeffirelli's 1960 London stage production and the subsequent film (pp. 82–123). Further information on the production of the film, including discussion of its shooting script, will be found in Jackson, *Shakespeare Films in the Making*, pp. 191–221.

3. See William Van Watson, 'Shakespeare, Zeffirelli, and the Homosexual Gaze', *Literature/Film Quarterly* 20/4 (1992), 308–325 and Peter Donaldson's chapter, '"Let Lips do What Hands Do": Male bonding, Eros, and loss in Zeffirelli's *Romeo and Juliet*', in *Shakespearean Films/Shakespearean Directors* (Boston: Unwin Hyman, 1990), pp. 145–188.

4. Franco Zeffirelli, *Autobiography* (New York: Weidenfeld and Nicolson, 1986), p. 225.

5. Baz Luhrmann, commentary on the DVD of *William Shakespeare's Romeo+Juliet* (Twentieth Century Fox, 2002).

6. Pam Cook, *Baz Luhrmann* (London: BFI/Palgrave MacMillan, 2010), p. 48.

7. Terry Coleman, *Olivier: The Authorised Biography* (London: Bloomsbury, 2005), p. 195.

8. Robert Hapgood, 'Popularizing Shakespeare: The Artistry of Franco Zeffirelli', in Lynda E. Boose and Richard Burt, eds, *Shakespeare, the Movie: Popularizing the Plays on Film, TV and Video* (London and New York: Routledge, 1997), pp. 80–94 (88).

9. Patrick J. Cook, *Cinematic Hamlet: The Films of Olivier, Zeffirelli, Branagh and Almereyda* (Athens, OH: Ohio University Press, 2011), p. 90.

10. Lisa Starks insists that 'Branagh's film continues in [the] conservative vein by further reinstating the Oedipal dynamic of desire', but also 'through the representation of sexuality and the use of cinematic conventions that reinscribes dominant ideology … reinforces puritanical attitudes of American (and, to a lesser extent, British culture at the close of [the 1990s]'. ('The displaced body of desire: sexuality in Kenneth Branagh's *Hamlet*', in Christy Desmet and Robert Sawyer, eds, *Shakespeare and Appropriation* [London and New York: Routledge, 1999], pp. 121–177 [172]). Starks's argument effectively accuses the director of a complex kind of bad faith. (It was simply decided not to go down a well-trodden path.)

11. Jack Jorgens, *Shakespeare on Film* (Bloomington IN: Indiana University Press, 1977), p. 96.

12. Mícheál MacLiammóir, *Put Money in thy Purse: The Filming of Orson Welles's Othello* (London: Methuen, 1952), pp. 26–27.

13. For a thoughtful discussion of this aspect of the film, see Virginia Mason Vaughan, 'Orson Welles and the patriarchal eye', in *Othello: A Contextual History* (Cambridge: Cambridge University Press, 1994), pp. 212–214.

14. Oliver Parker, 'Shakespeare in the cinema: a film directors' symposium', *Cineaste*, XXIV 1 (1998), 48–55 (51).

15. Ania Loomba, *Shakespeare, Race, and Colonialism* (Oxford: Oxford University Press, 2002), p. 91. Pascale Aebischer, in *Shakespeare's Violated Bodies: Stage and Screen Performance* (Cambridge: Cambridge University Press, 2004), examines the scenes in which sexual activity and the naked

bodies are shown, and argues that 'With its leads played by a real black man and a real white woman, Parker's film disturbingly naturalises racial and sexual inferiority by showing it embodied, not performed' (p. 150).

16. Burt (*Unspeakable ShaXXXpeares* [Houndmills and London: MacMillan, 1998], pp. 31–32) claims that 'Branagh plays Iago as a gay man', but accepts that in the 'handkerchief' scene he is about to have 'what *appears* to be anal sex' with Emilia (my emphasis); Carol Rutter is categorical in claiming that 'out of frame . . . he is sodomising her'. ('"Her First Remembrance from the Moor": actors and the materials of memory', in Peter Holland, ed., *Shakespeare, Memory and Performance* [Cambridge: Cambridge University Press, 2006], pp. 169–206 [196]).

17. Virginia Wright Wexman, *Roman Polanski* (New York: Columbus Books, 1987), p. 79.

18. Roman Polanski, *Roman by Polanski* (New York: William Morrow and Co., 1984), p. 332.

19. Polanski, *Roman by Polanski*, p. 333.

20. Kenneth Tynan, 'Magnetic pole: a portrait of Roman Polanski', in *The Sound of Two Hands Clapping* (New York: Holt, Rinehart, 1975), pp. 87–105 (103).

21. Tynan, 'Magnetic pole', pp. 100–101.

22. Wexman, *Roman Polanski*, p. 88.

23. Janet Adelman, *Suffocating Mothers: Fantasies of Maternal Origin in Shakespeare's Plays, 'Hamlet' to 'The Tempest'* (New York and London: Routledge, 1992), p. 131.

CHAPTER 5

1. Jan Kott, *Shakespeare our Contemporary*, translated by Bolesław Taborski (New York: Norton, 1974), p. 40.

2. Kott, *Shakespeare our Contemporary*, p. 147.

3. Douglas Lanier, 'Shakescorp Noir', *Shakespeare Quarterly* 53/2 (Summer 2002), 157–180 (169).

4. Raymond Durgnat, *Films and Feelings* (Cambridge, MA: MIT Press, 1967), p. 262.

5. Branagh notes in the published screenplay that the exchanges with Burgundy 'failed to advance the plot, and added little to the aspects of the play that we wanted to explore': *'Henry V' by William Shakespeare: Screenplay and Introduction by Kenneth Branagh* (London: Chatto and Windus, 1989), p. xv.

6. James Agee, *Agee on Film. Criticism and Comment on the Movies* (New York: Modern Library, 2000), p. 203.

7. On the reception of the film in the United Kingdom, see Jackson, *Shakespeare Films in the Making*, pp. 114–121.

8. Emma Smith, ed., *King Henry V* ('Shakespeare in Production' series) (Cambridge: Cambridge University Press, 1997), p. 75.

9. Donald K. Hendrik, 'War is Mud. Branagh's Dirty Harry V and the types of political ambiguity', in Lynda E. Boose and Richard Burt, eds., *Shakespeare, the Movie. Popularizing the Plays on Film, TV and Video* (London and New York: Routledge, 1997), pp. 45–66; p. 49. See also Chris Fitter, 'A Tale of Two Branaghs: *Henry V*, ideology and the Mekong Agincourt', in Ivo Kamps, ed., *Shakespeare Left and Right* (London and New York: Routledge, 1991) pp. 259–276.

10. Kenneth Rothwell, *A History of Shakespeare on Screen*, second edition (Cambridge: Cambridge University Press, 2004), p. 236.

11. Claire Bloom, *Leaving a Doll's House* (Boston, MA: Little, Brown, 1996), p. 91.

12. See Hugh Richmond's discussion of the script in *Shakespeare in Performance: 'Richard III'* (Manchester: Manchester University Press, 1989), pp. 58–61.

13. Jorgens, *Shakespeare on Film*, p. 144.

14. Christopher Andrews identifies the 'seductive' effect within the film and on the viewer of McKellen's performance and those of Olivier and Ron Cook (in the 1983 BBC TV production) in '*Richard III* on Film: the Subversion of the Viewer', *Literature/Film Quarterly* 28/2 (2000), 82–94.

15. *William Shakespeare's 'Richard III': A screenplay written by Ian McKellen and Richard Loncraine, annotated and introduced by Ian McKellen* (Woodstock, NY: Overlook Press, 1996), p. 54. Unless otherwise indicated, McKellen's comments are quoted from this source.

16. McKellen, p. 286. Peter S. Donaldson suggests that Richmond's 'shy smile of recognition, directed towards the camera', is accompanying 'the crucial moment at which the medieval becomes modern, in which a hellish, demonic rule yields to a new dynasty, one perhaps equally cold, more casual and banal in its evil' ('Cinema and the Kingdom of Death: Loncraine's *Richard III*', *Shakespeare Quarterly*, 53/2 [summer 2002], 241–259 [258]).

17. On the film's use of various genres, and the significance of the conclusion, see James M. Loehlin, '"Top of the World, Ma" *Richard III* and Cinematic Convention', in Boose and Burt, *Shakespeare, the Movie*, pp. 67–120.

18. On Brecht's *Coriolan*, see Margot Heinemann, 'How Brecht Read Shakespeare', in Jonathan Dollimore and Alan Sinfield, eds, *Political Shakespeare: New Essays in Cultural Materialism* (Manchester: Manchester University Press, 1985), pp. 202–230 (221–223).

19. Shooting script in New York Public Library, Performing Arts Division: Billy Rose Theater Collection, MFLM + [1952], pp. 55–68. (The scene is printed by Jorgens, *Shakespeare on Film*, pp. 103–104.) Houseman (*Front and Center*, p. 404) reports that Mankiewicz was incensed by a cut he regarded as the work of studio executives. See also Kenneth L. Geist,

Pictures Will Talk: The Life and Films of Joseph L. Mankiewicz (New York: Scribner's, 1978), p. 234. Jorgens, *Shakespeare on Film*, pp. 103–104, prints the scene from the shooting script.

20. Maria Wyke, *Caesar in the USA* (Berkeley: University of California Press, 2012), pp. 148–149 (155).

21. John H. Lenihan, 'English Classics for Cold War America: MGM's *Kim* (1950), *Ivanhoe* (1952) and *Julius Caesar* (1953)', *Journal of Popular Film and Television*, 20.3 (Fall 1993), 42–57 (51).

22. Jorgens, *Shakespeare on Film*, p. 100.

23. In addition to Wyke, *Caesar in the USA*, see Sarah Hatchuel, *Shakespeare and the Cleopatra/Caesar Intertext. Sequel, Conflation, Remake* (Madison and Teaneck, NJ: Fairleigh Dickinson University Press, 2011).

CHAPTER 6

1. Deborah Cartmell and Imelda Whelehan, eds, *Adaptations: From Text to Screen, Screen to Text* (London: Routledge, 1999), p. 24.

2. On *Gnomeo and Juliet*, see Abigail Rokison, *Shakespeare for Young People* (London: Bloomsbury, 2013), pp. 209–214.

3. Thomas Cartelli and Katherine Rowe, 'Surviving Shakespeare', in *New Wave Shakespeare on Screen* (Cambridge: Polity Press, 2007).

4. See the account of the scripting process in Peter Cowie, *The Godfather Book* (London: Faber, 1997), pp. 106–123.

5. Irene G. Dash, *Shakespeare and the American Musical* (Bloomington: Indiana University Press, 2010), p. 76.

6. Harwood's play *The Dresser* was first performed at the Royal Exchange Theatre, Manchester, in 1980; his biography, *Sir Donald Wolfit. His Life and Work in the Unfashionable Theatre*, was published in 1971.

7. Felicity Kendal describes her experiences and her, at times, troubled relationship with her father in *White Cargo* (London: Michael Joseph, 1998).

8. Kenneth Branagh, *The Shooting Script: A Midwinter's Tale* (New York: Newmarket press, 1995), p. vii.

9. Samuel Crowl, *Shakespeare at the Cineplex: The Kenneth Branagh Era* (Athens: Ohio University Press, 2003), p. 135.

10. John Madden, audio commentary on the DVD (Columbia Tristar/Universal Pictures, 1999). The dialogue of the omitted scene is included in the shooting script: see 'Final draft 22nd January 1998' (Shakespeare Institute Library, Stratford-upon-Avon).

11. On the film's depiction of Shakespeare in love (but not reading too much) see Michael Anderegg, 'James Dean Meets the Pirate's Daughter. Passion

and Parody in *William Shakespeare's Romeo+Juliet* and *Shakespeare in Love*', in Richard Burt and Lynda E. Boose, eds, *Shakespeare, the Movie, II: Popularizing the Plays on Film, TV, Video and DVD* (London and New York: Routledge, 2003), pp. 56–71.

12. On the net and the gross, see Edward Jay Epstein, *The Hollywood Economist: The Hidden Financial Reality behind the Movies* (Brooklyn, NY: Melville House Publishing, 2010), pp. 85–88.

13. Those who believe that 'Shakespeare' was a front for the true author of the works, the Earl of Oxford, have their own biopic, *Anonymous* (2012).

14. Gus Van Sant, interviewed by Graham Fuller in *My Own Private Idaho* (London: Faber and Faber, 1993), pp. xxiii, xxxvii.

15. Fuller, *My Own Private Idaho*, pp. xliii–iv.

16. Anthony Lane, *Nobody's Perfect: Writings from the 'New Yorker'* (New York: Knopf, 2002), p. 586.

17. This and other deleted scenes are included in the 2005 Criterion Collection edition of the film.

18. Scenes with the references to the maiden and the unicorn are included in the extras on the '30th Anniversary Two-disc Special Edition' DVD (2007).

19. Barry Keith Grant, '1956. Movies and the crack of doom', in Murray Pomerance, ed., *American Cinema of the 1950s* (New Brunswick: Rutgers University Press, 2005), pp. 155–176 (175).

20. Robert Warshow, *The Immediate Experience: Movies, Comics, Theatre and Other Aspects of Popular Culture* (New York: Atheneum, 1979), pp. 128, 129.

21. Janet Maslin, 'Car Bomb and Chianti in "Macbeth" Variation', *New York Times*, 18 January 1991.

22. Jack Shadoian, *Dreams and Dead Ends: The American Gangster Film*, second edition (New York: Oxford University Press, 2003), pp. 167, 169.

23. Poster reproduced on imdb.com (accessed 15 June 2013).

24. *The Taming of the Shrew*, Induction 2, pp. 133–135.

25. See Courtney Lehmann, *Screen Adaptations: Shakespeare's Romeo and Juliet. The Relationship between Text and Film* (London: Methuen Drama, 2010), pp. 103–133; and Irene G. Dash, 'The challenge of tragedy. *West Side Story* and *Romeo and Juliet*', in *Shakespeare and the American Musical*, pp. 77–121.

26. Kenneth S. Rothwell, *A History of Shakespeare on Screen*, second edition (Cambridge: Cambridge University Press, 2004), p. 259.

Further Reading

The pre-eminent survey is Kenneth S. Rothwell, *A History of Shakespeare on Screen: A Century of Film and Television*, second edition (Cambridge: Cambridge University Press, 2004). Rothwell covers television as well as cinema productions, providing a useful chronology and a filmography in which films are grouped according to the plays from which they are derived. The generosity of spirit and critical acumen of the author's comments make this an indispensable source. Robert Hamilton Ball's groundbreaking study, *Shakespeare on Silent Film* (New York: Theatre Arts Books, 1968), should be read alongside Judith Buchanan's *Shakespeare on Silent Film: An Excellent Dumb Discourse* (Cambridge: Cambridge University Press, 2009). Ball's account of films that survive only in summaries from the trade papers or reviews is especially valuable, but Buchanan's work corrects several errors in his account and brings a fresh critical sensibility to the subject. For films made before 1990, the authoritative reference work remains Kenneth S. Rothwell and Annabelle Henkin Melzer, *Shakespeare on Screen: An Annotated Filmography and Bibliography* (London: Mansell, 1990), but the first port of call (though it provides less detailed information on individual films) is an ongoing web resource, the *Shakespeare on Film, Television and Radio Database* of the British Universities Film and Video Council <http://www.bufvc.ac.uk/shakespeare/>. The editors and curators, Olwen Terris, Eve-Marie Oesterlen, and Luke McKernan, have produced *Shakespeare on Film, Television and Radio: The Researcher's Guide* (London: BUFVC, 2009). The earlier *Walking Shadows: Shakespeare in the National Film and Television Archive* (London: BFI, 1994), edited by Terris and McKernan, is limited to items held in the NFTA, but is valuable for its informative catalogue entries and essays. Among the online catalogues of archives and libraries, those of the Library of Congress and the Folger Shakespeare Library, both in Washington DC, are especially helpful. For American films made before 1978 the online catalogue of the American Film Institute has details of production and reception, in some cases drawing on studio archives. A useful source — though it lacks academic editorial oversight — is the *International Movie Database* <http://www.imdb.com>. In particular, users of all these resources should be aware of variations in the dates given for films and the often confusing identification of their nationality, usually ascribed to the sources of their finance.

Several recent critical overviews can be recommended as introductions, notably Deborah Cartmell, *Interpreting Shakespeare on Screen* (Basingstoke: Macmillan, 2000); Stephen M. Buhler, *Shakespeare in the Cinema: Ocular Proof*

(Albany: State University of New York Press, 2002); H.R. Coursen, *Shakespeare in Space: Recent Shakespeare Productions on Screen* (New York: Peter Lang, 2002); Michael Anderegg, *Cinematic Shakespeare* (Lanham, MD: Rowman and Littlefield, 2004); Sarah Hatchuel, *Shakespeare, from Stage to Screen* (Cambridge: Cambridge University Press, 2004); and Judith Buchanan, *Shakespeare and Film* (London: Longman, 2005). Samuel Crowl's *Shakespeare on Film: A Norton Guide* (New York and London, W.W. Norton and Co., 2008) and Maurice Hindle's *Studying Shakespeare on Film* (Houndmills: Palgrave Macmillan, 2007) address a specifically student audience, while the expert and pocket-sized *100 Shakespeare Films* by Daniel Rosenthal (London: BFI Screen Guides, 2007) can also be recommended as a supplement to the information available in such popular guides as those marketed under the 'Halliwell's' and 'TimeOut' brands. Rosenthal's *Shakespeare on Screen* (London: Paul Hamlyn, 2000) is an attractive and lavishly illustrated book aimed at the general reader with perceptive commentary on the films.

Earlier book-length critical works include Roger Manvell's *Shakespeare and the Film* (1971; revised edition Cranbury, NJ: A.S. Barnes, 1979) and the more sophisticated study by Jack J. Jorgens, *Shakespeare on Film* (Bloomington: University of Indiana Press, 1977). *Filming Shakespeare's Plays: The Adaptations of Laurence Olivier, Orson Welles, Peter Brook and Akira Kurosawa* by Anthony Davies (Cambridge: Cambridge University Press, 1988) complements Jorgens' work with a similar approach, informed by the tenets of literary 'new criticism' together with a keen eye for the specifically filmic interpretive strategies of the directors discussed. Similar critical and historical approaches characterize Ace G. Pilkington, *Screening Shakespeare from 'Richard II' to 'Henry V'* (Newark: University of Delaware Press, 1991); Lorne M. Buchman, *Still in Movement: Shakespeare on Screen* (New York: Oxford University Press, 1991); and Robert F. Willson, Jr, *Shakespeare in Hollywood, 1929–1956* (Madison and Teaneck, NJ: Fairleigh Dickinson University Press, 2000).

More radical analysis, taking account of issues of racial and sexual politics and the insights of psychoanalytical theory, is offered by Peter S. Donaldson, *Shakespearean Films/Shakespearean Directors* (Boston: Unwin Hyman, 1990); Kathy M. Howlett, *Framing Shakespeare on Film* (Athens, OH: Ohio University Press, 2000); and Courtney Lehmann, *Shakespeare Remains: Theater to Film, Early Modern to Postmodern* (Ithaca and London: Cornell University Press, 2002).

The sense that attention had been focused unduly on a few canonical films had been contested for some time by cultural materialist commentators, notably Graham Holderness, whose collection *Visual Shakespeare: Essays in Film and Television* collects essays written by him between 1984 and 1988. As its title suggests, Richard Burt's *Unspeakable ShaXXXspeares: Queer Theory and*

American Kiddie Culture (Houndmills: Macmillan, 1998) shifts the critical ground even more determinedly, aligning Shakespeare films with cultural movements beyond the relatively conservative mainstream. Richard Burt and Julian Yates have collaborated in *What's the Worst Thing You Can Do To Shakespeare?* (Houndmills and New York: Palgrave Macmillan, 2013), which moves in and out of the mainstream with dexterity.

On the films that go 'beyond Shakespeare', discussed in my Chapter 6, see Douglas Lanier's *Shakespeare and Modern Popular Culture* in the present series (Oxford: Oxford University Press, 2002). This is a sophisticated and concise overview of the field covered extensively in *Shakespeares after Shakespeare: An Encyclopedia of the Bard in Mass Media and Popular Culture*, edited by Richard Burt (Westport, CT: Greenwood, 2007), a collection of essays in two volumes and over 800 pages by experts in various aspects of the field. The richness of this aspect of Shakespeare studies is further reflected in Burt's *Shakespeare after Mass Media* (Basingstoke: Palgrave Macmillan, 2002) and essays in *The Cambridge Companion to Shakespeare and Popular Culture*, edited by Robert Shaughnessy (Cambridge: Cambridge University Press, 2007). The broader context of adaptation studies is well represented by Deborah Cartmell and Imelda Whelehan, eds, *Adaptations: From Text to Screen, Screen to Text* (London: Routledge, 1999), and in *The Cambridge Companion to Literature on Screen* (Cambridge: Cambridge University Press, 2007) and *A Companion to Literature, Film, and Adaptation* (Chichester: Wiley-Blackwell, 2012), the last two both edited by Cartmell. See also James R. Keller and Leslie Stratyner, eds, *Almost Shakespeare: Reinventing His Works for Cinema and Television* (London: McFarland, 2004). Abigail Rokison, *Shakespeare for Young People: Productions, Versions and Adaptations* (London: Bloomsbury/Arden Shakespeare, 2013) discusses 'teenpix' Shakespeare and other versions aimed at a young or 'young adult' clientèle.

In *New Wave Shakespeare on Screen* (Cambridge: Polity Press, 2007) Thomas Cartelli and Katherine Rowe offer stimulating responses to 'canonical' films — which by now include those directed by Kenneth Branagh — and to work outside the mainstream. (The first chapter's title, 'Beyond Branagh' announces in itself the book's agenda.) However, because the mainstream Shakespeare films are still, in industry terms, mostly for a 'niche' market but sometimes break through into wider popular currency, the work of oppositional filmmakers (such as Derek Jarman) can seem like a niche within a niche. Two recent studies contribute in different but analogous ways to widening the scope of the discussion, and of the field itself: Mark Thornton Burnett, *Shakespeare and World Cinema* (Cambridge: Cambridge University Press, 2012) and Pascale Aebischer, *Screening Early Modern Drama: Beyond Shakespeare* (Cambridge: Cambridge University Press, 2013). Branagh's own films and their significance in facilitating by example the producers' confidence in Shakespeare as a potential product, if only for prestige purposes, is examined by Samuel Crowl in *Shakespeare at the Cineplex: The Kenneth Branagh Era* (Athens, OH: Ohio University Press, 2003). Emma French's *Selling Shakespeare to Hollywood: The Marketing for Filmed Shakespeare Adaptations from 1989 into the New Millennium* (Hatfield: University of Hatfield Press, 2006) is a shrewd and well-documented analysis of its topic, with important implications for the assessment of the cultural work done by the cinema and the influence of commerce on the films themselves and their reception. Publicity (known in the Hollywood studios' heyday as 'exploitation') and distribution also figure in my own study *Shakespeare Films in the Making: Vision, Production and Reception* (Cambridge: Cambridge University Press, 2007), which draws on production records, script materials, publicity, and reviews to describe the evolution and reception of a number of important films: Reinhardt's *Dream*, Olivier's *Henry V*, and three versions of *Romeo and Juliet.*

Critical Anthologies

The growth of interest in Shakespeare on film as a subject of study at university level since 1970 has been reflected in a number of anthologies of commissioned or reprinted essays. An early entry in the field, including valuable material not easily found elsewhere, is Charles W. Eckert's *Focus on Shakespearean Films* (Englewood Cliffs, NJ: Prentice Hall, 1972). Almost two decades separate this from *Shakespeare and the Moving Image: The Plays on Film and Television*, edited by Anthony Davies and Stanley Wells (Cambridge: Cambridge University Press, 1994), which was followed by Robert Shaughnessy's *Shakespeare on Film*, in the 'New Casebooks' series (Houndmills: Macmillan, 1998). *Shakespeare, the Movie: Popularizing the Plays on Film, TV and Video* (London and New York: Routledge, 1997), edited by Richard Burt and Lynda E. Boose, was succeeded in 2003 by what was effectively a newly amended and augmented second edition incorporating some of its contents, *Shakespeare, the Movie II* from the same publisher. *The Cambridge Companion to Shakespeare on Film*, edited by Russell Jackson (Cambridge: Cambridge University Press, 1999) appeared in a second, revised edition, in 2007. *Shakespeare, Film, Fin de Siècle*, edited by Mark Thornton Burnett and Ramona Wray (Houndmills: Macmillan Press, 2000) sought a degree of distinction by situating itself at the turn of the century. Their *Screening Shakespeare in the Twenty-First Century* (Edinburgh: Edinburgh University Press, 2006) moves the debate further into the millennium. A number of authors appeared in more than one of these volumes, as well as in Diana E. Henderson's *A Concise Companion to Shakespeare on Screen* (Oxford: Blackwell Publishing, 2006), a valuable collection despite its limited claims to be a 'companion' — which implies an attempt at comprehensive coverage as well as a variety of viewpoints. James M. Welsh, Richard Vela, and John C. Tibbetts, in *Shakespeare into Film* (New York: Checkmark Books, 2002), offer a fuller overview of the field, achieved partly by the reprinting of important articles from *Literature/Film Quarterly*, partly by the participation of Kenneth S. Rothwell. Lisa S. Starks and Courtney Lehmann have edited two anthologies, *The Reel Shakespeare: Alternative Cinema and Theory* and *Spectacular Shakespeare: Critical Theory and Popular Cinema*, both published by Fairleigh Dickinson University Press in 2002. No less than three editors have combined to oversee *Reinventing the Renaissance: Shakespeare and his Contemporaries in Adaptation and Performance* (New York: Palgrave Macmillan, 2013), which includes a number of essays on film versions, among them a position paper by the veteran polemicist and deconstructor Charles Marowitz.

Among journals that regularly carry reviews and commentary on Shakespeare films are *Literature/Film Quarterly* and *Shakespeare Bulletin* (which incorporated *Shakespeare on Film Newsletter*, 1976–1992) as well as *Shakespeare Quarterly*, *Shakespeare Survey*, and the online journal *Shakespeare*. Among special numbers of other periodicals, the 'Shakespeare in the Cinema Supplement' in *Cineaste*, 24/1 (Fall 1998) is especially valuable for its virtual 'symposium' of notable directors, responding to questions posed by the editor.

Individual Directors

Michael Anderegg, in *Orson Welles, Shakespeare and Popular Culture* (New York: Columbia University Press, 1999), places Welles' Shakespeare films in the context of his other films and his theatre work. Among the many books devoted to Welles, the second volume of Simon Callow's biography, *Orson Welles: Hello Americans* (London: Jonathan Cape, 2006), provides details of the often tortuous production history of *Macbeth* and *Othello*. An outstanding (and often hilarious) account of the making of the latter is that by the Iago, Micheál MacLiammóir: *Put Money in thy Purse: The Filming of Orson Welles's Othello* (London: Methuen, 1952). Dale Silviria gives a shot-by-shot critical analysis of Olivier's *Henry V*, *Hamlet*, and *Richard III* in *Laurence Olivier and the Art of Film Making* (Rutherford, Madison and Teaneck, NJ: Fairleigh Dickinson University Press, 1985), and information from archive sources will be found in Terry Coleman's *Olivier: The Authorized Biography* (London: Bloomsbury, 2005). A persuasive reading of Polanski's *Macbeth* in the context of his career up to the late 1980s is given by Virginia Wright Wexman, *Roman Polanski* (New York: Columbus Books, 1987). Two accounts of Branagh's work, also up to date at the time of their publication, are Sarah Hatchuel, *A Companion to the Shakespeare Films of Kenneth Branagh* (Winnipeg: Blizzard Publishing, 2000) and Samuel Crowl, *The Films of Kenneth Branagh* (Westport, CT and London: Praeger, 2006). Pam Cook's *Baz Luhrmann* (London: Palgrave MacMillan, 2010) includes a substantial account of the production of the director's *Romeo + Juliet* as well as a lucid assessment of its interpretive strategies. Important discussions of Derek Jarman's *The Tempest* in the context of his other films are Michael O'Pray, *Derek Jarman. Dreams of England* (London: British Film Institute, 1996) and Rowland Wymer, *Derek Jarman* in the series 'British Film Makers' (Manchester: Manchester University Press, 2005).

Specific Plays

Volumes in two ongoing series on the performance history of individual plays — *Shakespeare in Performance* (Manchester: Manchester University Press) and *Shakespeare in Production* (Cambridge: Cambridge University Press) — include discussion of film versions of the plays. Virginia Mason Vaughan, *Othello: A Contextual History* (Cambridge: Cambridge University Press, 1994), a valuable overview of the play's critical and theatrical fortunes, is essential background reading for commentary on films of the play. The series *Shakespeare on Screen/Shakespeare à l'écran* (Publications des Universités de Rouen et du Havre), edited by Sarah Hatchuel and Nathalie Vienne-Guerrin, includes papers and proceedings from a series of conferences: to date the plays covered are *A Midsummer Night's Dream* (2004), *Richard III* (2005), *The Henriad* (2008), *The Roman Plays* (2009), *Hamlet* (2010) and *Macbeth* (2013). The essays and transcripts of some of the conference discussions are accompanied by very full 'annotated filmo-bibliographies' by José Ramón Díaz-Fernández. *Hamlet* has been particularly well served by Bernice W. Kliman, *Hamlet: Film, Television, and Audio Performance* (Rutherford, Madison and Teaneck, NJ: Fairleigh Dickinson University Press, 1988) and Patrick J. Cook, *Cinematic Hamlet: The Films of Olivier, Zeffirelli, Branagh and Olivier* (Athens, OH: Ohio University Press, 2011). Courtney Lehmann's *Shakespeare's Romeo and Juliet: The Relationship Between Text and Film* (London: Methuen Drama, 2010) appears in the context of a series 'Screen Adaptations', and situates its subject in terms of theories of adaptation. It can be read alongside the discussion of Luhrmann's film in her *Shakespeare Remains* (2002) and Thomas Leitch's *Film Adaptation and its Discontents* (Baltimore, MD: Johns Hopkins University Press, 2007). The 'Screen Adaptations' series also includes volumes on *The Tempest* by Lisa Hopkins (London: Methuen Drama, 2008), *King Lear* by Yvonne Griggs (London: Methuen Drama, 2009), and *Hamlet* by Samuel Crowl (London: Arden Shakespeare, 2014).

Printed and bound by CPI Group (UK) Ltd, Croydon, CR0 4YY